FILTHY FICTIONS

Critical Perspectives on Asian Pacific Americans Series

Critical Perspectives on Asian Pacific Americans aims to educate and inform readers regarding the Asian Pacific American experience and to critically examine key social, economic, psychological, cultural, and political issues. The series presents books that are theoretically engaging, comparative, and multidisciplinary, and works that reflect the contemporary concerns that are of critical importance to understanding and empowering Asian Pacific Americans.

Books in the Series:

1. Diana Ting Liu Wu, *Asian Pacific Americans in the Workplace* (1997)
2. Juanita Tamayo Lott, *Asian Americans: From Racial Category to Multiple Identities* (1998)
3. Jun Xing, *Asian America Through the Lens: History, Representations, and Identity* (1998)
4. Pyong Gap Min and Rose Kim, editors, *Struggle for Ethnic Identity: Narratives by Asian American Professionals* (1999)
5. Wendy Ho, *In Her Mother's House: The Politics of Asian American Mother-Daughter Writing* (1999)
6. Deborah Woo, *Glass Ceilings and Asian Americans* (2000)
7. Patricia Wong Hall and Victor Hwang, editors, *Anti-Asian Violence in North America: Asian American and Asian Canadian Reflections on Hate, Healing and Resistance* (2001)
8. Pyong Gap Min and Jung Ha Kim, editors, *Religions in Asian America: Building Faith Communities* (2002)
9. Pyong Gap Min, editor, *The Second Generation: Ethnic Identity among Asian Americans* (2002)
10. Susie Lan Cassel, editor, *The Chinese in America: A History from the Gold Mountain to the New Millennium* (2002)
11. Sucheng Chan, editor, *Remapping Asian American History* (2003)
12. Monica Chiu, *Filthy Fictions: Asian American Literature by Women* (2004)
13. Him Mark Lai, *Becoming Chinese American: A History of Communities and Institutions* (2004)
14. Daniel F. Detzner, *Elder Voices: Southeast Asian Families in the United States* (2004)

Submission Guidelines:

Prospective authors of single or coauthored books and editors of anthologies should submit a letter of introduction, the manuscript, or a four- to ten-page proposal, a book outline, and a curriculum vitae. Please send your book manuscript or proposal packet to:

Critical Perspectives on Asian Pacific Americans Series
AltaMira Press
1630 North Main Street, #367
Walnut Creek, CA 94596

FILTHY FICTIONS

Asian American Literature by Women

Monica Chiu

ALTAMIRA
PRESS

A Division of Rowman & Littlefield Publishers, Inc.
Walnut Creek • Lanham • New York • Toronto • Oxford

ALTAMIRA PRESS
A division of Rowman & Littlefield Publishers, Inc.
1630 North Main Street, #367
Walnut Creek, CA 94596
www.altamirapress.com

Rowman & Littlefield Publishers, Inc.
A wholly owned subsidary of The Rowman & Littlefield Publishing Group, Inc.
4501 Forbes Boulevard, Suite 200
Lanham, MD 20706

PO Box 317
Oxford
OX2 9RU, UK

A portion of chapter 5 appeared in *LIT: Literature Interpretation Theory*. Copyright 2001 from "Postnational Globalization and (En)Gendered Meat Production in Ruth L. Ozeki's *My Year of Meats*," by Monica Chiu. Reproduced by permission of Taylor & Francis, Inc., http://www.routledge-ny.com.

British Library Cataloguing in Publication Information Available

Library of Congress Cataloging-in-Publication Data
Chiu, Monica, 1965–
    Filthy fictions : Asian American literature by women / Monica Chiu.
      p.   cm.— (Critical perspectives on Asian Pacific Americans series)
    Includes bibliographical references (p.) and index.
    ISBN 0-7591-0455-7 (cloth : alk. paper)—ISBN 0-7591-0456-5 (pbk. : alk. paper)   1. American literature—Asian American authors—History and criticism.   2. Women and literature—United States—History—20th century.   3. American literature—Women authors—History and criticism.   4. American fiction—20th century—History and criticism.   5. Asian American women—Intellectual life.   6. Asian American women in literature.   7. Asian Americans in literature.   8. Body, Human, in literature.   9. Hygiene in literature.   10. Women in literature.   I. Title.   II. Series.

PS153.A84C483   2004
810.9'9287'08995—dc22   2003016791

Printed in the United States of America

∞ ™ The paper used in this publication meets the minimum requirements of American National Standard for Information Sciences—Permanence of Paper for Printed Library Materials, ANSI/NISO Z39.48–1992.

For my mother and father

Contents

Acknowledgments

I owe much gratitude to those who have encouraged, pressed, inspired, financially supported, and often cajoled me into completing what has been an immense project over the past nine years. An eternal debt to my father. He lovingly nurtured my interests in words and writing by presenting me with a gift of *The Compact Edition of the Oxford English Dictionary* when I was still in high school. If he were alive today, he would be as proud of this publication as he was of my first poem, my first essay, my first short story, all neatly filed in a folder marked "Monica." As for my love of literature, I recall my father's retort to my admission of boredom in the summer months of my childhood: he repeatedly stated, "Pick up a book and read." My mother possesses unflagging patience and faith in all my endeavors. Rather than tire of my enthusiastic discussions, she borrowed or bought the Asian American novels I recommended, taught, or merely mentioned. I am positive that she has read as many Asian American novels as I have. I am especially thankful for her numerous and lengthy visits, from Wisconsin to New Hampshire, to entertain my children with songs, stories, and creative play, to clean up their daily messes, and to prepare family meals while I labored over the final details of this book. My brothers Marcel and Michael humored me throughout the lengthy writing process, reminding me all too often to quit working so hard and to have some fun!

Although this project does not remotely resemble the dissertation from which it metamorphosed, I am obliged to my committee for guiding me smoothly and efficiently through the dissertation process: Angelika Bammer, Catherine Nickerson, and Sau-ling Wong, whose excellent suggestions have prompted my selection of novels to investigate and whose incisive criticism has shaped the book's revisions. I thank Jun Xing for his professional assistance throughout the years and especially for his warm friendship. Much gratitude to Michael Strysick for his encouragement and for reading and rereading the project when it was still a dissertation. A Minority Fellowship from Emory University enabled me to finish the dissertation with very few teaching obligations.

At the University of Wisconsin, Eau Claire, I was inspired and supported by my colleagues, most specifically Anna Brickhouse, Asha Sen, Jane Pederson, and Selika Ducksworth. William Kuskin and Richelle Munkhoff provided camaraderie. When I needed someone to talk to, Ron Mickel always saved me a chair at his kitchen table. Carol Fairbanks reignited my interest in Japanese literature in translation and wrote me many words of encouragement on her lovely, handmade paper.

Over the past two years, my reading group has buoyed me with intellectual curiosity and enthusiasm for my work when I thought I didn't have any left. My gratitude for constructive criticism, healthy doses of necessary comic relief, and fabulous food to Siobhan Senier (recognized also for her generous child care on occasion), Robin Hackett, Eve Raimon, Rebecca Herzig, Lisa Botshon, and Melinda Plastas. I gratefully acknowledge my colleague and generous friend Naomi Nagy, who knows the psychological benefits of chocolate desserts and has served them up at crucial times; she also has played with and happily rocked my children when I couldn't find a baby-sitter.

I have shamelessly used my American Studies colleagues at the University of New Hampshire to read chapters, the manuscript prospectus, and applications requesting funding for my project, even though they are always beleaguered by departmental commitments, teaching responsibilities, and their own scholarship. For their time and energy, and for their valuable insights, I am obliged to John Ernest, who received every one of my inquiries for a critical reading of the manuscript with a broad smile; to Briggs Bailey, for never saying no; to Lisa MacFarlane, who has the uncanny ability to successfully manage and complete an unusually large number of tasks and still accept one more; to Sarah Sherman, for incisive comments on my book prospectus and her thoughts about the politics of publishing; and to David Watters and Diane Freedman for their cheerful encouragement. It has always been a pleasure to have lunch or tea with John Archer, and I appreciate his advice on a variety of academic topics.

Jana French endured countless e-mails and phone calls about both seemingly enormous frustrations and many small victories. My heartfelt gratitude for her constant support, both voiced and intuitively felt, and for the gift of her close and enduring friendship on which I can always rely. Karen Severns's passion for film has provided me with an enjoyable means by which to escape my work, two hours at a time. Her friendship across the Pacific these past fifteen years has been invaluable.

I completed the book's fourth chapter with the assistance of a Gustafson Fellowship through the Center for the Humanities at the University of New Hampshire. I would like to recognize Burt Feintuch and Jennifer Beard, at the center, for their support before and during my semester sabbatical in 2002. Letters of recommendation from both Josephine Lee and Traise Yamamoto helped me obtain the Gustafson Fellowship.

Grace Ebron, my editor, had faith in my project, and my three anonymous readers offered both concrete advice for revisions and some very useful terminology. I would like to thank Brian Richards, my assistant editor, for fielding innumerable questions over the phone and by e-mail; and Carole Bernard, my copy editor. Others I fondly acknowledge for their friendship, enthusiasm, and guidance: Tim Engles for his endless supply of reading suggestions in the field of ethnic studies; Greg Choy for enlightening e-mail chats about the gratification and frustrations of simultaneously parenting, writing, and teaching; Rocío Davis and Sämi Ludwig for believing in my book and for encouraging me to publish; Carole Doreski for her insightful reading of an initial version of chapter 5; Michael Oishi for prompt clarifications of the term "Local" and for corrections to my use of the

ʻokina in "Hawaiʻi"; Kemp Pheley for moral support; the Association for Asian American Studies for its annual forums in which to present my work and meet other scholars; the friendly and efficient librarians at the University of New Hampshire (Deanna Wood, Deborah Watson, David Severn, Valerie Harper, Louise Buckley, and Peter Crosby); Health Services at the University of New Hampshire, which provided me with a small grant with which to buy books and to incorporate my ideas about pathology and dirt in the classroom; and all of my students throughout the years who have inspired and challenged me to teach, to read, to think, and to rethink my ideas.

I thank the following publishers for permission to reprint portions of my work: "Memory, Motion, and Conflict in Chuang Hua's Modernist *Crossings*," *MELUS* 24(4) (winter 1999), and "Postnational Globalization and (En)Gendered Meat Production in Ruth L. Ozeki's *My Year of Meats*," in *LIT: Literature Interpretation Theory* 12 (2001).

To my family, for joy. My daughter Ellie's smile has been utterly inspiring, and her fierce resistance to sleep has often rekindled my fortitude toward and determination to finish this project. To Roland, the sweet, new member of our family, I apologize if the tap-tap-tapping of my keys has been his afternoon lullaby. To Brian, for dancing into my life.

1

Introduction: Pejorative Matter

Contemporary Asian American literature is fraught with female characters that are situated within the troubled categorization of women's bodiliness. The literature references the cultural constraints of national and global racialization. It magnifies how Asian American female bodies refuse containment in discourses about sexuality and female propriety. It investigates the consequences of racial pathology and the messy, uncomfortable interconnections between humans and animals. Most significant, however, is the literature's unique approach to such categorizations. These female characters' acceptance arises through the ironic rejection brought about by their association with pejorative matter, what I loosely call filth or dirt.[1] The portion of the title *Filthy Fictions* suggests a slipperiness between literature about dirt and the concept of dirt itself as a national fiction about Others that conflates connotations of worthlessness and rubbish attached to the term "dirt" with the moral defilement inherent in the term "filth."

Racialized women in contemporary Asian American literature often admit to pejorative self-constructions, becoming "matter out of place," to borrow from Mary Douglas, who equates dirtiness with what is out of its proper place and residing in spaces where it does not belong, however these spaces may be defined ([1966] 1980:35).[2] Dirt, here, is a concept that encompasses the key terms filth, pollution, pathology, sexuality, toxins, and abjection. The terms shape and are shaped by a history of Asian American construction and Asian American wom-

1

en's belonging. The terms and their uses are influenced by corresponding literary responses to cultural constructions of race, gender, sexuality, and class; their uses reflect the changing foci and parameters of investigation within the field of Asian American studies itself, a topic I broach in the conclusion of this book.

My readings of dirt in racial and gendered contexts move beyond Douglas's definition of dirt, in her field of cultural anthropology, which she designates as matter out of place. Her definition has been both lauded and roundly criticized for its simplicity. According to my readings of contemporary Asian American literature, culturally defined dirt can be bound up in exactly the spaces where it does not belong, thus clear-cut divisions of what constitutes dirt and not-dirt are ultimately more complicated than Douglas's construction allows. My work focuses on the fractious divide, illuminated by poststructural theory, of binaries (in/out, clean/dirty, ill/healthy, men/women, natural/unnatural) whose intersections provoke, not prevent, a dismantling of their mutual exclusivity. The aim of *Filthy Fictions* is to interrogate the seemingly transparent—but hardly neutral or innocuous—designations between concepts and metaphors of what is considered dirty and what is considered clean. States Lawrence S. Kubie,

> [W]e scarcely know what is meant by the word "dirt," that there exists neither a psychoanalytic nor yet reasonable pragmatic definition of dirt, and that in general our behavior towards things that are usually thought of as "dirty" is replete with paradoxes, absurdities, confused assumptions, and mutually contradictory implications and premises. (1937:389)

He concludes that one can speak and write of "the *fantasy* rather than of the *reality* of dirt" (1937:388, emphasis in original). Such recognitions demand that we reconsider that the categories we take for granted are themselves in flux, allowing us to constantly re-imagine the meanings and the cultural work of the terms dirty and clean.

This book engages in three scholarly debates: feminist theory and the body; ethnic studies and the concept of race; and conversations about global and transnational concerns that are at the forefront of Asian American studies. Focusing on the provocative subject of culturally constructed and reconstructed perceptions of filth pertaining to racialized women's belonging, I address national and transnational preoccupations with what racial and gendered bodies signify *for* and *beyond* the nation— their facts and their fictions—and what the subjects within these bodies suggest *about* themselves. I interrogate who and what matters in Asian American literature, and in what places, in the often unread voice of Chuang Hua's *Crossings* ([1968] 1986) and in the very contemporary voices of Ginu Kamani's *Junglee Girl* (1995); Lois-Ann Yamanaka's *Wild Meat and the Bully Burgers* (1996), *Blu's Hanging* (1997), and *Heads by Harry* (1999); and Ruth L. Ozeki's *My Year of Meats* (1998). I pose questions that consider the wider implications of culturally accepted practices coupling race and filth. In what practices and in what spaces do we find filth? How do we and should we clean it up? If whiteness is inherently coded as cleanliness, and if class makes possible one's elevation from a dirty racialized person, then how do we categorize an honorary (clean) White/Anglo (Prashad 2000; Tuan 1998)? How, when, and where do white women's historic roles as gatekeepers of domestic cleanliness (Tomes 1998; Hoy 1995) reverberate for Asian American women? If cleaning assumes erasure (of dirt), then who is eliminated in the process (McHugh 1997), or what are the stakes in cleansing one's existence? How is whiteness itself not necessarily a transparent backdrop whose so-called purity highlights a racial taint? Do racial agents who perform society's manual labor recede as the backdrop by which whiteness is seen as untarnished? And why is a low-income designation often seamlessly equated with unsanitary domesticity, at the same time that low-income domestics perform sanitary practices elsewhere, usually in the houses of their so-called clean white employers? *Filthy Fictions* questions not only culturally constructed concepts of pathology, pollution, filth, or sexuality, but also the female characters themselves who remain either displaced or who transgress acceptable social borders in their so-called sullied states.

Such a study of dirt in Asian American literature runs the

risk of merely evoking a contemporary re-perilization, which is certainly not my endeavor. Rather, I acknowledge that the historical trajectory of the Yellow Peril, the quintessential strand of Asian abjection, has omitted input by and narratives of resistance from Asian Americans themselves about the insidious manner in which such stereotypes function. I contend that the subtle and overt references to Asian Americans as filthy that fill the pages of contemporary Asian American fiction offer counter-perspectives rejecting an Orientalism rooted in Yellow Peril rhetoric. The authors of the novels I discuss are wholly aware of their characters' tenuous acceptance. They cleverly use pathology, filth, pollutants, toxins, and other related matter to subvert the racial and gendered displacement that prevent their characters' belonging. Seemingly ahistorical references to the Yellow Peril prove to be salient and necessary gestures backwards as an egress into investigating contemporary and future pejorative matter.

The key terms in this book, revolving around concepts of dirt, are defined and maintained by a relationary progression of representations of impropriety, moving from degrees and kinds of national definitions to their global and transnational ones. The study's organization corresponds closely to how the field of Asian American studies itself has shifted from an exclusive concentration on domestic, national concerns to wider transnational ones. In attending to culturally constructed concepts of dirt and the mutually influencing field of Asian American studies, chapter 2 connects national and familial displacement to profoundly debilitating personal consequences. It is not surprising that Asian Americans who attempt to assimilate national forces prescribing racial-ethnic behavior and circumscribing women, while harboring individual desires to resist or acquiesce to those forces, exhibit pathological conditions in their fragmented, bifurcated, "polluted" states. This complicates accepted explanations of ethnic assimilation and integration, and it questions prescriptives that are demanded of Asian American bodies and of Asian American studies. Characters in chapters 3, 4, and 5 leave the continental United States—for Bombay, Hawai'i, and Japan, respectively—often circling back to the national American framework. The transnational and eventual national postnational leanings of the novels I discuss correspond neatly to the direction of Asian American studies, which can no longer concern itself only with how the national impacts the global terrain. Such studies must accept that "over there" shapes and *is shaped by* "over here," moving from the realm of what Shirley Geoklin Lim calls a "homogenizing" and universalizing globalism to "discrepant cosmopolitanisms," or to transnational considerations (1999:4). This book's progression from domestic to transnational concerns about dirt unfolds in a manner relevant to the direction of Asian American studies itself, as I outline in chapter 6, allowing me to embrace the pejorative matter of dirt at the same time that it has resulted in Asian America's profound rejection.

—〰—

I begin with a brief and necessary historical outline of the rise of a relationship forged between race and dirt via the Yellow Peril, the insidious strand of race abjection, where visible differentiation promoted the manufacture of "natural" narratives of so-called pathologized Chinese. Their cleaning up involved not necessarily instructions in bathing habits, but a socialization embodying racist, Western norms.[3] From fictions created about so-called diseased and dirty Chinese immigrants evolved spurious medical "facts" and eventually political acts prohibiting the legal and civil actions and national migrations of not only Chinese but other Asian immigrants as well.[4]

A sociohistoric categorization of Asians as harbingers of illness and progenitors of pollution was already deeply rooted in American rhetoric by the 1880s. San Francisco's Chinatown, for example, was regarded as "little more than a 'laboratory of infection' . . . distilling its deadly poison . . . and sending it forth to contaminate the atmosphere of the streets and houses of a populous, wealthy and intelligent country" (Kraut 1994:82). In the words of historian Arthur B. Stout, the locale became "'a cancer' in the 'biological, social, religious and political systems'" of America.[5] And for Gina Marchetti, the medical scare coupling Chinese immigrants with the bubonic plague resulted in "the notion that all nonwhite people are by nature physically and intellectually inferior, morally suspect, heathen, licentious, disease-ridden, feral, violent, uncivilized, infantile, and in need of the guidance of white, Anglo-Saxon Protestants" (1993:2–3). Indeed, the color yellow in the term Yellow Peril conjures up images of disease (the yellow of jaundice, the sallow tone of unhealthy skin) and putrefaction (the unsightly hues of abscesses, blemishes, and infections). The Chinese, said to possess "putrid flesh, poisoned blood, leprous bodies and leprous souls," documents Kraut, were thus a pathological assault on the health, wealth, and welfare of America, provoking a host of legal sanctions (1994:83).[6]

While being sick and being dirty are not synonymous by any means, an association between health and cleanliness in America was gaining acceptance as late as the mid-nineteenth century. It was rapidly adopted as a form of hygienic consciousness, *not* as a national undertaking for everybody's good health, but rather as a political tool wielded against unassimilated immigrants, the "great unwashed." An etiology outlining infection and contagion was slowly, and unevenly, affecting ideologies of cleanliness, themselves based on European practices that viewed bathing as a highly dangerous (disease-inducing) activity and cleanliness as the pursuit of nothing more than tidiness.[7] By the 1850s, the status of personal, bodily hygiene was such that many Americans found dirt "positive, even healthy" (Hoy 1995:3). I puzzle over a past logic that pressured immigrants for a standard of cleanliness to which the nation itself did not adhere, magnifying the imaginary status of unclean foreigners. Even more puzzling, the eventual feminization of domestic cleanliness[8] resulted in emasculated Chinese immigrant men who were tethered to so-called feminine forms of employment: busing tables, washing and pressing laundry, and cooking food. Given their social exclusion as unclean, it is ironic that Chinese immigrant men found their employment limited to work in restaurants and laundries, arenas that traditionally demand employees' overt cleanliness and good health in their covert connection to consumers' intimate personal hygiene.

Early in the twentieth century, immigrants' stance toward

personal hygiene was regarded as a visible indicator of their moral stance, outlines Suellen Hoy (1995), and immigrant morality was tantamount to good citizenship. English tutorials were eventually accompanied by instructions for daily cleansing routines, seemingly adhering to Douglas's (1980) theory of dirt as "matter out of place." Cleansing oneself, or removing dirt from its improper place on the body, in what Hoy deems "the American way," more smoothly paved an immigrant's transition into American society (1995:87–88).[9] Finding one's national, patriotic place involved putting dirt in its proper place, a national endeavor beyond the scope of Douglas's theory.

The attribution of "dirty" and "diseased" to the Chinese speaks more clearly to the nation's own preoccupation with moral and medical self-hygiene than to that of the Chinese and other immigrants. The nation's emphasis on cleanliness (moral, racial, physical) has concealed its perpetrators' own (self-) loathing of a potentially dark and dirty self. Therefore, what we now call Yellow Peril narratives—depicting "the sinister and evil character of the quarter [Chinatown] and most of its inhabitants"[10]— are described as "Anglo-American literature [that] does not tell us about Asians . . . but tells us about Anglos' opinions of themselves, in relation to their opinions of Asians," according to Elaine Kim (1982:20).[11] The initial Yellow Peril scare, despite its fictional basis, paved the way for a symbolic institutionalization of the Asian American corporeal within this peril/(para)lyzing paradigm. Its operative narratives rose from biocultural foundations that were derivative of the discursive intersections between fact and fiction that have plagued social reaction and attendant legislative action against Asian Americans, the same intersections with which I find contemporary Asian American authors wrestling. The Peril corresponds to a particular late-nineteenth-century moment in U.S. history that seems to have little bearing on the contemporary novels considered here. But in this book I take up how current and subtle manifestations of the Peril are a means by which the nation continues to work through notions of the Oriental and therefore the means by which contemporary authors draw sources of inspiration or protest.

The Peril references are, for me, the instigating element of a national Orientalism that profoundly influenced the subsequent creation and production of Asian American representation throughout the twentieth century as pollutants, enemy aliens, gooks, and model minorities, all of which express the nation's rejection or acceptance of its Asian American citizens based on cultural constructions of impropriety.[12] The Peril has left a linguistic, semiotic, political, and symbolically bitter trace within American culture, one that played out recently in the 1990s when high incidents of tuberculosis and HIV diagnosed in New York's Chinatown re-pathologized the community.[13] Contemporary Asian American authors address such embodiedness in their fiction, one in which Asian American bodies cannot escape their (mis)placement as biologically and bodily driven entities poised on the border between ill and healthy, dirty and clean.

At the very advent of Asian American rehabilitation—the now valid subject of the once invalid racial object[14]—Asian American bodies are plagued by what I broadly categorize as dirt. The pages of contemporary Asian American literature by women reference real and metaphorical dirt in the global circulation of tainted beef, in the gory practice of taxidermy, through class designations and servants' bodies, and in deracination as a means of self-cleansing. In my readings, race is no longer the problem. Dirt is. Patricia Yaeger's incisive comments from her *Dirt and Desire* resonates powerfully here: "[D]irt becomes the arbiter of cultural categories that are both offensive and arbitrary"; and "Dirt . . . becomes a site for restructuring the contamination associated with race-thinking itself" (2000:66–67, 274). Like Yellow Peril rhetoric, dirt is symptomatic of the nation's mediation of and constraints on Asian American somatic and psychic arenas, themselves based on troublesome, fluctuating definitions in which an irony emerges in a flexible fixity of racial and national meanings.[15]

Dirt is disjunction. It interposes in literature and theory in radical and fascinating ways. Dirt becomes an organizing principle that influences, and is itself tainted by, the changing parameters of racial and gendered acceptance. Dirt, like the Yellow Peril, suggests unassimilability and alienation, two elements experienced by all of the female characters under investigation.

Dirtying others involves scopic practices based on visible differentiation. Dirt's visibility (as, say, sand on the floor) and invisibility (as, say, microscopic germs) has an analog in the practice of racial acceptance in which visible difference provides grounds for manufacturing tarnished narratives. In Monique Thuy-Dung Truong's short piece "Kelly," for example, Vietnamese American character Thuy Mai blatantly states, "When [white] people like you looked at me and my yellow skin, you didn't see color you saw dirt, and I was a walking pile of it" (1996:290). For Asian Americans, belonging has been influenced profoundly by the changing linguistic, material, somatic, and social practices that define what is considered proper and acceptable and what is culturally rejected. *Filthy Fictions*, therefore, clarifies, not cleanses, the efficacy of using dirt to map shifts in scholarly fields and to reconfigure them in provocative ways.

—〰—

A somatic existence is a convenient launching ground for innumerable and complicated forays into how the body operates, not only in cultural and national contexts, but within global contexts as well. The material, biological body has always presented a thorny territory for theorists and critics.[16] Does the body exist? If so, how is it theorized? If race exists, by what definitions does it do so, and is it important or extraneous to corporeal theorization?

The relationship between the state and the body, between constructions of race and impropriety, is complicated by the inability to discern which bodies matter and by whose values. Consider filmmaker Michiko Omori's (1999) staunch refusal to produce a child destined to be trapped in an "alien body": "Why I didn't have children. I used to think it was not having a stable relationship or money. But since my childbearing years are over, another possibility came to light. Like me, my child would be an American trapped in the body of an unwanted alien race. Could I conceal from my child how I wished he or she were more white, so as not to suffer the rejection I had just because of my face?"

Etienne Balibar suggests that neoracism, "the insurmountability of cultural differences," is embedded in "so many intellectual elaborations of the phantasm of prophylaxis or segregation (the need to purify the social body, to preserve 'one's own' or 'our' identity from all forms of mixing, interbreeding or invasion)" (1991:21, 17). Clearly, Asian Americans have been strapped with stereotypes delineating a body at odds with contemporary American culture,[17] where dirt and attendant concepts of pollution, pathology, and sexuality have an analog in both "real" and literary histories, in Asian American belonging and displacement.

Globalization is one avenue by which the body's racialized and gendered meanings have been disseminated along narrow, often racial, trajectories. Anne McClintock, for example, illustrates how imperialist projects entangled global constructions of cleanliness with racial domestication by discussing representations of darker, therefore dirtier, African people through the lenses of more civilized British colonizers laden with boxes of soap: "Soap . . . persuasively mediate[d] the Victorian poetics of racial hygiene and imperial progress" (1995:209). David Palumbo-Liu addresses the more recent phenomenon of mass marketing and globalization of "cultural capital." On the one hand, globalization may contribute to "fetishized" commodities and people and may "alienate" labor, but in its recursive representatory mode—in which transnational images are appropriated, often against their original uses and meanings—it also can "reconfigure" and "recontextualize" identificatory avenues such as race, class, and gender (1993:3).

Referring implicitly to both McClintock's notion of global products as cultural baggage and to Palumbo-Liu's notion of the subversive qualities of transnational commodification, Shirley Geok-lin Lim in "The Center Can(not) Hold: American Studies and Global Feminism" encapsulates the pressing project of engaging "a critically reflexive global feminism" that confronts issues of the transnational, female body (2000:27). Her work revolves around the intersections of feminist studies, ethnic studies, and global studies with which I engage in *Filthy Fictions*.

Lim addresses worrisome images of women's bodies circulating globally, and the subsequent real, female, somatic damage such images provoke. Dangerous eating disorders, such as anorexia and bulimia, were once thought to be middle-class Western pathologies, but unfortunately they are also cropping up in locations around the globe whose populations suffer from famine or poverty. The irony of women intentionally starving themselves for beauty in countries rife with nutritional shortages is frightening. If feminist theories and criticisms of the 1980s and 1990s attempted to erase the biological body as a site of deleterious essentializing, Lim's example speaks to the material body's necessary resurrection. The body's rematerialization amid an impasse in feminist theorizing over the value of emphasizing a somatic existence has always been central to those scholars who are invested in difference—as visible bodily inscriptions—for ethnic and racial bodies (Lim 1999; hooks 1998; Roof and Wiegman 1995; Mohanty, Russo, and Torres 1991; Anzaldua 1990; Glenn 1986). Certain stereotyped images of the female body may be commodities, but their worldwide circulation as cultural capital can produce damaging material consequences.

Participants uneasy about a reintroduction of the material body fear that a corporeal emphasis will reposition this body within just the biological arguments that resist more complicated views of a dialogically constructed one.[18] This has been especially true for feminist theorists bent on dismantling entrenched concepts of sex and gender, first by destroying their natural or biological inventions, then by illuminating social and dialogic constructions.[19] Furthermore, although the concept of a biologically "natural" racial body has been debunked, there exists a tendency to embrace simple, stereotypical (read: natural) designations and attribute them uncritically. Other debates accused feminists' discursive theorizing of ignoring social and economic factors contributing to gender and race oppression.

The fallout in feminist theory of overlooking "colored" bodies in a so-called white feminist practice, coupled with their dissenters, prohibited narrowly individualized narratives of the minority few from speaking for the many, and the (namely white) many were prohibited from speaking for the few. Far from prohibiting further work, this impasse has conveniently provided me with tools with which to move forward. Female bodies intervene in discursive debates, thus prompting me to ask: Are these bodies a site marking cultural trauma, bearing "the function and burden of cultural memory," as in interviews with Korean, Filipina, and other comfort women?[20] How are state politics enacted on citizens' bodies?[21] To what degree is naming, accepting, or rejecting racial bodies as filthy not merely about the body but rather about what racism itself embodies?[22]

New gendered explorations in Asian American studies revisit women's roles out of urgency as articulations of globalization and transnationalization gesture dangerously toward revisiting a masculinist cultural nationalism.[23] Additionally, consider the circulation of mobile food toxins, passed via international food imports and exports, or the difficulty in finding "suitable" dumping grounds for nations' nuclear trash, which cannot help but categorize trash-receiving communities, as well as citizens of those nations, as less valuable than trash-donating communities. The mobility of filth circulates back to Lim's anxiety over Western bodily images in destructive, transnational circulations. My study examines the troubling and fascinating intersections of body, gender, dirt, and the global as they pertain to shifts within these fields of study and how they might contribute toward new understandings of gender and ethnic identity. My work maps and illuminates concerns over women's bodiliness and impropriety by allowing concepts of dirt to challenge vexing binaries endemic to national and global debates about women's bodies and to work through theoretical impasses.

More current gendered articulations in the field complicate a process of subject formation formerly viewed as a linear trajectory from majority dictation to minority adoption, from white ascription to varying forms of racial resistance, both successful and devastating. Yet the most current readings push the borders of these accepted interpretations of gender and racial formation. The most recent explore not only how culture is analyzed through Asian American literature, but how Asian American literature rereads gender, sexuality, homosexuality, and subject formation (Bow 2001; Eng 2001; Patricia Chu 2000; Wong and Ana 1999; Traise Yamamoto 1999; Eng and Hom 1998). Such work propels Asian American studies from the margins to the mainstream. Coupled with other so-called marginal studies—marginal in both context and within disciplinary perimeters—academic terrain once considered mainstream is re-viewed from refreshing and necessary new angles as in the exploding field of white studies, gender studies (including those in masculinity), and work in transsexuality and transgenderism. That which traditionally has been displaced is earning placement within the changing parameters of the field.

—◊◊◊—

In his discussion of an Asian American "body politic," Viet Thanh Nguyen's response to a "rhetoric of demonization, marginalization, and exclusion" is to acknowledge that "Asian American culture is characterized by this constant tension between American racism's efforts to construct Asians as a singular body and the Asian American response that there are instead multiple ones" (2002:vi, 17). My readings attest to the multiple ways in which Asian American literature responds to the politics of dirt.

Chapter 2 of Chuang Hua's *Crossings* ([1968] 1986) addresses the phenomenon of displacement through the itinerant, but profoundly depressed, protagonist Fourth Jane. She moves physically but is stagnated psychologically within cross-cultural narratives that are encoded by socially ascribed abjection. The chapter also establishes Chuang's transnational character as an apt precursor to globalization and its effects. "Abjection, Displacement, and Psychological Dissonance in Chuang Hua's *Crossings*" is thus a case study of Jane's attempts to cleanse her existence of racial markers, specifically that of her overbearing Chinese father and of his gendered restrictions, at the same time that she is bound to them. The act produces devastating consequences to her agency. Jane lives the "place" of race and gender in an unyielding familial structure and in a stagnating love relationship; she experiences the "place" of deracination as an Asian immigrant in America and as a Chinese émigré in Europe in the 1960s. Chuang's inclusion of Jane's numerous crossings from China to England, then from the United States to Paris and back, reflects her attempt to displace static notions of race and to dismantle herself of the burdens of being a Chinese American woman. Such an endeavor—perhaps even a subversive "betrayal" (invoking the work of Leslie Bow [2001])—takes its toll on Jane, and her perpetual motion, mirrored in the novel's meandering narrative structure, references the intersections rather than the gaps that bind together nations, genders, races, and politics. Her emotional paralysis, which I illuminate through Anne Anlin Cheng's (2000) theory of minority "hypochondria"—a residual melancholic grief—is emblematic of a larger national paralysis.[24] Jane's deracination reverberates with troubling consequences for individual agency.

Kamani's collection of sexually racy stories, *Junglee Girl* (1995), straddles the fine line between socially constructed illness and culturally defined filth, thereby situating this collection as a bridge between Asian America's pathologization and what I deem its present focus on filth. In chapter 3, "Ginu Kamani's Crass, Classed, and Incurable Female Bodies," so-called filthy rites associated with menstrual taboos, women's lust and sexuality, as well as attention to women's breasts, buttocks, and pubic hair, introduce such female "products" as impure and volatile.[25] The fear and loathing of women's bodies in Kamani's story "The Cure," for example, illuminate how natural female maturation is unnaturalized through hyperbole: South Asian character Baby's fantastic growth is diagnostically equated with perverse sexuality. Her aberrant body thus "leaks" beyond, or opposes, accepted patriarchal boundaries and poses a threat to her family's social status, familial interpersonal relations, Baby's marriageability, and, according to her physician, even herself. As a female grotesque, she embodies a fear of women's bodies, an unnaturalizing of the natural. Yet as much as "The Cure" sets the feminist tone for the remainder of Kamani's collection, the stories embedded within its interior mask a classed regulation of female embodiedness. That the stories outline the sexual and daily corporeal functions of Indian cooks, servants, and nannies establishes dirty, somatic necessities as potential class equalizers. But told from the point of view of wealthy employers' daughters, the latters' growing acknowledgment of their powerful place vis-à-vis the hired help establishes a cycle of sexism and classism practiced by women, on women. The stories eventually capitulate to just the paradigms from which Kamani attempts to extricate them, re-miring women in filth. Kamani's work exposes Asian American authors' own vexed positioning within larger social narratives, highlighting an inadvertent self-pollution, here in Kamani's unself-conscious slippage from Asian American cure to an unintended besmirching of the lower classes.

Chapter 4, "Animals and Systems of Dirt in the Novels of Lois-Ann Yamanaka," considers the significance of the many mangy animals that dominate three novels by Local Japanese[26] author Yamanaka: *Wild Meat and the Bully Burgers* (1996), *Blu's Hanging* (1997), and *Heads by Harry* (1999). Hers are not the groomed and manicured pets of the immaculate show dog arena, but the wild boars, feral cats, tick-infested dogs, and taxidermally preserved creatures that share the Hilo, Hawai'i, locale of Yamanaka's Local Japanese, female protagonists. I read the animals, initially, as anthropomorphized and superficial placeholders of race, class, and gender among and between Locals and *haoles* (Whites), both of whom occupy "illegally" partitioned Hawaiian land in a historical reference to its colonization, annexation, and neocolonization. But such a reading becomes increasingly complicated and difficult to sustain in the arenas of taxidermy, dog breeding, and the pets-to-dinner fare of Yamanaka's world, for their material use serves the necessities of food and income. The chapter uses an actual controversy over Euro-Polynesian wild pigs in Hawai'i Volcanoes National Park to make theoretical use of terms such as "natural," "native," and "exotic" within the historically conflicted space of Hawai'i and amid the equally contested Local and *haole* issues surrounding race and class. The pig and all of Yamanaka's animals magnify the Local Japanese protagonists' struggles to balance the cerebral and corporeal halves in an already racially divided community: to conceal, if not purge, constructed notions of contamination and pollution from their everyday existences is, in essence, to disparage their Local Japanese designation and their gender. Far from reading Yamanaka's characters as victims of a system, however, I view animals as enabling them to come to practical terms about economic inequity in their homeland as well as to discover sexual and self-acceptance.

As a transition into chapter 5, "Inside the Meat Machine: Food, Filth, and (In)Fertility in Ruth Ozeki's *My Year of Meats*," I use food prohibitions and pollution in Ruth L. Ozeki's novel (1998), many of which vacillate around the contested binaries of edibility/inedibility or cleanliness/filth. Her novel addresses the pathological consequences of eating tainted beef for two Japanese/American female characters as well as for a host of minor characters.[27] I begin the chapter, via Doris Witt (1998), through a reference to the African American soul food chitterlings, or hog intestines, which retains an unstable qualification as "food." If intestines are the location in which hogs winnow usable protein from waste, or where the good and clean are meticulously separated from filthy excrement, chitterlings straddle a tenuous border embedded in the dividing slash (/) of the binary, a liminal space useful for the novel's many unstable binaries that inform and ground my interpretation: edible/inedible, fertile/infertile, clean/dirty, natural/artificial, true/false, and the inextricable link between the constructed division of men and meat and that of truth and fiction.[28] The chapter answers Sau-ling Wong's invitation to investigate references to food and eating in Asian American literature as ethnogastronomic semiosis and to regard ingestion as "the physical act that mediates between self and not-self, native essence and foreign matter, the inside and the outside" (1993:26).[29]

I conclude *Filthy Fictions* with such racial- and gender-inflected discussions of foodways (Inness 2001; George 2000; Counihan 1999; Scapp and Seitz 1998; Adams 1998) because Ozeki's (1998) emphasis on classed constructions of cuisine speaks to how pathogens have shaped and shadowed not only images and definitions of Asian Americans, but those of minorities in general, in order to forge connections within ethnic studies. Take, for example, the Environmental Protection Agency's 1990 report that promised a closer adherence to issues of environmental justice, citing studies that indicated how much of the nation's toxic wastes have been, and still are, dumped in or near low-income and/or minority neighborhoods. According to Ruth

Rosen, who has traced a history of America's pernicious environmental racism, "poor communities [often a coded phrase meaning raced communities] are disproportionately harmed by industrial toxic pollution and . . . corporations and government . . . build their worst toxic sites and store their most hazardous chemicals in and around these low-income neighborhoods" (1997:64).[30] Robert D. Bullard's *Dumping in Dixie* concentrates on how African American communities in the South are considered "throw away communities" (2000:xvi). "[B]ecause of their economic and political vulnerabilities, they have been routinely targeted for the siting of noxious facilities. . . . People in these communities, in turn, are likely to suffer greater environmental and health risks than in the general population" (2000:xv). Such a calculated inclusion of minorities—other than Asian Americans—and their polluted status at my project's conclusion invites forays into a necessary "literary transethnicity."[31] Therefore, I anticipate future collaboration among scholars of ethnic studies interested in investigating how cultural fictions can become biological and social facts, how the abjected becomes the adopted norm—a conduit for pathologizing and dirtying others.

I intend to expose the deceptive simplicity between concepts such as ill and healthy or clean and dirty within disciplinary borders in the fields of feminist theory, ethnic studies, and global studies in order to expose how scholars and writers have sanitized ethnic experience. Further, my analysis of the provocative concept of filthy fictions within a collection of Asian American texts by and about women that have received little critical attention provides an original and contrapuntal view to those who may deem this investigation a dangerous foray into debilitation. Others might consider the project's premise a wholesale reduction of the ethnic subject to illness and pollution, to suffering and invalidity.[32] On the other hand, I agree with Sheng-mei Ma's simple and efficacious statement that "in order to retire racist stereotypes, one is obliged first to evoke them" (2000:xi).[33] The ruminations these stereotypes generate about a body's value, and in what context and by what existing racial-, sexual-, or class-based paradigms,[34] unfold in a collection of Asian American novels where the female body is circumscribed by rules of belonging. In essence, these Asian American bodies matter deeply, to borrow from Judith Butler, as a reminder of how abstract political concerns play themselves out on concrete, somatic existences.[35]

Notes

1. While filth references moral implications and dirt does not, I use the terms interchangeably.

2. I refer specifically to Douglas's discussion of dirt in the chapter "Secular Defilement," where she states,

> If we can abstract pathogenicity and hygiene from our notion of dirt, we are left with the old definition of dirt as matter out of place. This is a very suggestive approach. It implies two conditions: a set of ordered relations and a contravention of that order. Dirt then, is never a unique, isolated event. Where there is dirt there is system. Dirt is the by-product of a systematic ordering and classification of matter, in so far as ordering involves rejecting inappropriate elements. This idea of dirt takes us straight into the field of symbolism and promises a link-up with more obviously symbolic systems of purity." (1980:35)

Robert G. Lee, in *Orientals: Asian Americans in Popular Culture*, also references Douglas's notion of pollution as "[m]ere presence in the wrong place" (1999:2–3): "Orientals represent a present danger of pollution. An analysis of the Oriental as a racial category must begin with the concept of the alien as a polluting body" (p. 2).

3. See Nayan Shah's (2001) *Contagious Divides: Epidemics and Race in San Francisco's Chinatown*.

4. "[R]acial stereotypes have been linked with images of pathology, especially psychopathology," from the mid-nineteenth century, says Sander L. Gilman in his *Difference and Pathology: Stereotypes of Sexuality, Race, and Madness* (1985:129). Gilman explains how medicine, a field perceived to be founded on objective fact and thus substantially fortified against critique, helped establish a pathology of race. Medical essays in the mid-1800s, for example, documented a disease called "Drapetomania," which was claimed a biological cause of slaves' desire to run away (p. 138). In addition, the "discovery" of the illness "dysaethesia aethiopis" explained acts of slave "rascality" (p. 138) and in

the 1840s, statistics proved the predominance of insanity in free Blacks to be "eleven times higher" than in Whites (p. 137), which encouraged white supremacists to extrapolate that the preservation of the institution of slavery would spare the entire nation emotional and monetary burdens of caring for freed, "crazy" Blacks (p. 138). Jews, Gilman continues, were also diagnosed as exhibiting disproportionately higher instances of madness than Whites. Anti-Semitic explanations attributed Jewish mental infirmity to their "cosmopolitanism"—pressures of their professions—and their racial inbreeding, which manifested themselves in deviant sexuality (p. 154). Such narratives critiqued Jewish self-exclusion and their perceived economic success.

5. Arthur B. Stout is quoted in Ronald Takaki's *Iron Cages: Race and Culture in 19th-Century America* (1991:219).

6. "Indeed, early germ theory was intermixed with racial, anti-immigrant, and xenophobic rhetoric" says John Kuo Wei Tchen, and "the call [by the federal government] to protect the national body politic from the attack of the impending 'Yellow Peril' proved potent" (1994:18).

7. Marilyn Thornton Williams, in *Washing "The Great Unwashed": Public Baths in Urban America, 1840–1920*, mentions the influence of "the water cure craze of the 1840s and 1850s, which reinforced the association between bathing and health" (1991:12). Williams reports that health care workers began emphasizing the necessity for both water and soap in the mid-1800s, but it was not until the 1890s that "most Americans had come to believe, as we do today, that the desire to be clean was almost innate and that to go without bathing for any length of time voluntarily was inconceivable and repugnant" (1991:5–6). For other supporting materials, see Martin V. Melosi's *Pollution and Reform in American Cities, 1870–1930* (1980); Alain Corbin's *The Foul and the Fragrant: Odor and the French Social Imagination* (1986); Suellen Hoy's *Chasing Dirt: The American Pursuit of Cleanliness* (1995); Georges Vigarello's *Concepts of Cleanliness: Changing Attitudes in France since the Middle Ages* (1988); Lawrence Wright's *Clean and Decent: The Fascinating History of the Bathroom and the Water Closet* (1960); and George Ryley Scott's *The Story of Baths and Bathing* (1939).

8. See Hoy's subchapter in *Chasing Dirt*, "The Domestic Woman, Agent of Cleanliness" (1995:15–19).

9. Hoy focuses on Eastern European immigrants whose categorization as diseased and dirty—an ideology of cleanliness embraced by female social workers and educational and sanitarian leaders—was far more benign than that ascribed to Chinese immigrants. Cleanliness be-

came "the American way," Hoy discovers. See her chapter "The American Way" (1995:87–121). Also see Juliann Sivulka's (2001) book *Stronger Than Dirt: A Cultural History of Advertising Personal Hygiene in America, 1875–1940* for a cultural trajectory of cleanliness in American advertising.

10. Quoted in Annette White-Parks, *Sui Sin Far/Edith Maude Eaton: A Literary Biography* (1995:2). She speaks of "the 'Yellow Peril' literature popular in [Eaton's] era" (p. 1). For plot summaries of much Yellow Peril literature, see William F. Wu, *The Yellow Peril: Chinese Americans in American Fiction 1850–1940* (1982).

11. Amy Ling considers Helen Clark's *The Lady of the Lily Feet and Other Tales of Chinatown*, published around 1900. Ling suggests that Clark, armed with missionary intentions, illuminated the cruelty of Chinese footbinding, the immorality of Chinese opium addiction, and the enslavement of Chinese women by Chinese men in prostitution rings. Clark, according to Ling, intimated that these combined atrocities demanded a form of white Christian succor for their Chinese perpetrators (1990:48). For William Wu, Atwell Whitney's *Almond-Eyed: The Great Agitator; a Story of the Day* (1878) depicted the "solid heathenism" of Chinatown immigrants and illuminated "the concept of the Chinese contaminating [the fictional] Yarbtown . . . [which] grows into a noxious hilltop slum, with a stream of refuse rolling down toward Aristocracy Street" (1982:31–32).

12. See Robert G. Lee's *Orientals: Asian Americans in Popular Culture* (1999).

13. Shah's *Contagious Divides* (2001) is an apt example of a recent, scholarly revisitation of the Yellow Peril in order to excavate how Chinese American activists, up to the mid-twentieth century, rallied against their communities' constricting pathological designations and for their full, civic inclusion within U.S. society.

14. I use Diane Price Herndl's notion of "invalid," signifying women's illness and invalidity, in her *Invalid Women: Figuring Feminine Illness in American Fiction and Culture, 1840–1940* (1993).

15. Robert Joseph Priest discusses dirt as "cultural symbolism" (1993:567).

16. The backdrop for my arguments arises in the context of persistently shifting categories and connotations of race and gender in American discourse, categories that routinely organize the boundaries of valid, embodied social constituency. "[R]ace is not a category of nature," an idea amply delineated in cultural studies, feminist studies, and multicultural studies; "it is an ideology through which unequal

distributions of wealth and power are naturalized," says Robert G. Lee (1999:2). As Michael Omi and Howard Winant state, it is not something to which we are born, but rather what we learn: "Race becomes 'common sense'—a way of comprehending, explaining and acting in the world" (1994:62).

17. Take the seemingly positive myth of the model minority, in which the celebratory status of Asian Americans as hardworking, educated social exemplars conceal biased policymakers' ulterior motives of upholding "good" Asian Americans against other "bad" ethnic minorities. That is, there exists a concern about Asian American bodies in the disjunction between their "enjoyment" of model minority status and the fact that Asian American intellect has never eclipsed historical stereotypes surrounding their bodily presence as a threat. The recent rescinding of affirmative action policies at universities in California and Texas belies a current strain of the Yellow Peril: even though Asians and Asian Americans have been tethered, of late, to the brain drain, they remain a bodily threat to white admissions and to the overall fair operability of these campuses. Proposition 187, an anti-immigration policy proposed only ten months after governmental approval of the January 1994 North American Free Trade Agreement, illuminates the nation's oxymoronic stance between "transnationalism on the one hand, and xenophobic retrenchment on the other," states Stacy Takacs (1999:592). Popular culture also reifies the so-called unassimilability of Asian American bodies. Consider the racist narratives manufactured over John Huang's political contributions to the Clinton campaign and spying allegations against Wen Ho Lee.

18. Of the burgeoning literature that complicates the divide between biomedical and cultural interpretations of the body, I suggest Julia Epstein's *Altered Conditions: Disease, Medicine, and Storytelling* (1995) and Kathryn Montgomery Hunter's *Doctors' Stories: The Narrative Structure of Medical Knowledge* (1991).

19. For more on this debate, see anthologies such as Katie Conboy, Nadia Medina, and Sarah Stanbury's *Writing on the Body: Female Embodiment and Feminist Theory* (1997); Elizabeth Grosz's *Volatile Bodies: Toward a Corporeal Feminism* (1994); and Janet Price and Margrit Shildrick's *Feminist Theory and the Body: A Reader* (1999).

20. Quoted from Wendy S. Hesford (2001:x). She discusses the "material body as a site marked by the trauma of cultural and national conflicts" (p. ix).

21. See Amy K. Kaminsky's *Reading the Body Politic: Feminist Criticism and Latin American Women Writers* (1993:xv).

22. Gloria Anzaldua (1990).

23. See Rachel C. Lee's *The Americas of Asian American Literature: Gendered Fictions of Nation and Transnation* (1999:10).

24. Other invalid characters in Asian American literature (among a proliferation) include Mrs. Yamada of John Okada's *No-No Boy* ([1957] 1976) whose untenable position as a fanatic Japanese nationalist after World War II in an anti-Japanese country prompts her depression and eventual suicide; Wendy Law-Yone's central, unnamed character in *The Coffin Tree* (1983) emigrates from the political turmoil of Myanmar to the United States in the 1970s, falls into poverty, and attempts suicide; Mrs. Oka, from Wakako Yamauchi's "And the Soul Shall Dance" ([1966] 1994) is forced into an arranged marriage with a man she does not love, becomes an immigrant to the hardscrabble farm life of America's dusty West, and remains childless, eventually becoming an alcoholic; and Holly Uyemoto's *Go* (1995) maps the recovery of a Japanese American woman after severe depression and her conflicted relationship with a post-internment camp mother.

25. I borrow the term "volatile" and its attendant meanings, as well as the sense of a body "leaking" from its borders, from Elizabeth Grosz's *Volatile Bodies* (1994:viii).

26. For an excellent discussion about what Local means, the ideologies surrounding these meanings, as well as the conflicts involved in maintaining them, see Jonathan Y. Okamura (1980). I thank Michael Oishi for refining debates concerning Natives, Locals, and Caucasians (private correspondence, September 24, 2001). Also see Edna Bonacich (1984).

27. I use the slash (/) in Japanese/American to denote that the character Akiko in Ozeki's novel relocates from Japan to the States at the novel's conclusion, thus she is not strictly Japanese American. Such complicated categorization illuminates recent debates in Asian American studies concerning if and how to "denationalize" its borders amid theoretical discussions and economic considerations over globalization and transnationalism (see, for example, Wong's "Denationalization Reconsidered" [1995], Koshy's "The Fiction of Asian American Literature" [2000], and Ma's *Immigrant Subjectivities* [1998]).

28. See Doris Witt's "Soul Food: Where the Chitterling Hits the (Primal) Pan" (1998).

29. See Sau-ling C. Wong's chapter "Big Eaters, Treat Lovers, 'Food Prostitutes,' 'Food Pornographers,' and Doughnut Makers" in her *Reading Asian American Literature: From Necessity to Extravagance* (1993:18–76).

30. Rosen cites black, Latino, Native American, and low-income white communities in her study. Is her exclusion of low-income Asian American neighborhoods indicative of an inherent model minority mentality?

31. I borrow this term from Kathleen Brogan, who discusses the use of ghosts in ethnic literature through such transethnic affiliations in her *Cultural Haunting: Ghosts and Ethnicity in Recent American Literature* (1998:27). For Timothy Burke's fascinating work on the "critical nexus for the intimate interpenetration of race, bodies, and hygiene" as a "distinctive aspect of colonial racism," see his *Lifebuoy Men, Lux Women: Commodification, Consumption, and Cleanliness in Modern Zimbabwe* (1996:20, 21). See Megan Vaughan's *Curing Their Ills: Colonial Power and African Illness* (1991) on biomedicine's construction of African subjects and their ills, or, the social construction of medical knowledge, and Deepika Bahri's "Disembodying the Corpus: Postcolonial Pathology in Tsitsi Dangarembga's *Nervous Condition*" (1994).

32. Others critical of my project may ask, like Rey Chow, "what politics is in play" when academics discuss the term "ethnic"? (1998:100). Chow takes issue with the current institutionalization of multiculturalism, which she finds unfortunately dedicated to "liberating" a repressed ethnicity from ethnic texts. My critical praxis is not complicit in such a plot. Rather, I find that her argument begs pressing questions that are relevant to my work: Why was ethnicity suppressed in the first place and by whom—the ethnic Other or the society othering that other that have promoted just the conditions that advocate its reappearance?

33. Furthermore, the "'futures' of American studies" depend on interrogating a history of Asian American "racialized immigration," according to Lisa Lowe (1998), which "highlights the convergence of nationalism with racial exclusion, gendered social stratification, and labor exploitation" (pp. 29, 30).

34. Important to this argument is a rapidly emerging body of work about queer Asian America that destroys established borders and boundaries of ethnicity, sex/gender, and heteronormativity. See, for example, David L. Eng and Alice Hom's *Q&A: Queer in Asian America* (1998); Eng's *Racial Castration* (2001); Russell Leong's *Asian American Sexualities: Dimensions of the Gay and Lesbian Experience* (1996); Sharon Lim-Hing's *The Very Inside: An Anthology of Writing by Asian and Pacific Islander Lesbian and Bisexual Women* (1994); and Prakesh Ratti's *A Lotus of Another Color: An Unfolding of the South Asian Lesbian and Gay Experience* (1993).

35. That Asian American bodies matter in the field of criticism is evident in this very recent spate of related publications: see much of David Palumbo-Liu's *Asian/American: Historical Crossings of a Racial Frontier* (1999); Shah's *Contagious Divides*; Lee's *The Americas of Asian American Literature* (2001); Traise Yamamoto's *Making Selves, Making Subjects: Japanese American Women, Identity, and the Body* (1999); Leslie Bow's *Betrayal and Other Acts of Subversion: Feminism, Sexual Politics, Asian American Women's Literature* (2001); Viet Thanh Nguyen's *Race and Resistance: Literature and Politics in Asian America* (2002); and Sunaina Maira's *Desis in the House: Indian American Youth Culture in New York City* (2002).

2

Abjection, Displacement, and Psychological Dissonance in Chuang Hua's *Crossings*

Filthy Fictions takes as its premise the abjected, rejected, defiled, or in-validated women of contemporary Asian American literature. Their self- and societal rejection is brought about via the dominant population's need for "cultural and national homogeneity," according to David Lloyd, which necessitates rooting out a contamination "from an original essence, the recovery of which is the crucial prerequisite to the culture's healthy and normative development."[1] The process of alienating others, as in the case of Asian Americans, is understood as a cultural re-authentication based on fictions about a pure essence, which I will take up in chapter 5 regarding food pollution, race, and gender; or it exemplifies a societal establishment via a rejection of who we think we are not. According to David Leiwei Li, Asian American subjectivity is marked by alienation and what he deems "Asian abjection" (1998:6). Society has named Asian otherness as one particular, even necessary, defilement against which to promote its own fictitious purity. Thus, the Asian American self constitutes and establishes itself by "willfully discard[ing]" aspects of itself that are on "the other side of the border, the place where I am not and which permits me to be," Li quotes Julia Kristeva (Li 1998:6). The Asian American abject is, therefore, an essential social product driving the construction of a dominant self and, in its wake, producing the negative construction of an Asian American self. The existence of the latter provides the possibility of the former, contributing to the "in/out position of the Asian American abject, as formal nationals and cultural aliens" (Li 1998:12).

Chuang Hua's *Crossings* ([1968] 1986) presents the consequences of racial and gender abjection through the character Fourth Jane. Extra-textually, the novel's position within Asian American studies illustrates the field's own negotiation with (literary) acceptance and reception, an issue I address below. Despite the frequency with which Jane crosses international borders, alluding to the novel's title, the book is freighted by the protagonist's unsettled grieving, or what I deem a pronounced depression, a malady rising from her national, community, familial, and identificatory placement within arenas of abjection. "On certain days," writes Chuang, "moving from one room to another in her apartment was the only displacement she felt capable of undertaking" (1986:116). Jane is unable to transgress boundaries that define and confine her as a woman, a Chinese American, an émigré, a daughter, and a lover. Bound by the deleterious effects of constantly accommodating cultural and familial expectations, Jane is unmoored in both body and psyche, crossing and recrossing international boundaries trying to find a place of belonging. Her embodiment of multiple identities provides her with no solace, roundly defying poststructural views of a subject's ability to cross and recross borders and remain psychologically unscathed. By the novel's end, Chuang presents no resolution to Jane's state, leaving unanswered questions of her state of health and any possible cure. Coupled with the difficulty of the novel's form, the book resists a coherent conclusion in which loose ends are tied up and identity issues are neatly resolved. Such a conclusion, however, is indicative of and highly apropos to the complexity of these issues that have always defied, and should defy, any easy resolution.

At the same time, scant academic attention to the novel illuminates other, extra-textual issues associated with notions of belonging that are significant to the field of Asian American studies. Even though the field eagerly embraces challenging texts that address women's identity in flux, exemplified in the flood of academic praise garnered by Theresa Hak Kyung Cha's eclectic *Dictée* (1995), Chuang's novel (equally fascinating in form and character) has generated little pedagogical attention or criticism, either in print or at academic conferences. In spite of its concentration on form-as-function, its complicated uses of memory, its depiction of the personal toll that cultural assimilation and resistance take, and its emphasis on gender, race, and deracination, *Crossings* has remained obscure after its initial 1968 Dial Press printing followed by its 1986 Northeastern University Press republication. In other words, the novel itself is bound by and to the *place* that academia creates for fiction that falls within or outside the purview of what is considered accessible and what is deemed appropriate material for the (Asian American) academic mill. The novel offers plenty of grist for this mill, especially in its unusually difficult form, one that critics have attributed to Chuang's modernist leanings.[2] Modernism often has been chastised as a masculine form privileging an elite class. This grates against readings that invoke a form's fluidity and disjunction as a type of female prose (here I reference not only the work of French feminists such as Luce Irigaray [1985], Hélène Cixous [1991], and Julia Kristeva [1982], but also that of bell hooks [1984], Gloria Anzaldua [1990], Cherríe Moraga [1983], and Trinh T. Minh-ha [1989], all of whom promote certain types of feminist reading practices). Or, Asian American studies, which may pride itself on reading the literature of an oft-overlooked group of writers, practices similar acts of elision in bypassing important works such as Chuang's. Similar to my attempts in chapter 3 to reposition Kamani's *Junglee Girl* (1995) as a collection containing pressing and important insights for American and Asian American studies, so I urge a reconsideration of *Crossings*.

Jane's locutionary experiences—the novel catalogues "seven crossings of the ocean and four cultural changes," states Amy Ling (1982:30)—exemplify a larger realm of Asian Americans' continued displacement, from their forced and voluntary immigration—especially in the late 1800s, which resulted from employment restrictions—to changes in economic class.[3] While the parameters of racial acceptance are often defined by the state for its raced constituents who live and negotiate in a constructed, national space, *Crossings* illuminates a tropic sense of racial dislocation. On the one hand, Chuang's novel encompasses how circumstances of dislocation affect individuality, or how the individual is interpolated by the terrains through which she moves. On the other, Jane's decisions and movements are attempts to undermine a paradigmatic sense of national, ethnic, and patriarchal order. What Ling deems her "emotional and physical torpor" arises from Jane's efforts to achieve self-individualization in her father's regimented Chinese American family (Ling 1986:4). Jane's turmoil is echoed by Kingston's protagonist in *Woman Warrior*: "Chinese-Americans, when you try to understand what things in you are Chinese, how do you separate what is peculiar to childhood, to poverty, to insanities, one family, your mother who marked your growing with stories, from what is Chinese? What is Chinese tradition and what is the movies?" (5–6). The difficulty of choosing one's alliances, or even distinguishing choice from what is dictated, is symptomatic of the national, cultural, and political hierarchies that bind and define individuality. As Wendy Ho states, they represent "the complicated struggles women confront in naming desire, self, and community" (1999:22). Yet how and to what degree can the abjected individual impact established place and form? And is relocation *as* deracination a betrayal of one's race? This chapter addresses such questions arising from social and self-abjection as they play out in Jane's numerous displacements.

—\\\\—

As a Chinese émigré in America via England, Jane's personal and national loyalties have been harmoniously and securely embedded in the microcosm of family, carefully groomed by its domineering patriarch, Dyadya, or father. However, family loyalties eventually divide over her brother James's marriage to a white woman, or a "barbarian" as the family has been taught to regard Caucasians. With the birth of their son, Dyadya revises his racist codes and eventually accepts the grandson and James's wife as family. Jane is enraged at her father's unfathomable inconsistency amid his usual implacable strictness and his request that Jane, too, accept her new sister-in-law. In anger, she relocates from America to France, where she agonizes about the mutually exclusive union of a traditional Chinese family, demanding female obedience, and her personal desires to be an independent woman unfettered by Dyadya's dictates. In her rebellion, she wonders if, in her haste to leave home, she has reacted against a so-called innate and abjected Chinese self by criticizing the strictures of her heritage. In an uncalculated defiance against Dyadya, she takes a white Parisian lover who is both an Orientalist and an adulterer.[4] Chuang presents a paradoxical tension between Jane's desire to be freed of personal ties while simultaneously embracing that which she rejects.

Jane attempts to remove herself from, and remove from herself, those familial, national, and even racial moorings that she finds debilitating. Yet fierce emotional ties, and even more so her visible racial markings, prevent any easy dissolution of her past. Jane is suspended between anger at and love for her judgmental family, between deracination and others' categorization of her as Oriental. That which abjection demands she cast off is also that which constitutes her subjectivity. Her desire for individuation cannot be freed from cultural baggage. She therefore belongs neither at home nor away from it. The title of Chuang's *Crossings* announces just this tension between embracing and rejecting places and abstractions of identity. Jane is both the Asian American formal national and the cultural alien named by David Leiwei Li (1998).

Crossings' fluid form is itself an unusual play on and with nonlinear literary space that supports readings of the character's, the text's, and ethnic identity's displacement. *Crossings* references actual geographical locations as Jane travels from one continent to another. Yet each new location is only vaguely distinct, demanding that the reader work to disentangle "here" from "there" in the book's stream of ordered and chaotic life experiences, where Jane's memories, unfolding at revelatory instances, confuse or blend those experiences occurring in one location with those that occur within another. Additionally, Chuang's prose allows colorful but sharply contrasting detail to resound with meaning as well as to transport the reader across emotional landscapes, fusing events that may have occurred at different times and in varying locations. The results are confusing but nonetheless effective in exemplifying a type of psychological dissonance. Take the passage in which mourners at a funeral "filed out of the room past curtained windows of flowery chintz and chintz-upholstered armchairs, descended the narrow stairs carpeted in red and emerged into sharp wind and brilliant sunshine" (1986:35). While the flowered curtains and chintz chairs reflect a domestic realm of safety and comfort (an arena connoting "home"), the sudden and uncomfortable confrontation of the wind's sharp edges and the sun's blinding light sublate one mood for another: contentment for a piercing grief, domestic familiarity with death's remoteness. Life's unexpectedly sharp edges prevent the characters from sinking into emotional complacency. In keeping with the novel's unsettling qualities, the already unconventional narrative is interrupted by horrific images—bloated bodies clogging waterways, torture victims flayed alive—that recall past events committed in Jane's former home, China, from which the family has emigrated. They introduce the element of trauma, itself a mediation on how past atrocities negatively impact and continuously disrupt an individual's present psychology.

In fact, the entire novel exists uneasily on shifting grounds, allowing neither protagonist nor reader to rest as it undulates on a current of conflict.[5] In its challenging prose style, it demands that the reader decipher, at every turn, what the novel narrates in the present and what the protagonist remembers from her past and where these events have taken place. Its vague temporal and spatial cues, sudden interruptions of pleasant images by displaced violent memories, and juxtaposition of brilliant colors laid against sharp sounds all represent a type of literary motion that mimics Jane's psychological dissonance.

It is no wonder, then, that if readers are consistently denied emotional complacency, Jane remains entirely ungrounded in the novel's locutionary flux, a direct parallel to her unmitigated consternation over identity. The family has been successfully transplanted from China to England, at unspecified times, and finally emigrates to America for unstated reasons; they have not returned to China in over twenty years. Chuang couples the instability of self-placement with the ways in which place attempts to fashion identity. In Jane's individual displacement (crossing from America to Paris as a Chinese), she lives cross-cultural narratives about the "place" of gender in an unyielding familial structure and in a stagnating love relationship, as well as the "place" of a Chinese émigré in Europe in the 1960s. In many ways, the novel is Chuang's artistic attempt to displace static notions of the "place" of race—its place of abjection—through a disobedient Chinese daughter and her overbearing Chinese father.[6] Jane both accepts and refuses her named places through emotional mechanisms that are as ethereal as memory and as solid as the lived pressures she encounters from family and lover. Not knowing one's place—or knowing and remaining resistant to its adoption—engenders intense internal and external friction. In Jane, they prod a paradoxical coupling of motion and stagnation, of aggressive psychic locution and passive corporeal submission. It is no wonder that she attempts to separate herself from elements of racial and gender rejection.

In this dynamic *place* of emotional frisson, Jane lives intensely within stagnation. It is this juncture of numerous crossings that I want to investigate as related to Jane's psychic wounds prompted out of infidelity to her (patriarchal) heritage and a concomitant yearning for (male) acceptance amid the waning desires of her lover. After a brief historical survey of the lay of the novel's political land, my interpretation begins with a careful analysis of Dyadya's debilitating control in the architectural engineering of his so-called human extensions (his children), articulated in language that is representative of his penchant for exactitude in form, function, thought, and deed. The specter of her father embodied by her lover constructs a condition whose seeming distance between duty and desire map similar territories of restriction and confinement. Jane's belated apology to her father, who is deceased by the end of the book, and her decision to terminate her relationship with her lover raises more questions than answers about resolution and reconciliation, whereby my reading is again a displacement, here of easy resolution.

The novel's schizophrenia, a word I use cautiously as a metaphoric reference to the multiple forms that nationality can take, is attributed to the political events and national attitudes leading up to and defining *Crossings'* 1960s time frame. As meticulously outlined by Robert G. Lee (1999), World War II set the stage for national, moral conflict. On the one hand, the Allies condemned the Nazis' ruthless ethnic cleansing; on the other, the U.S. incarceration of over 120,000 Japanese Americans (dubbed "enemy aliens") underscored the contradictions between U.S. beliefs and its actions (Lee 1999:145–46). Such an ironic stance was exacerbated by the ongoing discriminatory treatment of Blacks, still separate and unequal, whose "containment" in the army only undermined the government's proclamation that "Why We Fight" rested on the elimination of the racial superiority practiced by Hitler's Nazis (Lee 1999:149). While the Yellow Peril often lumped all Asians as threats, the end of World War II marked a dizzyingly complex categorization of "good" and "bad" Asians, based on factors such as the release of traumatized Japanese Americans who had been interned on the West Coast, "postwar Japan" as "America's junior partner [while] the People's Republic of China became its principal enemy," China's immersion in the Korean War, the hunt for "Red" Chinese in American communities during which the FBI enlisted cooperation from the "pro-Chiang Kai-shek Chinatown elite," thereby pitting many Chinese Americans against each other (Lee 1999:148, 152). Included in this messy terrain of conditional ethnic acceptance was a series of bills surrounding Asian immigration: the repeal of both the Chinese Exclusion Act (instigated in 1882 and barring most Chinese immigrants from entry) and the Asiatic Barred Zone (passed in 1917, which limited immigration of those from the Philippines and South Asia), and the 1952 McCarran-Walter Immigration and Naturalization Act, which opened up Asian immigration.

Amid this imbalance of acceptance of and resistance to the Other, Lee discusses the rise of the Model Minority Myth, a persistent fable of ethnic assimilation that inaccurately assessed Asian silence (especially Japanese American silence) as thoughtful acquiescence to American values while it pitted so-called

Asian success against an increase in black reliance on welfare (1999:150–151). This consternation over the minority question complicates the status of the Asian immigrant woman. The War Brides Act of 1945 had already invited the immigration of many Filipina wives of American GIs to enact what Lee calls the "Americanization of the Asian war bride—Orientalism domesticated" (1999:162).[7] By the 1960s and 1970s, an era of revolution and revision was ushered in with the rise of the Civil Rights, Black Power, women's, and antiwar movements. These conflicting currents exposing how national repression contested individual expression render characters' so-called contradictory actions in *Crossings* part and parcel of the norm. If Dyadya's attitude, for example toward James's wife, is a "perverse product of racism in the form of ethnic pride," says Shu-yan Li (1993:99), that works to self-alienate, or deracinate, the family, it is no different from the nation's perverse inclusion of some racial constituents at the same moment it excludes others. Similarly, Jane's racist adherence to Dyadya's anti-Anglo teaching reflects a nation's inability to unlearn the racist narratives it has written over time. If a national process of becoming is fraught with progression and regression, as well as attachment and detachment, so, too, is Jane's search for individuality from coerced conformity.

Through the use of a timepiece Dyadya gives to Jane, the novel's major themes arise: time, represented by the round face of the watch as it fuses past, present, and future; the importance of family lineage as it is circumscribed by cultural inheritance; the irrepressible presence of Dyadya as the crucible of Jane's actions; and the physical and psychological spaces of Jane's journeying.[8] "[Jane] glanced at her watch, a round gold face with thin round numerals which Dyadya had bought on a holiday in Geneva the summer of 1938" (p. 7). Dyadya, a medical doctor by training whose current stateside position is grounded in finance and the stock market, uses the exactitude—represented by the Swiss watch—in both professions in a prescriptive arrangement of his Chinese family. Borrowing numerical accuracy from his financial position, he orders family chaos numerically as a means to arrange his own head and heart: "*Account 595223.* . . . Completely out of the running in this system of balances and counterbalances I have devised over the years to maintain harmony and equilibrium between the head and my extensions and the extensions among themselves" (pp. 176–177, emphasis in original).

Both James and Jane, two of these extensions, have tipped his carefully calculated family equilibrium, the former by marrying a "barbarian," the latter by adamantly refusing to accept her, despite Dyadya's eventual heartfelt capitulation to the white wife after she produces a grandson. For Jane has adopted Dyadya's adamant articulations against biracial unions. Dyadya's debilitating *control* overshadows a useful, yet still organized *guidance*, for the seven children are fortified by Chinese custom in spite of their itinerant globetrotting. The children, for example, are named numerically by birth order, typical of Chinese families: First Nancy Chen-Hua, Second Katherine Kwang-Hua, Third Christine Tswai-Hua, Fourth Jane Chuang-Hua, Fifth James Chuang-Shin, Sixth Michael Chuang-Chu, and Seventh Jill Lo-Hua (p. 31). Birthright organizes the siblings by age and gender: "Nancy you are my firstborn and you are to lead Dyadya said. James you are my firstborn son and you are to lead" (pp. 57–58). According to Amy Ling, "Jane's middle position . . . its very centrality . . . makes it vulnerable to pulls from both ends: the responsibility of the older child as well as the deference and dependence of the younger sibling" (1982:30). Additionally, says Ling, Fourth Jane Chuang-Hua belongs "in name both to the male attribute [in the male name Chuang, denoting patrilineage] and the female [in the given name Hua]" (Chuang 1986:31).[9] Jane will be shaped by female prescriptives from which she attempts a masculine form of escape—leaving home.[10] As well, her Western inscription ("Jane") chafes against an Eastern one ("Chuang Hua"), as father and lover demand mutually exclusive assumptions about the nature of fidelity and that of ethnic affiliation. The conflicting elements of Jane's namesake mirror seemingly irreconcilable extremes: family bonds and female independence, Chinese strictures and American affiliations, national expectations and personal allegiances. Furthermore, the children are educated to respect patriarchal authority ("Listen to me I am your father and I know what is right for you. . . . How dare you question me! I am Father I can do no wrong" [pp. 195–196]) and insulated against "barbarians" despite a life among white neighbors in an unspecified U.S. location. "Dyadya," writes Chuang, "kept his First and all his rest in self-raging love and self-sweet bondage" (p. 57).

Most essential to the children's sturdy growth are their Chinese roots, planted carefully yet firmly in three different types of soil: Chinese, English, and American. The novel is filled with references to roots, transplantation, and growth: "They scattered wet [lichee] peels and stones in the gutters as they strolled through the dusk crowded neon-lit streets of the Chinese quarter, silently following Dyadya who led the way" (p. 17). The discarded rinds represent those aspects of the *new* American culture they are requested to reject ("barbarians" and their customs being exemplary) as they suck the meat of this Eastern fruit and wander, literally and figuratively, through the *old* culture of Chinatown. "Dyadya said imagine the Chinese have brought the lichee tree to America and have planted it in American soil," alluding to his own family's transplantation and his own fierce decisions regarding where and how his children should take root (p. 17).

Dyadya's myopic view prohibits an adaptation of Chinese customs to an American environment, thus promoting the personal struggles his acculturating family experiences. When James marries a white woman, crossing his Chinese roots with her Anglo ones, the son commits the ultimate act of familial betrayal. Chuang's description of the incident references internment, enclosure, and illicit entrance: "The barbarian stood outside the barred gates of the wall. After fruitless years of patient search, with gnawing heart, she found a weakness along the immense wall encircling the garden, found, followed, married Fifth James and entered the garden at dusk" (p. 50).

Allusions to walls—their solidity, their defense, their ability to crumble—bolster the novel's literal and figurative definitions of groomed space. Shu-yan Li presents an interesting exegesis of "architectural closure" through a discussion of a record that Jane plays of "a famous Chinese opera based on a story from the classic *Romance of the Three Kingdoms*," in which the military wit of one commander-in-chief, concerning the defense of the city walls and gates, effectively staves off an impending city siege (Li 1993:107). The recorded opera plays in the background, while Jane and her lover debate the inevitable conclusion of their affair, the opera's events resonating with their present circumstances. Li writes:

> Read in this context, the opera is the projection of Jane's mental activities. Under a calm surface, she is experiencing a violent inner struggle. Her mind and ethnic pride tell her to end the relationship, but her heart yearns for the man. When the opera comes to its end, proclaiming the successful defense of the city, Jane declares that she wants to return home to the United States, thus disengaging herself from the affair. Given her perspective on her brother's marriage (infiltration), it seems that she has just played a war of wits with the unsuspecting Frenchman [who intimates another infiltration] and, unlike her brother, has successfully defended the purity of the family. (p. 107)

Indicative of Dyadya's penchant for order—self, familial, and professional—is an office with neatly stacked piles of newspapers and magazines, wall-to-wall bookcases arranged according to subject matter, a desk drawer holding "documents and papers such as certificates of medical studies . . . assorted travel documents, and official papers, military decrees" along with "watches purchased in Geneva, cameras, old sturdy Parker fountain pens, stamps and paper clips, a rubber doll . . . a thank-you note . . . his Zeiss microscope" (pp. 71–72). The collection references those brands deemed superior: a Zeiss microscope, a Parker pen, and a Swiss watch and camera. They illustrate his worldliness and his intelligence.[11] Likewise, his children receive French, piano, and dance instructions. But the aforementioned objects also refer to his limited vision. For if other cultures produce perfection, what is his resistance to intercultural alliances, to the "barbarian" from whom he protects and forbids his children? It is not surprising that Jane attempts to unclutter her life of things and objects, an inheritance of orderliness, once in Paris where she has self-exiled "to rest, to remove myself from ties for the moment" (p. 121). She seeks a place with "white walls and not too much furniture" in contrast to her family home's "mantel [that] is crowded with . . . a carved miniature table of teak and ebony and rosewood on top of which rests a miniature silver melon with stem leaves and vines. There is a measuring tape encased in silver, a French crystal vase etched all over with vines, picture cards . . . [and] a soapstone bust" (pp. 11, 170). Physical objects are nonetheless replaced by a myriad of mental obstructions that crowd her thoughts and hinder her daily movement.

Spatial arrangement, as a trope for family control, occurs in the strategic placement of Dyadya's living room chair from which he is able to observe the entrance hall as well as the corridor into the children's bedrooms, part of the dining room, and the pantry entrance. His other armchair offers a view of "the corridor, the entrance hall, all the way to the music corner of the living room and the violet armchair" (p. 71). In such panoptic positions, he surveys the children's "comings and goings," exemplifying some of the crossings indicative of the novel's title (p. 70). He not only sees but also eventually dictates his children's behavior even when he is not looking.

In much Asian American literature, ethnic scrutiny stems from a dominant community, wherein Asian American subjects internalize the potential for observation and subsequent reprimand—when it exists and even when it does not—in order to police their actions. These subjects attempt invisibility within their communities, but their visible racial trace invites constant surveillance. In Monica Sone's *Nisei Daughter* ([1953] 1991), the protagonist

> had been warned [after internment] over and over again that once I was outside, I must behave as inconspicuously as possible so as not to offend the sensitive public eye. I made up my mind to make myself scarce and invisible, but I discovered that an Oriental face, being somewhat of a rarity in the Midwest, made people stop in their tracks, stare, follow and question me. (pp. 219–220)

In Sui Sin Far's "Leaves from the Mental Portfolio of an Eurasian" ([1909] 1995), the young protagonist is subjected to inspections, becoming an inhuman "specimen" to be observed beneath a white gaze. While family demands shape Jane's national (Chinese and American) allegiances, she also acquires them differently than many of her Asian American literary counterparts as she lives an existence of deracination.[12]

In a reversal of the tendency for minorities to lose themselves in a crowd—the penchant for Chinese Americans, for example, to live among "their own" in Chinatown—Jane's family profiles their nationality in their financial ability to move away from other Chinese. Dyadya's medical education at a German university, the family's ability to afford a variety of Irish, English, and Scottish nannies during their tenure in England, as well as the purchase of a second home somewhere in the American countryside, remove them from the usual confines of Chinatown to which they return only to celebrate special occasions via Asian food, aligning them more closely with Whites than with other Chinese. Their deracination demands that Dyadya, who is already self-exiled from one home, manipulate the terms of the children's so-called independence and individuality by engineering their relationships and marriages in their new homes. *Crossings* pages are devoid of any other Chinese American characters beyond Jane's family members. In addition, their solidly upper-middle-class wealth separates them from other, poorer Chinese immigrants.[13] Jane's removal from other Chinese, along with her upper-middle-class privileges, can more easily bolster her national, American pride: "America is a good place to live for oneself and for others, to live fully, with dignity, and to work in the main current of life" (p. 122). This grates against a majority of Asian American characters' more bitter expressions of a constricting and judgmental America, expressed in John Okada's *No-No Boy* (1957) or Carlos Bulosan's *America Is in the Heart* (1946).

Jane's deracination begs many questions. If, as outlined above, Jane finds security and dignity in America, it does not explain her extreme removal to Paris. Could she not have relocated to another American city? Why must she "escape" across the globe? The book suggests Jane's complete disconnection in Paris from other Chinese, or from any other Asians. Is this a self-imposed deracination? Yet why, one might ask, would she seek solace in other Asians, a form of essentialization, if her American life has been happily removed from any concrete center of Chinese American lives? Chuang's use of dislocation, therefore, becomes a useful trope for reading race, raising numerous unanswered questions that address individual choice amid self- and social rejection, and the dictates of socially constructed spaces. Removal can be politically defined, as in the family's emigration from China's burgeoning civil war; but it need not be confined solely to political interests, as evidenced in the text's unanswered questions.

That Jane turns away from Dyadya and toward her lover speaks to a patriarchal web from which and to which Jane journeys, nuanced with subtle shades of a burgeoning feminism. Initially, Jane is scrutinized and categorized by her father, instilling within her an innate sense of proper daughterly (read: feminine) behavior and Chinese superiority and aloofness. When her father changes his views about James's wife, Jane announces her bitterness at his traitorous decision and her resolve to follow his original, racist edict:

> I played my part in your system of balances, forever ready to forfeit what was to my own advantage so as not to shake that first principle, the essential mode and core of my existence. It was a hard lesson to come by and you required it of me. By now it has become a necessity, I hardly know how to be without it and I'm not prepared to throw it out for their sakes for their child. I want to go away. I want my separateness for a time. I don't know who I am outside of the old context and I'm afraid I might not survive the new. . . . The oneness of you and Ngmah [mother] you have built so tightly you can't undo overnight just to accommodate them. You taught me that first hard lesson, I survived the trial and accepted my place. It's unfair to try me a second time. I can't help. (pp. 196–197)

Jane's "terrible danger crossing" (p. 196)—reflecting both her removal to Paris and her refusal to capitulate to Dyadya's new demands—is prompted by the ways in which personal space is always already circumscribed by inherited, familial self-definitions. For Jane's removal to Paris interrupts social custom in which Chinese daughters are often prohibited from leaving home except to attend college or to marry into their husbands' families. If Dyadya represents an immuring of sorts, then Jane's daily glances at his watch, as heirloom, constantly confine her within that (paternal) tradition. In refuting Dyadya's accepted orders and thus also her own culture, she must create her own borders, evidenced in her lover (a married, white Parisian journalist) whom her father would consider a barbarian.

Jane's reaction to the unnamed lover's initial, assertive behavior reinvents the specter of paternal control to which she is drawn in her escape from it. She seeks her father in her lover. Later, the Parisian lover waxes considerably less aggressive and more unreliable, mirroring the change occurring in Dyadya's attitudes toward interracial marriage when he exudes initial, fierce objections toward James's wife, only to relax his convictions. The lover rarely phones to establish or confirm appointments. "I've lost it," he claims of her telephone number, "otherwise I would have telephoned." Or, "Look here. I got the days confused. I did come on Friday. I heard voices from your apartment and thought you were giving a party." Jane replies in disappointment, "I never give parties. You were invited for Thursday" (pp. 128, 129). In the novel's total topology of imagined and actual wanderings, Jane is stopped by desire in Paris, compelled to wait for her lover to phone, to return from work, to institute the machinations that would physically move the plot along. In fact, Chuang explicitly equates him with suspended action when, in a taxi together, "They approached the Avenue by a narrow side street but found the entrance blocked by huge red and white striped barricades on account of construction underway" (p. 11). Only sentences earlier, the man is described as "tieless and his shirt was unbuttoned at the neck, a red and white checked shirt under a slightly limp dark blue suit" (p. 11). Like the red and white striped barricade, the lover prohibits her progression toward a goal, whether the trivial one of getting to her appointment via bus or the more important one of nurturing personal growth in order to arrive at self-understanding. Eventually, their dispassionate romance retains little emotional direction, resting instead on a weak current of stagnating desire.

As an Orientalist, Jane's lover contributes to her consternation over ethnic affiliation, reinventing a type of ethnic rigidity practiced by her father. "You should return to China. . . . America is not your country," he admonishes her. "You are an exile in America as you are in exile here [in Paris]" (pp. 120, 121). He conflates Jane's Chinese parentage with an obligatory Chinese nationalism. He promotes not only ethnic assimilation (i.e., as a Chinese, Jane should return to where she belongs) but also insinuates similar monoracial liaisons as those expressed by Dyadya, for if Jane belongs in China, and he in France, then what would such a removal demand of their relationship? One questions, then, if he is attracted to Jane the woman or Jane the Oriental woman. Because Jane is pregnant via this lover by novel's end, his views also demand answers about where, indeed, this child belongs. If Jane were to return to her country of origin (China), what would the mixed-race child's origin be? To what country would this child return and belong? The pregnant Jane dissolves their relationship and returns to the States, suggesting that she will raise the child alone. Jane's response to the lover's admonitions encompasses how memory and her lived experiences collapse a Chinese and an "American landscape. I can't separate any more . . . I belong to both, am both" (p. 125). She concludes that "both parts equally strong canceled out choice" (p. 122). National identity hardly satisfies individual yearning; nation, part of a community, is thus also contingent on family. As an Asian American in Paris, this sense of duality is not liberating; rather, it reestablishes Jane's need to acknowledge ethnic and familial ties. And so the novel's intertwined notions of belonging and exile, of racial marking and deracination, of patriarchy and denial, are sedimented within the perimeters of family, itself a conflicted territory.

If the lover possesses essentialized notions of what it means to be Chinese, he similarly categorizes gender: "You must always be amusing and sweet and never ask why," he declares. "I don't come here for lunch. I come here to learn and be amused" (pp. 118, 123). Whether "Oriental" or "woman," he insinuates that she must adhere to what is "natural" to her sex. Thus alienated by lover and father, Jane is incapable of confronting and resolving her own difficulties in an ever-widening space between lover and loved and between Dyadya and daughter. While her physical escape from home is liberating, the visible traces of her race prohibit clean separation from her Chinese background, strengthening the ties between identity and race at the same time that she attempts to dissolve them. In consciously disordering her known existence—seemingly unemployed and unoccupied in Paris—Jane no longer knows herself: "[S]he saw her image cut off at the waist . . . her face [in the mirror] appeared intolerably alien and unclaimed as the space and light around her" (p. 40). She exists in suspended time, whether sleeping or taking extended baths. For a woman whose defiance against paternalism once crackled with spirit, Jane's listlessness magnifies the psychologically debilitating effects of being bounded by and bonded to others' construction of her self-identification.

Jane's captivity by familial and social boundaries is referenced in the captivity narrative of John Ford's 1956 *The Searchers*, a film that Jane views repeatedly. A white man in this American Western "rescues" a white woman from Indians who had kidnapped her. Before plucking the resistant young woman from the camp, he urges her to voluntarily cross, a term indicating both the fording of a river as well as the divide between Indian and white worlds, advocating the mutual exclusivity of the territories they inhabit: "You don't belong there [among Indians]. You belong with us," he declares, emphasizing her "place" with "right/White" people (p. 105). Jane weeps at the conclusion of each showing when the male protagonist gathers the woman onto his saddle, carrying her away from her Indian family, thus rendering her twice kidnapped. The words "I have brought her home" close the film in an unsatisfactory conclusion about crossing and returning "home," but apropos to Chuang's project of exposing various types of crossings (p. 105). The film, produced in the "nostalgia" of the Cold War era, complicates images of the white nuclear family and the concept of going home, says Karen A. Lee, wherein the protagonist "is not brought back to the nuclear, racially homogenous home at the outset of the film, but a new kind of home that is ethnically mixed," an oblique reference to *Crossings'* themes, especially Jane's "worries concerning the changing ethnic and racial face of her family" (1997:81–82).[14] Both home and away in Chuang's novel elicit profoundly melancholic reactions from Jane. She succumbs to her lover's tepid affection and vague itinerary of direction only because she is puzzled about how to effectively rally against culturally inarticulable definitions—captivity narratives in their own right.

My argument about displacement and dissonance benefits from two recent dialogues in Asian American studies: Leslie Bow's (2001) notion of Asian American women's sexuality as betrayal of traditional, ethnic, and national allegiances and Anne Anlin Cheng's (2000) investigation into what she names a melancholy of race. The former explains the relationship between a construction of Asian American women's identification through subversions of political or ethnic affiliations, or says Bow, how "feminism mark[s] ethnic or national betrayal, particularly as sexuality mediates between progress and tradition, modernity and the 'Old World,' the United States and Asia" (2001:11). Women's disloyalty to ethnic affiliation, to tradition, and to nationality is evidenced in how they "perform" their sexuality (Bow 2001:10). But sometimes, subversions come with a price, as when sexual transgressions (such as interracial interrelations) come to be regarded as assaults against national identification, a metonymous relationship wherein the offending (female) individual is representative of a community's, a state's, a political organization's morality—and is expected to uphold it, no matter the personal cost.

Cheng (2000) mediates on the "psychical injury" attendant in such negotiations: defying the strictures of one's sex or ethnicity becomes pathological. Cheng's reading does not cancel Bow's discussion of feminism's potential subversion, but illuminates that acts of betrayal all too often enact incidents of what Cheng deems hypochondria. It is this juncture between the two readings that is useful for my analysis: Jane is poised between a betrayal of Dyadya on the one hand, and of self on the other, resulting in psychical injury.

Dyadya's definition of love incorporates devotion and allegiance to ethnic identity. His children are rooted in his ethnically charged definitions of marriage, of filial piety, of woman, and even of self. Jane accommodates herself to these codes, adopts them as her own, but at a price. Demanding to go her own way instantiates a betrayal against the father, the family, and therefore her Chinese affiliation. James, like his sister, has crossed his father, but the announcement of his wife's pregnancy resolves the conflict. In other words, sexuality exhibits the curious potential for being both punishable and celebratory. Dyadya's seemingly unassuaged anger at James's marriage to a "barbarian" exemplifies that the codes by which the family operates are nonnegotiable—until the arrival of a male heir. According to much Asian American literature, women often obtain privilege and power through reproduction. But this power is double edged, rendering it both an effective tool that exists beyond patriarchal control (encompassing the invisible, private, and subversive act of sex) as well as an incriminating violation in the very visible results of pregnancy. "[W]omen at sex hazarded birth and hence lifetimes," writes Kingston (1989:7). Engaging in sex purely for enjoyment is punishable, especially premarital sex, yet in much Asian American literature, pregnancy becomes fundamentally less disturbing when its attendant (unintended) product is a child, preferably a male one. Note the progression of events in Louis Chu's *Eat a Bowl of Tea* (1961) that adeptly illustrate how male and female sexuality and infidelity are differently used and assessed. A long-awaited child is conceived through recent immigrant Mei Oi's infidelity to her husband Ben Loy, whose formerly active, sexual life among white prostitutes, regarded with impunity, grates uncomfortably against his present impotence with his Chinese wife. At the same time that Ben Loy's potency is revived, partly by eating a bowl of fertility tea—not to mention the couple's relocation away from New York City's Chinatown, a site of paternal authority and social conformity—Mei Oi's sexual infidelity is easily forgotten with the birth of an illegitimate baby boy.[15]

Mei Oi transgresses in both positive and negative ways. What Bow would deem Mei Oi's act of female sexual transgression offends her Chinese community, which therefore condemns her. At the same time, it also subverts traditional forms of marriage that advocate female fidelity, especially provocative in a novel of self-sacrificing women, like Ben Loy's mother, who raises children single handedly in China in order to send them to their stateside husbands. Men like Ben Loy are culturally licensed to avail themselves of prostitutes, in their sexual frustration, whereas women are denied such privileges. Thus, Mei Oi's character commits a betrayal out of extravagance, to borrow from Sau-ling Wong (1993). That is, a bold reading of female desire would squarely place Mei Oi's's infidelity in her desire for sexual satisfaction—she seeks pleasure, not reproduction.[16] Or, in an alternate reading, she transgresses out of a necessity to manipulate the terms of her marriage. She prompts a reaction from her husband and from the culturally (narrowly) circumscribed Chinatown community by rallying toward a different vision of women's desire and sexuality. Mei Oi betrays and liberates simultaneously.

Sexuality, however, remains limited to punishable transgression for Kingston's pregnant No Name Woman in *Woman Warrior* ([1976] 1989), a comment on the fluidity by which sexuality-as-sign is interpreted. The eventual charge of infidelity is leveled not only at the offending woman, but also at her family, whose home is burned and the family excised from further community inclusion; the aunt's male lover, complicit in the pregnancy, remains unpunished. That is, he disappears from any accusatory discussions as the visible roundness of No Name Woman's belly marks her act of betrayal against family and community. She commits suicide by throwing herself into the family well, taking her newborn with her; not only does her ghostly presence—a community (and communal) punitive trace—haunt the village girls into chaste submission as a warning against women's dangerous transgressions, but her revenge suicide has poisoned the family well. As Bow (2001) thoroughly investigates, women's sexuality is used as both cultural regulator and as patriarchal subversion; its management negotiates the terms of its naming and its use for social or political reasons, while women's covert actions elicit a challenge to embodied confinement, but one that rarely escapes with impunity. This is evident no more clearly than in Brave Orchid's oft-quoted injunction against her daughter—"Don't tell"—marking not only the weight of the aunt's infidelity, but the commencement of the daughter's menstruation and present potential for burgeoning (dangerous) sexuality and its attendant communal offenses.

Crossings alludes to Jane's first pregnancy, followed by either an abortion or a miscarriage—Chuang never clarifies—suggesting sexual transgressions similar to that of Mei Oi and to that of No Name Woman. But what prevents this novel from sliding into a comfortable, even complacent, Asian American tale outlining how a rebellious daughter eventually pleases her father and the traditions for which he stands is its subtle allusion to cultural taboos like abortion or miscarriage.[17]

A novel read through a similar rubric of paternal, authorial limitation and the woman who strains against them is Jade Snow Wong's *Fifth Chinese Daughter* (1945), punctuated by many of the same issues evident in *Crossings*: an overbearing father; sexism against daughters and wives; a strong-willed Chinese American woman who defies paternal edicts; and resolution through the protagonist's ethnic reacceptance.[18] When Jane attempts "a terrible danger crossing," her father's anger may stem less from her rejection of the "barbarian" than the visible trace of a premarital affair—her pregnancy. Dyadya retorts, "I forbid you to leave. . . . You have failed me. You are a failure. . . . Go. I don't want you to stay. You are not my daughter" (pp. 195, 197). That he begins his tirade with "I forbid you to leave" and concludes with the curt "Go" reflects his ambivalent stance toward dispossessing the daughter he once so fiercely possessed, perhaps less so for her obstinacy than for her sexual indiscretion. Much of Jane's time in Paris thereafter is spent in a brooding depression. Yet she hardly heeds her father's words, not only by engaging her lover in an extramarital affair, but by becoming pregnant again. In this manner, *Crossings'* iconoclastic form parallels its surprisingly unusual subjects—such as feminist issues of premarital sex, abortion, adultery, hybrid children, and Asian re-masculation in the marriage between Chinese American James and his Anglo wife, subjects that do not arise in *Fifth Chinese Daughter* (Wong 1945), despite the novels' contextual similarities.

Cheng's project on the melancholy condition of ethnic categorizing investigates the hypochondria I see arising in Jane, evolving when self (sexuality and individuated desire) challenges proponents of ethnic belonging (filial and cultural piety, among other implied and coerced allegiances). Cheng's close reading of Kingston's protagonist uncovers the "melancholy of race," an "internalization of discipline and rejection—*and* the installation of a scripted context of perception" (p. 17, emphasis in original). The protagonist is narrativized through embodied betrayals: culturally accepted behavior supports oppressive national and political behavior, but at the expense, according to Cheng, of individual mental health. Cheng taps into the psychic impact of hypochondria on a racialized subject, as in the strange illness striking down Kingston's female protagonist and how such illnesses manifest themselves in both metaphor and bodily consequence.

Most relevant for Jane, the literally and figuratively dislocated protagonist, is Cheng's announcement that "[T]he dream of a culturally healthy body defines itself through displacement," in which Kingston's protagonist, according to Cheng, is "most at home when not at home" and therefore is rendered a body in "perpetual unease" (pp. 66, 67). Cheng's allusion to displacement as the act of positioning oneself "elsewhere" in the throes of "bodily malaise" underscores Jane's peripatetic existence (p. 72).[19] On the one hand, Chuang's novel may evoke the displacement of accepted notions of racially placed women, but on the other, such displacement has been detrimental in other arenas, including but not limited to the relevance of raced authors to literary canon placement; the incorporation of affirmative action (the placement of minority employees that can belie institutional advancement).[20] Resisting authority and playing out personal desires, Cheng suggests, have their consequences; subversion is dangerous on many fronts.

Crossings' dispossessed protagonist lives no jubilant liberation in Paris, adrift in mental agitation: "[I]n the center of the square carpet of faded reds greens and blues and whites . . .

[Jane] discerned oases and deserts, scorpions and camels, departures, wanderings and homecomings woven inextricably there" (p. 187).[21] Her reaction illustrates a hypochondriachal response to culturally groomed perceptions, inherited through paternal orders and schizophrenic, national constructions of race that become historically accurate when she lives the existence of the "problem" her sexuality and her race imply. While Dyadya's disapproving words have exiled his daughter, she "wanted both my worlds," referring to her existence in America (as a family member) as well as to that in Paris (as a single woman). But Jane exhibits a sexuality beyond the appropriate security and approval of wedlock, and she further insults her family by failing to accept her father's prearranged (Chinese) match for her first pregnancy. The tension the novel establishes delineates seemingly impossible places: being an independent woman and a "good" daughter, and expressing pride in her Chinese heritage amid her lover's Orientalist views. Again, compare this novel with Wong's *Fifth Chinese Daughter* (1945), where Jade Snow's reactions to sexist edicts and Chinese prescriptions are embedded in clear purpose: she proves the existence of female intelligence, especially to her father, by graduating from college, and she illustrates an American marketing acumen by starting a successful Chinese American business.

But *Crossings* is hardly a narrative with such subversive purpose. The novel boasts motion, but to what end? Unlike Jade Snow, Jane does not envision an identity of female empowerment or national belonging; rather, she escapes from a stifling allegiance that demands impossible loyalties. If the novel suggests any intentionality at all in its itinerancy, it resides in Jane's statement "I want to get married" (194).[22] The novel's upshot, however, is not her marriage but her pregnancy. So even intended purpose is subjected to unexpected consequence and other loyalties. Yet her pregnancy introduces a third element and therefore a third option to a kinetic weariness entangled in crossings: a cross-cultural child who will, by nature of his or her parentage, cross boundaries of race; and conceived in defiance, the child transgresses parental approval. While the novel expresses ambivalence about its protagonist's ability to resolve her racial

and gendered conflicts successfully, perhaps her unborn, biracial child represents the potential for familial and cultural re-
union. The arriving child, like that of Mei Oi's in *Eat a Bowl of
Tea* (Chu 1961), exists to unify cultures and families. Jane may
never be healed, but her child may instigate long-awaited dialogues addressing racial and gendered pathologies.

The figure of the mother is curiously absent in this novel of
female self-placement, female rebellion, maternity, and pregnancy. Within contemporary literary criticism, scholars continue
to discuss the maternal figure as a generational, cultural guide
to their daughters. Maternal guides figure largely in Asian
American literature and criticism: from the four mothers in Amy
Tan's *The Joy Luck Club* (1989) to the war-traumatized mother in
Nora Okja Keller's *Comfort Woman* (1997), from the iconoclastic
grandmother of Cynthia Kadohata's *The Floating World* (1989) to
the absent mother in Joy Kogawa's *Obasan* (1982), and to the
yearning women of Hisaye Yamamoto's "Seventeen Syllables"
(1988) and "Yoneko's Earthquake" (Yamamoto 1988), to name
only a few. According to Patricia P. Chu, "The Asian or Asian
immigrant mother who adapts well to change appears in many
women's texts; this trait both enhances the Asian American offspring's capacity to construct an ethnicized American identity
and reduces the offspring's incentive to engage in the distancing
psychic or symbolic operations of maternal objection"
(2000:105). *Crossings*, however, delineates a father-daughter narrative, and in this novel of a woman's journey toward self-placement, the figure of the mother remains faint but not without
influence. Or, the changing patriarchal loyalties exhibited between Ngmah's (Jane's mother's) dutiful acquiescence to her
husband and Jane's rebellion catalogue, if quietly, the impact of
women's desires on family organization. Dyadya demands that
his children "Honor Ngmah . . . who has never left my side" (p.
18). He highlights not only spousal devotion, but also national
devotion in remembering his former medical position and their
shared attention to the wounded at "the beginning of hostilities"
in China (p. 18). As such, Jane and her constant movement away
from paternal direction (and from national/ethnic affiliation)
present a stark contrast to the more traditional women of the

novel (such as Ngmah and Jane's paternal grandmother) who remain bound to husbands and family. Yet Jane's activities revolve around just the domestic duties practiced by her foremothers: cooking and pregnancy. In fact, the novel's meticulous attention to Jane's culinary activities render it nearly an Asian cookbook at times. Likewise, it is the children's female amahs who bathe them and recite bedtime stories, rendering the act of narrativization female.

Bound up in *Crossings* are acts of maternal/domestic attention and affection that illustrate women's continued (expected) adjustment to familial revisions and thus their duty to just the traditions that Jane resists. Chuang writes, "She [Ngmah] had spent more than twenty years letting out a fraction of an inch here, taking in a fraction there, lengthening and shortening. . . . She threaded the needle and continued to stitch at the point where she had left off. Days, weeks, months, years, the pains of birth, absences, voyages, wars, losses, solitude, storms at sea" (pp. 15–16). In adjusting an inch here and there, the hemming process is an oblique allusion to the calibration necessary in cultural adjustment, an immigrant's self-accommodation, often at the resistance of the communities into which she moves. But "[w]hat a relief finally to go to the Far East to have clothes cut expertly and sewn to measure" (p. 15). This latter phrase suggests two readings: either the unique (read: "strange") Chinese figure cannot be accommodated by Western dress, rendering Chinese bodies unassimilable, or the West underestimates the cultural value (economic contributions) of an increasing Chinese American population, echoed through their invisibility as community, civic, or political constituents. The process of cultural accommodation, therefore, requires patience, a constant refitting and recrossing, a form of self-fashioning reflected in Chuang's musings: "Borders or no borders . . . and hours and hours of fitting" (p. 16). That the novel's women engage in such fitting along racial and gendered lines illuminates Jane's difference in resisting self-revision at the behest of communal systems inimical to her individuality.

The image of Jane's paternal grandmother as both regal (the honored family matriarch) and infantalized complicates the novel's images of accommodating women. At her eighty-fourth birthday party, the grandmother mutters the only English word she remembers—"machine gun"—because "the sounds pleased her" (p. 26). The utterance offers seemingly little connection to the surrounding festivities. Yet "connection"—embodied by the notion of crossings—is the operative term, for perhaps the trauma of emigration from China amid communist atrocities is encompassed in the term "machine gun," announced in English yet harkening back to a former place affiliated with a pre-immigrant life. The grandmother's birthday party is thus contaminated by bitter memories, evident also in how the novel is studded with Jane's own unexpected images of communist atrocities. In these ways, the women, like the conflicted Jane herself, embody notions of cross-culturalism and the difficulties of "crossing" as a woman, a minority, a foreigner, a wife, a mother. Jane's return to her father (her reconciliation and her bedside vigil in the hospital) is also a return to the mother, not only through Jane's pregnancy, but also through the maternal performance of adjustment, the novel's acknowledgment of the necessity of crossings, always contaminated by difference, whether one's own or those of the community in which one lives.

Jane's father, righteously adhering to his ethnic strictures, is not immune to the toll that such rigidity takes, prompting his own crossings. Even though his eventual hospitalization results from a literal heart attack, this ascription overlooks other emotional, psychological, and figurative readings that may have contributed to his condition: anxiety over berating his daughter and an immigrant parent's intense feelings of obligation to instill the tenets of a native culture within increasingly Western-acclimatized children. Indeed, his heart has been broken. Jane comes to terms with Dyadya's affections, and finally accepts her sister-in-law and nephew, only after her father has passed away, offering no clear narrativization of wholeness (whatever that may be) as cultural "cure."

Because Jane's rebellions make her ill, and because her understandable inability to act with purpose once in Paris prevent any concrete solutions to her problems, I turn for answers to the novel's other characters. While much Asian American literary criticism has tended toward defining cultural acceptance as a mediation between or among several ethnic affiliations, resulting in characters who accept their contested condition as exigent for cross-cultural adaptation, *Crossings* defies such a standard interpretation. In fact, if form functions as meaning, then the novel's unique narrative quality opens, rather than closes, possibilities about Jane's continued irresolution to questions of ethnic and gendered fidelity. I find *Crossings'* strongest gestures toward reconciliation in the novel's minor characters—whose major transgressions prompt iconoclastic reactions from Dyadya and the tradition he represents—and in the novel's unborn children, their hybridity demanding a reevaluation of accepted notions of racial demarcations.

If *Crossings* remains more conventional in addressing conflicted female identity as in-validity, it certainly defies established boundaries of East-West unions with the introduction of James's marriage to a white woman. The West's persistent sexualization of the Oriental exotic as female has worked to erode Asian men's masculinity. David Henry Hwang's transgendered character in *M. Butterfly* (1989) clarifies what David L. Eng (1998) names "racial castration" when Song wonders why we find it compelling and beautiful if an Asian woman falls in love with a white man, despite his cruel treatment of her, and then kills herself when he marries a white woman. Yet a similar scenario, one in which "a blonde homecoming queen fell in love with a short Japanese business man," and committed suicide at his remarriage, would be considered ludicrous (Hwang 1989:17).[23]

Feminist theory has led us to expect female rebellion, especially by minority women, against what has been deemed a double oppression of patriarchy and racism. But here, it is James, an Asian man, and not Jane, an Asian woman, who breaks patriarchal codes of acceptable behavior. The legal/nuptial union between James and the barbarian intimates the necessity of their sexual union with the pending arrival of a child, buttressing Asian American re-masculization at the same time that it dismantles cultural borders. James's rebellion thus fulfills his father's hopes: "James you are my firstborn and you are to lead."

While such an argument overlooks James's patriarchal privileges, inaccessible to Jane, Dyadya's final capitulation to accepting his son's wife and hybrid child is done in concert with a woman, and a "barbarian" at that. The joint effort points to the second generation's more equitable distribution of cultural work within the family. First, when family reproduction overturns racial prejudice, and the barbarian is invited inside the family's walled city, one might concede that in finding the weakness along the wall and garnering James's affections without parental permission, this woman has already infiltrated the sacred, culturally exclusionist "inside." She does not need Dyadya's help in her attack and forbidden entrance. And despite caveats arising in her own culture concerning the myth of the emasculated Asian man, she boldly risks marriage to Chinese American James, finds love, and eventually familial acceptance. Far from defying Dyadya, this woman echoes his paternal edicts about loving one's family as "possessions" when, on first meeting the family, she articulates a similar albeit more enlightened position: "I will share him with you fair and square" (p. 55). She uses Dyadya's tools and words to destroy his racist stance and to win his affection. Ultimately, their deviation foreshadows Dyadya's own potential flexibility on the race question, while Jane—who as woman would seem more pliable in her lived understanding of racial and gendered constraints—remain stalwart, until after Dyadya's death, in refusing the barbarian's love.

That James and his wife do not fit the norms adumbrated by feminist and cultural studies allows them to liberate the family from ethnic self-exclusion. In addition, the wife's unnamed status, referencing her spousal relation and not her individuality, contributes to my argument that minor characters carry much of the book's mediation of race, gender, miscegenation, and the hope of a pliable patriarchy. In American literature, unnamed female figures are so (un)marked in order to highlight their inefficacy in changing a system inimical to them (note Kingston's No Name Woman and Charlotte Perkins Gilman's unnamed narrator in "The Yellow Wallpaper," to name two). In many ways, the novel's difficult form asks that we read its contrasting images—and the spaces between them—by dislocating accepted notions of an abjected self, ethnicity, and gender.

Chuang allows those at the margins of the text to become central. And she repositions the stalwart man at its center to eventually acquiesce to the new forms and conditions represented by his children and his adopted nation.

By the final page, the novel is still a disjointed mosaic that the reader must assemble, offering up slightly different versions of the protagonist's current grounding and placement. Chuang concludes with an appropriate image that mimics the novel's constant motion:

> Grandfather practices calisthenics. In the yard of his former gate keeper's house he makes studied movements of limbs and body. He is frail and each gesture is very precise. His eyes squint in the sun. His sight is clear. He retreats, advances, and with each change of movement he inhales and exhales. The air comes out of his mouth in puffs of vapor which dissolve in the morning air. (p. 215)

The interpretive possibilities of such an image are manifold. First, the novel's form throughout has defied the smooth motion of "limbs and body" that rhythmically advance and retreat; it has refuted the calm existence exhibited in steady inhalation and exhalation. It is important that grandfather, a man, engages in this soothing activity, questioning its relevance as a potential solution to Jane's (a woman's) mental chaos. A more viable reading regards the practice of calisthenics as a formal structure that can be embellished with personal flair.

The cultural and familial structures that render Jane melancholic are not dismantled; rather, she accepts them and revises her attitude in varying degrees of self-accommodation and resistance. Duty and desire are not mutually exclusive, represented by Jane's concluding return to America and to her family despite being pregnant with her lover's child. She reconciles her emotional connection to the past, not necessarily to its strict tradition, but at least to the loving father, dead by novel's end, at the center of that tradition. She decides that if love for Dyadya and her family is an obligation, then it crosses all boundaries: physical, ethnic, familial, and emotional. The novel does not close with a smooth rhythm, but with the hopefulness of "progress, change, growth, life" (p. 17). Disjunctures are undeniably necessary as a measure of continually questioning ourselves and defining our futures here or elsewhere. Chuang's critique lies in recognizing a fluidity within rigidity, an emancipation within boundaries, a critical self-acceptance amid social rejection, and the positive consequences of complicating the borders of ethnic affiliation and cultural citizenship.

Notes

1. Quoted in Susan Y. Najita (2001:100, 112).

2. *Crossings* is considered Asian America's first modernist text. In her foreword to the novel, Amy Ling calls it "Asian America's first modernist novel" (1982:2); Sau-ling Wong, in her *Reading Asian American Literature*, labels it "the first modernist Asian American novel" (1993:120). Thus, while other Asian American authors before Chuang recorded ethnic American experiences through fiction or autobiography that progressed in a linear fashion—from a character's birth through adulthood—Chuang breaks from her predecessors to use modernism's highly experimental and often erratic form to map Jane's physical and psychological motion. It is impossible to speculate whether Chuang did so as a rebellion against traditional forms or whether the modernist form best accommodated her alienated, displaced character. These suggestions are not mutually exclusive, for they both characterize modernist tenets by avoiding traditional, linear avenues. A modernist reading of the novel prompts "crossing" into new territories, forcing the reader to rethink and redefine traditional ethnic notions. For an exploration of race, gender, and modernism in *Crossings*, see Monica Chiu, "Motion, Memory, and Conflict in Chuang Hua's Modernist *Crossings*" (1999). Also see Vera C. Wang on issues of self-identity, race, and class in her "In Search of Self: The Dislocated Female Émigré Wanderer in Chuang Hua's *Crossings*" (1993).

3. While it is impossible to list all those Asian American novels that address displacement, whether centrally or marginally, Sau-ling Wong's "The Politics of Displacement," in her *Reading Asian American Literature* (1993), is helpful in situating some of the ideas involved.

4. Besides his extramarital affair with Jane, the novel hints at others: "Among your lovers am I your favorite?" Jane asks him (1986:117).

5. The book catalogues numerous similarly coupled images, most of which underscore the novel's emphasis on conflict. Take the following phrases, for instance, all of which can be obliquely interpreted within the rubric of the novel's many themes of duty, desire, conflict, and patriarchy: "unending cycles of debt and repayment" (p. 182); "In its length, the river [the Missouri] flowed through seven states, she traced the course of the water . . . linking names of colors beasts saints trees ideas Indians rocks the names of men, holy procession signifying man's enduring tenure" (p. 185); "storerooms of visibles and invisibles of your life" (p. 188). Says Ling of such interesting passages, "Chuang Hua's synthetic vision and her acute sense of oppositions are also sharply realized in her most graphic images . . . These disparate images, mixing decay and life, ugliness and beauty, horror and nourishment, reveal an unflinching, unrestrained vision, one that recognizes the harsh reality of coexisting opposites" (Ling 1986:5–6).

6. Ling names Chuang's style an "artistic coherence through images" (Ling 1986:6).

7. What was ultimately constructed was the rise of a paternal America whose mission advertised acceptance and democratic treatment. This paternalism, or what Lee calls "restored postwar patriarchy," was supported by an emphasis on the nuclear family and its values, redomesticating (or dismissing them from labor) those women who had joined the war effort in its labor forces and thereby doubly feminizing the Asian/American woman, already Orientalized as submissive even though she had been viewed, pre-war, as "dangerously transgressive" (1999:162).

8. Says Ling of this same passage, referring to the watch (in *Crossings*, p. 7), "It [the novel] begins . . . with Jane at a bus stop in Paris looking at a pocket watch that had once belonged to her father. . . . Time present is being told by time past, and the power of the father, despite his physical absence, is concretely present in his timepiece, a progressive image" (Ling 1982:34).

9. While it is clear that Chuang uses her own surname in the novel, and it is therefore a form of veiled autobiography, I continue to call it a novel and not an autobiography.

10. This idea is partially informed by Jane Tompkins, in her *Sensational Designs: The Cultural Work of American Fiction, 1790–1860* (1985), where she argues that male literary characters who leave home (such as Huckleberry Finn or the crew pursuing Moby Dick) were accepted as thoroughly engaged in the world. On the other hand, those female characters in women's "sentimental fiction," obligated by societal dic-

tates to remain at home where they faced disappointments and personal battles, were projected as using domesticity to escape the so-called real world outside the home. Tompkins points to the irony of this designation, for these women, she argues, were explicitly confronting "real life," while Twain's character Huck Finn, for example, avoids his problems by traveling down the river (p. 175).

11. Dyadya keeps "documents and papers such as certificates of medical studies completed in China, Germany and America" (p. 71).

12. Sau-ling Wong says that *Crossings* refers "to the deracinated protagonist's trans- and intercontinental wanderings" (1993:120).

13. Sui Sin Far's character Mrs. Spring Fragrance, also a deracinated character, resides adjacent to white homeowners and is therefore uniquely positioned in acceptance and wealth at a time when most Chinese were confined to Chinatowns, a so-called dirty space once avoided by the majority population except as areas of amusement and leisure. In fact, Mrs. Spring Fragrance reverses the notion of the inscrutable Asian in her proclamation that "[s]he would write a book about Americans for her Chinese women friends. The American people were so interesting and mysterious" (Sui Sin Far [1912] 1995).

14. "As a matter of fact," states Lee, "every surviving character in the family at the end of the film is some sort of ethnic: Martin Pawley is one-eighth Cherokee, Mose is a light-skinned Black whose racial difference is ethnicized through his stereotypical black mannerisms, Debbie [the protagonist] is racially transformed from her experience with the Comanches, and Jorgenson is a stereotypical Swedish yokel" (1997:82).

15. When Ben Loy leaves New York for a weekend trip to Washington with Mei Oi, "he rediscovered his manliness. . . . [But to] his dismay and disappointment, he fell back into the old rut of incompetence at his own apartment on Catherine Street in New York" (Chu [1961] 1995:85).

16. Chu writes, "When Ben Loy had turned away [in bed], she felt unwanted and useless . . . his monk-like behavior had begun even before she set foot on the airplane [two months prior, but] . . . Ben Loy had failed miserably at making love. He was no more successful on subsequent nights" ([1961] 1995:65). Waiting for her lover to call on her in her new Stanton location, she takes pleasure in other men's gazes upon her: "She privately entertained the fantasy that he, Chin Yuen [Ben Loy's friend], might eventually seek some sort of relationship with her" (p. 173).

17. Few Asian American novels address abortions or miscarriage; it is only with the recent publication of Lois-Ann Yamanaka's *Father of the Four Passages* (2001) that the subject is treated frankly and graphically.

18. Jade Snow Wong's proclamation of her parents' irrefutable obedience structures her desires to live an existence outside the strictures of a home that denies the democracy of the America in which the family lives. Despite similarities between Jade Snow's and Fourth Jane's hierarchization beneath the gaze of an autocratic (Chinese) father, their rebellions differ on one major front: while Jade Snow seeks an American independence more akin (or more assimilated) to those who enjoy similar benefits within the nation, Fourth Jane harbors no such clearly articulated and strong desires. Her resistance is not shaped by an urge to become independent or even feminine-American; nor is it clearly articulated that she recognizes, as does Jade Snow, an inherent gender inequity within the family. As a matter of fact, all the children are urged to attend college, unlike the disappointed Jade Snow, who learns that the education of daughters is significantly less important—and financially unsupported—than that of sons. When Jade Snow is upstaged by the arrival of a new baby brother, she sets her sights on proving her worth to her family and to herself. Rather than repeat an argument already done well, I recommend Bow's "The Celestial in Our Midst: Jade Snow Wong's *Fifth Chinese Daughter*" (2001:77–91).

19. Cheng says, "the ability to claim health is *articulable* specifically under and only through the shadows of bodily malaise and displacement (physically putting herself *elsewhere*)" (72, emphasis in original). She concludes that "the racial question is an issue of *place*" (12, emphasis in original).

20. Part of this project, according to Cheng, involves the "wish to maintain the other within existing structures," such as those of segregation and colonialism (p. 12). Palumbo-Liu (1995) discusses minority texts and pedagogy as "recognizing that minority discourse, *once visible* as a represented and representative object, can indeed be stabilized and forced into a particular relationship with the hegemonic." As well, he outlines how the role of recruiting and diversification has been restructured as "a necessary economic consideration" over and above "a desirable goal in itself," yet the former can hide within the foregrounding of the latter (Palumbo-Liu 1995:17, emphasis in original).

21. See Ling's reading of this quote in her "Foreword" to *Crossings* (1986:1–6, specifically p. 6).

22. Even this intention is fraught with question: "Whom do you want to marry?" asks Dyadya. "I don't know," Jane responds (p. 194).

23. See David L. Eng's project of resurrecting Asian American masculinity in his *Racial Castration: Managing Masculinity in Asian America* (2001).

3

Ginu Kamani's Crass, Classed, and Incurable Female Bodies

In her collection of short stories *Junglee Girl*, author Ginu Kamani's (1995) hyperbolic linguistic and visual representations of women's sexuality as pathological and as filthy expose intense cultural anxiety over and aversion to bodily matter such as hair, menstrual blood, sexual fluids, body odors, and breast milk. These reviled elements are doubly castigated when attributed to servant bodies, allowing Kamani to introduce class hierarchies into discussions about women, illness, and dirt. Persistent incursions into and permutations of cultural constructions regarding what is considered clean and acceptable allow me to expose how binaries like clean/dirty work in Kamani's stories.[1]

Through such feminist reading practices I reveal how she both upholds and questions demarcated but ambiguous borders: ill/healthy, Asian/American, national/transnational, and masculine/feminine. Aided by poststructural theory that dismantles such binaries, I unpack the linguistic, material, somatic, and social practices from which definitions of filth emerge. I examine how the natural occurrence of dirt—as earth, clay, and the matter from which living things emerge—evolves to suit political denaturalization in racial and gendered terms.[2]

In the story "Waxing the Thing," for example, the "thing" remains unnamed throughout but it is hardly a textual secret amid Kamani's sexually explicit stories. "[S]he was already lying there with her sari pulled up to her stomach, and her legs bent at the knees . . . when suddenly she stuck one finger inside of her panties and pulled the material down and showed me all her hair *there*. . . . All this time, I didn't know that the ladies wax down there"—she did not know that they waxed the "thing" (p. 118, emphasis in original). *Junglee Girl*'s provocative book cover announces the graphic nature of Kamani's narratives about young South Asian women who come to consciousness about their bodies and their sexuality. A woman reclines promiscuously against a tree trunk, arms above her head, knees bent. She wears a gauzy vestment whose red polka dots on sheer fabric render her, at first glance, seemingly covered with blemishes and serve as the only solid portions of the fabric that "cover" her underlying naked body. Kamani's irreverent visual and textual content attempts to overturn the cultural constructedness of women as sickening, dirty, or reviled by highlighting women's bodies in a "natural" state (naked, sexual, hirsute), the state itself resting on a highly conflicted notion of natural as clean and good. To keep the skin "cool and clean," the hair on the "thing" demands routine removal, denaturalizing the body at the same time that frequent shaving naturalizes women's smooth and hairless skin (p. 118). "Mrs. Nariman and Mrs. Dastur say that it makes them feel clean, because there's no hair for anything to get stuck to down there" (p. 119). Then there is the odor: "And definitely [after waxing], the smell is also a little less" (p. 118). Hence, the "thing" is rendered filthy, a theme that the collection destabilizes only to eventually uphold, as I will argue, attesting to how meaning is accrued, used, disseminated, and recreated, often at the expense of women's bodies.

That "Waxing the Thing" is one of the collection's midtext stories confirms that its central taboo image will serve as the book's striking and driving visual metaphor, blatantly announcing the unutterable throughout, and proceeding to say much about it. Yet Kamani's work presents more troubling questions than answers concerning women's pathogenic condition. Her concentration on twinning numerous seemingly mutually exclusive territories is alluded to via the collection's cover, illustrating the tenuous divide between clothed and naked as an introduction to her work's evocation of similar paradoxes: women's irreverence within modesty; the exploitation of women by women via the tools of patriarchy; women's promiscuity amid an authoritarian adherence to tradition. In thumbing her nose at the rules, questioning the divisibility and simultaneous inextricability of terms such as clothed/naked, proper/improper, rebellion/acquiescence, Kamani attempts to untether women's bodies from traditional adherence to forms and practices.

Feminist theory has long grappled with revising socially constructed views of women's bodies as aberrations, or as dangerous and volatile, what Elizabeth Grosz considers a "leaking" beyond established cultural borders (1994:viii).[3] In acknowledging how women are construed as female biology to male culture, feminists reconfigure the so-called epistemologically natural female body and its sex (Irigaray 1985; Butler 1990).[4] *Junglee Girl*, whose title comes "from the Sanskrit root, 'jungle' [and] is used in India to describe a wild and uncontrollable woman," suggests just this female uncontainability that portends imminent "leaking" or "flowing" of forcibly obedient, restrained, but manipulable female bodies.[5]

Because all of Kamani's strong female characters reside in Bombay,[6] one might question the collection's suitability to Asian American studies, which has been concerned with predominantly Western-centric and U.S. domestic issues. Yet, Asian American literature increasingly addresses global territories through which its characters roam (for example, Yamashita's *Brazil-Maru* [1992] or her *Through the Arc of the Rain Forest* [1990] and Monique Truong's *The Book of Salt* [2003]). Subsequently, cultural relativity within this global sphere affects approaches to the criticism of such literature and has been shaping the field of Asian American and feminist studies. Speaking of "trans/national feminist perspectives," Leela Fernandes discusses how "texts, theories, and cultural commodities circulate and 'travel' . . . [and] the consumption, meanings, and power effects of such forms are contingent on the local and national historical and political boundaries of the 'audience' in question" (2001:48). Bodies that are in constant flux between two or more nations confront a dizzying set of assumptions about how they should function and how they should be categorized, outlined clearly by those who discuss the liberation and constraints of being national citizens of one country and working citizens of another (Parreñas 2001; Choy 2003). That these transient citizens perform sweatshop labor or the work of in-home nursing in countries not of their citizenship internationalizes practices that can be used to address the concept of filth. Forgetting such diasporan labor—while concomitantly recognizing wealthier Asian American international mobility as a necessary "bridge" to transnational capital—is subsequently erasing an Asian American consciousness that arose from a grassroots level, a past foundation that constituents have laid for present Asian American success.[7] Thus Elena Tajima Creef can certainly claim that "There is no escaping this [Asian American] body made out of history,/war and peace,/two languages,/and two cultures," which speaks to both the exciting outcomes as well as the dangerous consequences of transnational practices (Creef 1990:84). It is at the intersection of body, gender, and the global that pathology and dirt intervene in Kamani, allowing me to map shifts within these fields of study as well as to reshape such fields toward new understandings of women's bodies and of ethnic identity.

—⁂—

Kamani's female characters protest, either verbally or through their "silent" daily actions, a socially constructed fear and loathing of women's bodies as well as those cultural expectations that dictate "good" women as submissive sexual and marriage partners, as tractable servant "hands," no matter how inconsiderate partners, husband, or employers may be. In "Tears of Kamala," the eponymous protagonist is raped nightly by her husband. If she cannot protect her physical being from violence, she shields her inner being by *"shut[ting] off her skin"* (89, emphasis in original). Only after counting out one hundred tears during her morning routine at the office—a daily and necessary ritual of mourning for her abused psyche—does she allow an alternate, happy self to emerge: after emptying her bowels, she eats ravenously; then, "her skin is on fire with feeling. Her body burns with a desire of such strength that she has to sit down to keep from falling over. . . . In these moments Kamala can no longer remember what has come before, so easy is it to sink into the net of vibrating sensation" (p. 93). Kamani suggests that women can reconstruct themselves but not without immense emotional suffering. In "The Cure," which I discuss in detail below, women are cautioned against their own sexuality at the same time that men are handed legal and liberal access to it. Kamani criticizes the idea that women, who seemingly pose a danger to themselves, can be cured or tamed of their pathological sexuality by only men. In numerous other stories, the bodies of female domestics (specifically their breasts, buttocks, and menstrual blood) are curiosities to young, developing girls from upper-middle-class households but considered dangerous and dirty to the girls' mothers; women's milk and blood are both nourishing and reviled; offensive body hair is waxed and plucked; and tears—blatant symbols of women's deep emotional vulnerability and abuse—are ironically the only acceptable female fluids.[8]

On the one hand, Kamani's bold and refreshing literary moves address sexuality openly, destabilizing readerly expectations about how gender is—or should be—approached, neither surreptitiously nor delicately alluded to. On the other, they consistently retreat from enabling female characters to defy their captors, which include mothers and peers who accept established systems of sexism and classism. Such conclusions unfortunately cancel out potentially affirming revisions of women that Kamani so boldly imagines, and her stories retain the potential of returning women to their socially imagined in-validity.

I begin by delineating Kamani's gesture toward reimagining South Asian women's social (and sexual) positions of inferiority through a close reading of "The Cure," facetiously alluding to women as diseased objects who necessitate a cure, reminiscent of the be-spotted woman gracing the collection's cover. Then I reevaluate Kamani's commitment to allowing women's bodies to surreptitiously leak beyond culturally defined borders by concentrating on the collection's female domestic laborers in stories such as "Shakuntala" and "Maria." In the end, class—inextricably tied to racial and gendered constraints—becomes the book's stumbling block whereby servants' unabashed flaunting and enjoyment of their bodies and sexualities limit their employability. To earn one's keep is to relinquish one's body. The collection thus poses intriguing questions about the intersection of class and gender: Is Kamani sensationalizing and hyper-sensualizing working-class bodies by creating close affinities among servants, their bodily pleasures, and their manual labor? Is this a devaluation of their humanity that is simultaneously an overt suggestion of what Kamani might deem an animality? Or is the corporeal and sexual repression practiced by their employers less human than the bodily pleasure attributed to Kamani's domestics? Such questions resound in a larger inquiry: What does capital embody? While the book focuses on bodies, pleasure, sexuality, and menstruation, it reestablishes the filthy women it cleans up by putting dirt (female bodies and their fluids) into its "proper" place—whether relegated to invisibility, to unutterability, or whether acknowledged only in relation to laboring, female bodies. In the end, Kamani's textual cure is allopathological, the results resisting their initial intent.

Wealthy women in Kamani's collection stigmatize corporeality not because they are unencumbered by bodily predicaments, but because they unconsciously practice socially accepted definitions of women's bodily pathology. In "The Cure," protagonist Baby's shocked and ashamed mother is disinclined to leave her daughter's condition well enough alone: teenaged Baby is blossoming into a veritable giant. Her body will not stop growing. Her mother fears not that this developmental atrocity will emotionally traumatize her daughter, but that it will prevent her marriageability and detrimentally affect the family's reputation, and she drags her to the clinic for a cure. Kamani's tongue-in-cheek story encourages us to laugh at the mother's antics—for what teenaged girl does not grow?—and roll our eyes at the doctor's outrageous diagnosis of Baby's hypersexuality. Beneath the humorous exaggeration lies Kamani's critique of the grave consequences of naming female sexual maturation as a natural process gone awry, encouraging us to sympathize with a character whose difference brings derision. Women like Baby's mother practice naturalizing sexism, eliminating the seam between proper action and complicit behavior, and rendering acceptable and invisible the continued pathologization of women.

In asking "What does exaggeration, as a mode of signification, exaggerate?" Susan Stewart's question about literary miniatures and giants turns our attention to the social inscription of women's bodies (1984:ix). Baby can be viewed as a blatant touting of a female grotesque, challenging women's confinement to established bodily parameters by outgrowing them—an *enormous* project, Kamani implies—at the same time that social reaction to her condition attempts to rehabilitate wayward corporeality. In tandem with Elizabeth Grosz's consideration of the liberating but culturally reviled female body, Stewart states that "[T]he giant . . . [is] a violator of boundary and rule; an overabundance of the natural and hence an affront to cultural systems" (1984:73). She concludes that "the gigantic presents a physical world of disorder and disproportion" (p. 74). Womanhood, or what Baby's mother views as an interior and harmful pathology, becomes exteriorized in gargantuan proportions. Baby's imagined disproportion represents the social rejection of her impending sexuality, itself a so-called dirty and disordering phenomenon. If the miniature is coded as feminine and therefore "idealized," its opposite is the gigantic, a dangerous "symbol of surplus and licentiousness, of overabundance and unlimited consumption" (Stewart 1984:80). It is no wonder that Baby's pediatrician derogatorily remarks that her patient is "Fundamentally over-sexed!" and "[A] danger to society. Sex hormones out of control. Shameless and uninhibited. Look how she tempts!" (Kamani 1995:49). In fact, the female doctor "shrieked as I entered her office. . . . She waved her arms about, as if asking the universe to explain my presence" (1995:49). With the introduction of the male Dr. Doctor, a "licensed sexologist" whose medical cure includes invasive sexual practices, Kamani probes into definitions of women's bodies, their pathologization and medicalization, illuminating how Baby's condition is erroneously attributed to women's bodily irresponsibility; Kamani troubles Baby's so-called disturbing natural immodesty and shameless flaunting.

Baby's condition, diagnosed as pathogenetic, becomes Kamani's allegorical narrative of the difficult transition from girl to woman in a culture that seemingly appreciates women's diminuation and miniaturization, both literally and figuratively. Kamani's hyperbole is the author's criticism of society's discomfort with sexuality, a discomfort inherited by a woman from her mother, and in this fashion passed from woman to woman. Baby's mother and her peers first accuse the towering girl of overweening pride that they themselves desperately desire: "They [the mother's female friends] wanted mother to take me on a pilgrimage, because I was obviously *too proud*, standing tall over all men, my elders, the gods and all" (Kamani 1995:47, emphasis in original). As well, mother and doctor unite in solidarity against the daughter, the doctor comforting her for her daughter's aberration, the mother appreciating a sympathetic shoulder. Baby's mother exhibits complicity in her daughter's oppression, unequivocally accepting her so-called abnormality as an irresponsible show of sexuality and unable to entertain any other conclusions for her otherwise healthy daughter.

Baby herself experiences no bodily discomfort, exhibits no signs of thelarche (premature maturation) or acromegaly (the medical term for giantism)[9] except when others attribute them to her. Baby is completely oblivious to her illicit behavior until its announcement-as-pathology. Rather, her condition is her parents' desire to stave off their daughter's natural maturation, exemplified in the infantilizing name "Baby." Her father's rationale for such a daughterly aberration is to accuse his wife; either the mother's genetic constitution or that of a lover's contributes to Baby's condition. He conveniently excuses himself from any biological or behavioral responsibility toward his daughter's illness.

The social constructedness of women's ills has long been attributed to women themselves and their unique bodily constitution, hence the ease in blaming women's biology and not the cultural construction of that biology. The creation and perpetuation of women's hysteria in the late nineteenth century is a case in point. Thus, to render the body unnatural is to deem it pathological. But to cure what is natural is itself unnatural. Baby's parents and her doctors construct larger-than-life narratives to console themselves about the inevitability of their charge's maturation.

Baby is depicted as a young woman physically, if not psychologically, molded into spaces where she no longer fits: her desk scrapes the tops of her knees; her legs no longer dangle from chairs; she bends herself in half climbing in and out of the car. Only at the Worli Sea Face does she feel uninhibited, scrambling out of the automobile and onto the sea wall, watched over by her approving chauffeur, Ramdass. "He didn't care that I was too tall, in fact it had never even entered his consciousness. To him, I was still 'Baby,' still the young child of his employer" (Kamani 1995:47). During such excursions he pays no heed to the speed limit, "rac[ing] the car down the usually empty road," and "the breeze would whip up my [Baby's] hair like a shredded black flag," illustrating a sense of liberation (p. 48): Ramdass is liberated from the boundaries of class with this free-spirited and easygoing charge (a tenuous liberation, I fully acknowledge, and to which I will return), and Baby is freed from the constraining judgments over her ungainly body. It is also at Worli that Baby first meets Dr. Doctor, a regular at the sea wall, who seems a grave but sophisticated man in his three-piece suit. He routinely nods politely at the two other visitors with his "long thin face" (p. 48). Yet on being hired as Baby's sexologist, his namelessness and facelessness come alive with a patriarchal genealogy conveniently and practically outlined on his calling card: "Dr. Cyrus Rustom Doctor, M.D., F.R.C.S. Son of Dr. Ardeshir Mehli Doctor, M.D. Grandson of Dr. Kekoo Naoriji Doctor, M.D." (p. 53). The repetition of titular authority in "Dr. Doctor" as the official title he claims pokes fun at a patriarch who takes himself too seriously—and doubly so.

Hiring Dr. Doctor cements the mother's relationship to—and blind acceptance of—a medical system sometimes inimical to women's health. For example, Kamani renders this licensed sexologist Baby's physical opposite. Baby may be a towering giant, a "jumbo child" who eats too much and grows too fast, yet she radiates health and unflagging energy (1995:47). Dr. Doctor, who seems solidly girded by a foundation of esteemed (male) professionals as exemplified on his calling card and in his appellation of "Dr. Doctor," is physically pathetic: "His face was hollow-cheeked with dark slashes for eyes and mouth. His legs were no thicker than bamboo poles and his cadaverous frame stooped forward, as though unable to support his narrow torso" (p. 51). During his visits, though, this usually reserved and seemingly fragile man whom Baby associates with the cadaverish figure at Worli becomes highly animated, probing Baby's genitals and vagina, collecting her womanly "essence" for perusal under the microscope.

Kamani suggests that men reap their health and well-being from women's debilitation, for Dr. Doctor's once passive body blossoms with vigor and strength vis-à-vis Baby's prostrate body. His seeming schizophrenia—from weak and wan gentleman to an aggressor performing medically sanctioned pedophilia—warns against the dangers lurking beneath a passive male exterior. Furthermore, Dr. Doctor's increasing familiarity with Baby precludes professionalism, indicating a growing sense of disregard for the patient whom he is violating for her female fluids, to "capture [her] essence" (Kamani 1995:58). This is aptly illustrated in his progressive dressing down at each appointment, from a suit and tie to, eventually, "an old short-sleeved shirt and floppy pants" (p. 61).

Baby does not recognize her sexuality as inappropriate or pathological, evident in her view of Dr. Doctor's initial appointment as a friendly visit. "I have a friend coming today!" she excitedly declares to Ramdass (Kamani 1995:54). Together they purchase a welcoming box of sweets, after which Baby agonizes over what to wear. His visit is hardly that of a revered friend. Rather, he implores his young patient to relax as he yanks off her panties and places his fingers inside her vagina. The usually modest Baby literally spreads her legs for Dr. Doctor's examination—doctors cannot but appreciate such pliant patients, Kamani seems wryly to suggest—both curious about and pleasured by the new bodily sensations he arouses within her. At first, "I could feel his thumb and two fingers pushing against my thighs. The other two fingers were pushing inside me, but I couldn't quite understand where. Was he trying to find my stomach from the inside?" (p. 57). She soon discovers that "his fingers slowly, gently, going round and round and up and down inside my pouch of skin" allowed her body to feel as if it were "floating away into the air" (p. 57). "Suddenly the tickle inside became very strong, burning me, and I had to put a hand on the doctor's head to keep from falling. I couldn't keep my legs bent any more, they were trembling" (p. 58). She believes the sensation is one of imminent urination, but a few moments later, her vagina closes tightly around Dr. Doctor's fingers in an orgasm. They both scream—Baby in surprised pleasure and the latter in plain surprise. That Baby can mistake pending urination for a pending orgasm reverses her diagnosis as oversexed and clearly illuminates medicine's role in constructing both knowledge and meaning.

Dr. Doctor's cure exacerbates just the oversexed condition her mother abhors. "I wondered whether I [Baby] should tell my mother that I could now do to myself what the doctor was supposed to" (Kamani 1995:64). Baby hardly protests her treatments. Rather, she becomes more adequately and efficiently self-prepared for the routine, removing her underpants without prompting, spreading her legs, relaxing, and enjoyably participating in the medical routine by delighting in her sexual self-discovery. Following her doctor's orders garners results that replicate just the pathological behavior that he has come to cure: *"immodesty and [propensity to] nakedness"* with *"no resistance to contact with her female chamber"* (p. 60). Dr. Doctor recommends that Baby commit herself to *"lifelong celibacy,"* even *"early sterilization in case of accidental penetration"* because *"coitus or other sexual stimulation will be deleterious to the patient's health"* (p. 60, emphasis in original). The respected physician introduces Baby to sexual pleasure at the same time that he strictly prohibits the patient from her own body, or from the so-called unhealthy environment of her genitals and of self-pleasuring. Baby adopts what has been denied to her, and in that adoption of learned sexuality she is pathologized. Meanwhile Dr. Doctor retains unlimited, licensed access to her genitals and to his own pleasures as he elbows his way between her thighs, licking his fingers and literally burying his arms inside of her.

Baby is eventually punished for transgressions of self-pleasuring, and for her continued growth, when she becomes Dr. Doctor's intended bride. Her mother hopes to resolve all of her daughter's medical and sexual problems (which are inevitably the mother's own) by securing her future through marriage to the first man who has violated her innocence. Baby's confirmed pathology becomes the mother's most valuable commodity. From her daughter's reviled condition arises a practical, even lucrative, solution that unfortunately perpetuates female disempowerment. The mother's consent to Baby's medical treatment and her assent to marriage are the affirmation of an ideology whose intent to in-validate women is adopted, inherited, and disseminated by women. The mother's rights to her daughter's body and bodily transgression become emblematic of Baby's disempowerment.

Baby's emotional needs are best met through the family chauffeur Ramdass, subtly illuminating Kamani's use of working-class bodies as essential ingredients to their employers' well-being but, ironically, their bodies become inessential to the laborers themselves. Baby feels the least self-conscious in Ramdass's company. He offers no commentary on Baby's growth nor any edification concerning her sexuality. Baby fantasizes about marrying this widower and discovering, on their nuptial bed, that he has promised his first wife fidelity. In her dreams, she dismisses such concerns, stating proudly that her detailed knowledge in self-pleasuring eliminates her desire for marital intercourse, allowing Ramdass to honor his first wife's promise of fidelity. On the one hand, Kamani eradicates the necessity, and the desire, for women's sexual intercourse with men, obviating a system where sexual pleasure is often gleaned by men through women. On the other hand, we must consider Ramdass's state as a widower and its troubling implications within a system of pleasure (not necessarily sexual) and class privilege. Without a wife and family of his own, he devotes his energy and attention to his employers, regarding Baby as "his own" in ways that encourage her fantasies to pivot on class privilege: How is she able to "use" Ramdass, to possess him as her own? Or, Baby—as the wealthy, privileged employer's daughter—can create narratives, benevolent to patriarchal desires, about other bodies that benefit her own desires. The specter of privilege and oppression creates an endless circuit, effectively obscuring who is culpable for each restrictive narrative and why.

Ramdass eventually discovers and weeps over Dr. Doctor's actions against Baby when he illegally enters the physician's house during a personal investigation for Baby's sake. He reveals the physician's numerous house calls to the same *memsahibs*[10] and "girls of good family . . . for ten, fifteen, twenty years. . . . What kind of doctor keeps his patients sick forever?" (Kamani 1995:65). Caught on the premises, he announces that Dr. Doctor would make an admirable husband for Baby, thus capitulating to the accepted view of her female abnormality, not because he believes it, so Kamani's story implies, but because he has no choice. As an employee tethered to pleasing the hand that pays him, he must betray Baby in articulating what his employer, Baby's mother, desires to hear. Ramdass cannot protect Baby and himself in the same way that wealthy and professional men, like Dr. Doctor, are able. The doctor's subsequent marriage proposal suggests that women's incurability is not a liability as long as men, or rather a certain type of economically solvent men, can protect them. Dr. Doctor states, "[W]here I cannot change the ways of nature in mending your daughter's body, at least I can offer my humble self as husband and protector of her womanhood" (p. 77). I suggest that Ramdass is enlisted in Baby's care and protection through avenues antithetical to himself. His revelation of Dr. Doctor's covert operations should alert Baby's mother to medical malpractice. Instead, the information places Ramdass, and not her mother, in a position dangerous to his own employment, for it is she who hires the exploiting doctor to her daughter's detriment. Ramdass's power of discovery is overturned by his disempowered class position.

Appalled and dismayed at her mother's easy consent to Dr. Doctor's proposal, Baby rebels in a sudden growth spurt: she feels her limbs itch and stretch, as if this last offense against women, like all those that came before, is a final provocation to the seemingly abnormal evolution of her bodily self. "Stop," she screams "at my limbs and at my mother. . . . Stop it now! . . . None of you can decide for me. None of you. I know what I am.

Not you . . . I am not an animal. I do not belong to you. I am not a slave. I am not scared of you" (Kamani 1995:78). At this outburst, her limbs are released from a tight grip, her muscles and flesh relax. She claims that her "body would no longer grow" and maturely recognizes that *"I'm bigger than all of you"* (p. 78, emphasis in original). Her understanding of the work of social construction surpasses that of her now figuratively diminutive mother and doctor, still adhering to their small-minded diagnoses, and she cures herself. But whether Kamani can sustain such a cure becomes the collection's challenge.

Stories like "The Cure" propose women's acquired, bodily self-regulation, but only at the same time that they distinguish among categories of bodies and attendant types of regulation. While Baby and her mother possess the luxury of obsessing, if detrimentally, over the body's natural maturation, servants' and maids' constant physical use of their laboring bodies prohibits such corporeal musings. Furthermore, the *memsahibs* who *oversee* their work also *see over* their employees' bodies: they demand and pay for the products of manual labor at the same time that they condemn the sweaty, dirty bodies that such production creates. They erase the corporeal they depend on in their own liberation from physical, bodily work. Corporeal labor and public respect occur in inverse proportion: the more the physical body is used in employment, the lower its class standing; the further the laboring body is removed from domestic ease, the more it is reviled. In desiring to escape their conditions of labor by working harder for more money, Kamani's servants only mire themselves more deeply in just the so-called shit from which they are powerless to extract themselves.

In many of Kamani's stories, the corporeal contest between upper and lower classes is voiced by naive narrators who are fascinated with the bodies of their families' domestic workers. In peeping at servants showering or in probing beneath their skirts with their toes, these young charges allow other bodies to do the work of sexual self-discovery, for the girls harbor an implicit sense that their prurient knowledge is taboo. On the one hand, the girls are awed by the corporeal presence of their maids and caretakers (rendering the latters' menstrual blood and breast milk fascinating) and the hushed but exciting references to the sexual activities of cooks and servants, both of which galvanize the girls' own ruminations over the mysteries of sexuality. On the other, the girls explicitly understand the unbreachable power structure erected between themselves and the effectively dehumanized notion of the "help," gleaned from their mothers' own classist attitudes that hierarchize their daughters' bodies as cleaner and more acceptable than that of their servants. Using this endowed privilege at the expense of their servants, girlish innocence remains suspect. Young women like Baby who are mired in a web of familial expectations, which are themselves culturally defined, often replicate their own sense of disempowerment *as* children vis-à-vis their family's servants and maids, positioning Kamani's collection as both a resistance and an acquiescence to gendered and class expectations. The privileged young women act; their poor servants are acted on, inviting one to easily conclude that women contribute to their own problems, thus overlooking other attendant cultural, patriarchal contributions to this phenomenon.

The story "Shakuntala" is a case in point: it collapses the distinction between upper- and lower-class bodies while re-erecting it by the story's conclusion, prohibiting any amelioration of societal, economic rifts. Shakuntala is charged with watching the *memsahib*'s unnamed daughter. Prohibited from playing in the filthy servant sleeping quarters and tethered to Shakuntala's side as she works, this daughter discovers pleasure in wiggling her toes beneath Shakuntala's large domed skirt, feeling the servant's wet and slippery "tortoise" inside (p. 107). In Kamani's typical cheeky manner, the scene explores amusing appellations for and visualizations of female genitalia and foregrounds female pleasure wherein both prober and probee gain some satisfaction from their pseudo-sexual "games." The "hands" and "heads" are momentarily united.

The girl's explorations may be amusing to her, but have devastating consequences when the young girl tests the extent of her social and domestic power over an employee. She reports Shakuntala's forbidden forays into the cook's quarters, for example, which seals Shakuntala's dismissal. The hired help, who are described as "help" and not human beings, are forbidden from mingling, denying them a very human need for companionship. Shakuntala's sexual play with the unclean cook, as the mother deems him, is regarded as a transgression of decency. This charge is exacerbated by the knowledge that Shakuntala has been nurturing, on her own milk and blood, a blind kitten beneath her skirt, with which Kamani puns on the doubled meanings of "pussy." The use of servants' corporeality as labor vis-à-vis the secreted "pussy" reveal what the *memsahibs* attempt to self-conceal—sex and sexuality. Shakuntala is dismissed less for her sexual liaison with the cook than for revealing too much about women's natural functions to her employer's daughter: her breasts constantly dribble milk in the absence of a nursing infant, until she relieves them against a tree trunk; the daughter's toes become covered with menstrual blood when Shakuntala's "pussy" bites them.[11]

Kamani delineates the more tenuous than rigid division between classed female bodies by exhibiting how corporeal functions and fluids—whose commonality among seemingly divided women—unite them. Shakuntala leaves; the "pussy" stays as an unintended legacy of her corporeality and her labor. In retaining the "dirty" aspect of her servant's body (in raising the kitten as her own) the mother offers it a new meaning. While it served as a surrogate child for Shakuntala, all of whose daughters were buried at birth, then perhaps this *memsahib* is pleasantly reminded of her own bodily functions, of blood that embodied and birthed her daughter, of milk that nourished her.

Embodied by Shakuntala, the pussy is both playful and annoying—it bites. It is also regarded as unclean at the same time that the kitten becomes a metaphor for women's natural sexuality in its nourishment via Shakuntala's blood and milk. In her employer's possession, however, the kitten becomes a toy, cute and cuddly, but is endowed with a specific cultural meaning that the mother passes along to her daughter. For soon after Shakuntala is fired, the girl places the kitten between her own thighs. She replicates the servant's actions, suggesting the girl's own burgeoning sexuality as well as her affinity, across class lines, with all women. The blind pussy is not indicative of solely

Shakuntala; it surpasses all class boundaries by representing universal female anatomy, literally blind to class differences. While the girl wields power over the family "hands," she reconstructs their bodily play, engaging in just the behavior her mother finds so reprehensible. As such, Kamani draws parallels to "The Cure" by illuminating the hypocrisy of learned behavior through women who erase the shame of bodily functions only to reerect them. The pussy symbolizes how fixed meanings are destabilized and, here, restabilized to restitute classist categorization.

Despite Shakuntala's easy dismissal, her servant body serves as a convenient catalyst by which mother and daughter confront each other. The girl is poised in a space between obedience to her mother and power over Shakuntala; she explores the vast new world of sexuality at the same time that she is limited by her mother's prudence. She acknowledges that she should be repulsed by Shakuntala's "dirty" body, but this recognition only fuels her fascination with it, a daring confrontation of her mother's dictates. In this sense, Shakuntala erects a bridge between mother and daughter (the girl defies her mother via the domestic) at the same time that the daughter unwittingly connects mother to servant (the girl's transgression beneath Shakuntala's skirt provokes the mother's confrontation with the domestic). But finally, loyalty to Shakuntala is disloyalty to her mother. Relationships across class boundaries cannot exist simultaneously. Thus, the girl must betray Shakuntala to retain her mother's respect, as Ramdass in "The Cure" must betray his charge in order to retain employment.

Shakuntala's body announces the idiosyncrasy of a repulsion and fascination with the body. Because Shakuntala is dressed in mirrored blouses and long skirts, she sweats profusely, "a thick band [of sweat] reaching down to her navel" (p. 103). *Memsahib*, who orders labor but performs none of it herself, dons "a much shorter blouse, which left a wide band of skin exposed from her ribs to her waist," indicating that the body is employed in inverse proportion to its sartorial revelation (p. 103). The exposed body becomes a decorative luxury; the laboring body conceals the corporeal mechanism of its survival. Yet

Shakuntala, seemingly bundled up in her long skirts and blouses, exhibits a bodily ease that defies the nature of her modest dress. *Memsahib* in her crop tops lets it all hang out, so to speak, through her constant nagging: "Shakuntala! Ehh Shakuntala! . . . Go on now, leave the peas alone. Go get those two children and give them a bath. . . . Arrey woman! At least put the peas away. You don't want the birds to eat them. Where are you putting the peas? Put them in the fridge . . . but cover them first!" and so on (p. 102). If it is on and through Shakuntala's body that the mother finds the pussy and metes out punishment, then the domestic becomes the dramatic externalization of the mother's repression of bodily self-acceptance and enjoyment. And, while Shakuntala may be obedient in principle to her employer's demands as a seemingly silent presence, her body "speaks" loudly, and with frenzied action, as she scratches the "irritated skin" beneath her ankle rings, which sound against each other like "muffled temple bells" (p. 102); she rips open the pea pods, finding embedded worms and cracking them between her nails; she snaps her skirt smartly, sending peas dinging into a metal bowl; she places large peas beneath her tongue, "sucking [them] with hissing sounds" and "[s]macking her lips loudly" (p. 102). The sounds and actions of Shakuntala's restless body harangue and compete with the mother's noisy, nagging rants, themselves filled with allusions to the dirt banned from the family's interior: worms that eat furniture, grit beneath Shakuntala's nails, the "dirty mouth" and stealing hands of the cook (p. 105). The girl is nonetheless attracted to Shakuntala's "secret skin" and "the heat of her legs on my feet and calves," rendering the servant more fleshly human than the mother, whose intermittent ravings signal a disembodied voice, cold and harsh against Shakuntala's warm legs (p. 106). Shakuntala provides the affection the girl expects, but never receives, from her mother. The warm and filthy domestic body both destabilizes and reinforces differences between the classes.

Kamani may have named her character after the classic South Asian "dramatic" *kavya* (lyric poetry) called *Śakuntala*, sometimes written "Shakuntala.")[12] Penned by fifth-century poet Kālidāsa, the poem chronicles the process by which "gross

sensuality" becomes both "domestic felicity" and "divine ecstasy" (K. Krishnamoorthy 1972:213), where Śakuntala is the
personification of the "natural" and her lover, King Dusyanta,
of the "social" (Barbara Stoler Miller 1994:206). Kamani's story
hardly transforms sensuality into domestic felicity. For while
Shakuntala's cat/crotch alludes to the natural processes of menstruation, breastfeeding, and sexuality, the girl and her mother
are loath to accept them as anything but filthy, and the processes
come to represent the social (re)construction of the natural: "You
people," the mother says, categorizing all the hired help, "are
like animals, you can't control yourself" (Kamani 1995:114).
Shakuntala's sexual exploits and her improper sensuality engen-
der domestic unrest. If any divine ecstasy exists, it is that of the
young girl's fascination with and enjoyment of the black cat/
crotch, the turtle hidden under Shakuntala's domed skirt, and
the curious nipping at the young girl's toes.[13] Shakuntala's so-
called mysteries elevate her in the girl's eyes at the same time
that they degrade Shakuntala. Variations of what is considered
filthy can elevate or degrade her body (as laborer, as sexual object) depending on one's economic position.

Kamani's story "Maria" repeats threads of "Shakuntala"
when a young charge, as voyeur, watches the family servant
Maria make liberal and pleasurable use of her employer's
shower. "Normally, she [Maria] bathed out of a bucket in the
servants' quarters, squatting down fully clothed, sloshing water
over her head with a tumbler, just as she had always done in her
village" (p. 127). Immediately, the story establishes gradations
of hygiene according to the accessibility of running water and
categorizes degrees of undress during cleaning routines as
classed: the poor clean themselves "fully clothed" while the rich
enter their showers naked. As a forbidden zone, the shower de-
marcates clear boundaries between class and cleanliness. The
domestics, already discerned as filthy—the protagonist's mother
calls the servants' rooms "filthy" and a "pigsty"—are economically prohibited from becoming clean in the absence of their own
showers and in their habit of bathing fully clothed (p. 132).
Aware of the irony, Maria remarks to her charge, "You people
grow up in these big-big houses and you don't know which hole

is what!" (p. 133). "You people" may be clean and wealthy, she suggests, but "don't know shit," announces the hypocrisy and narrow-mindedness of these upper-class employers.

In her spying, the girl becomes a voyeur of her own body, its sexuality deemed off limits, reminiscent of Baby's predicament. While peeping at Maria's illicit showering, the girl is both un-nerved and excited: "My legs shook and my head swam so I had to lean forward and rest against the frosted glass. Maria spread her buttocks to let the water in, arching her back, then bending forward. I felt her fingers moving as though they were my own and I suddenly wanted to share with Maria how excited I was" (p. 127). The girl comes to appreciate not necessarily her own body, but the power structure that divides her "clean" self from the "filthy" bathroom intruder, for soon after, the narrator threatens to inform her mother of Maria's hygienic transgression "unless she did what I wanted"—allow her to play with Maria's nipples (p. 131). Curious and soon bored with this activity, she is eager to see what Maria houses below her breasts. "Same as you, baby, only same as you," says Maria, squeezing her thighs and iterating what the girl and her mother cannot see or refuse to acknowledge: that she is the same as they, a woman in a body (p. 131).

When Maria refuses to indulge the girl's pleasure, like Sha-kuntala she is eventually dismissed for both expressing sexual desire and for refusing to submit to the girl's demands; the girl replicates her mother's power by clinching Maria's dismissal. In similarly concluding both "Maria" and "Shakuntala," Kamani suggests that economic power and sexual maturation are inter-related. The more the girls learn of sexuality, the more their mothers suppress their knowledge, marking Maria's overt refer-ences to corporeality crass and the mothers' silence sophisti-cated. The conclusion to "Maria" bears this out when the young narrator insists that she name the succeeding "girl," or "ser-vant," Maria as well. Her mother replies, "You can call her any-thing you want" (p. 137). That the mothers and daughters remain unnamed in both stories attests to the power of privilege and its attendant act of naming others.

In her glowing review of *Junglee Girl*, Patricia Holt of the *San Francisco Chronicle* quotes Kamani on the subject of class:

> When I went back to Bombay, I couldn't stand the arbitrary way in which a lot of people I knew treated their servants, cursing the whole lot of them as unreliable and stupid and illiterate. A lot of the rage and anger that should be going upward in the hierarchy ends up going downward. It goes from men to women, from parents to children, from humans to animals, from rulers to servants. (p. 2)

The passage reveals Kamani's sympathies for those at the "bottom" of the hierarchy in a system with "no sense that two unequal people can come to some kind of understanding" (p. 2). In the collection's examples, the abject is a woman of a lower class who, unlike Baby verbalizing her anger or unlike Kamala shutting down her skin, cannot and do not rebel. Rather, as their bodies become unintentional rebellions against sexual prudery, they are cursorily dismissed. If this collection is a textual window into what Kamani views as the way things are, does it stand as such a simple revelation—of things as they are—or does it move toward (quiet) revolution? The paperback version of the book's back cover claims the novel as "a rightful space for Indian women to define themselves," invoking the notion of liberation. Yet my critique questions who, indeed, are the "junglee girls" of the book's title: the "innocent" girls or the domestic laborers? Who is more wild than the other and why? And are these junglee girls ultimately tamed by those who attempt to validate the in-valid?

Kamani positions divisions between notions of health and illness, purity and dirt, innocence and experience on a tenuous divide. Reconsider, for example, the novel's cover image: while the featured woman is certainly clothed, the sheer fabric exposes more than it conceals. Is she nude (provocative) or is she dressed (modest)? Dismantling the mutual exclusivity of these terms becomes the collection's most interesting proposition: Can one be both? And if so, how is such a space inhabited? Sonia Shah, in her autobiographical essay "Tight Jeans and Chania Chorris"

(1995), offers a sartorial example of the ability to straddle two seemingly mutually exclusive spaces.[14] Sonia, a freshman at Oberlin College, is steeped in her first dose of feminist consciousness raising and thus disapproves of her younger sister's sexual flaunting in tight jeans and midriff tops that are met with approving male glances. The young women's mother, an emigrant from a small Indian town, is outraged at her younger daughter for cultural reasons, while Sonia is chagrined for feminist reasons. The younger sister is eventually subjected to a three-month "exile" to India (Shah 1995:117), presumably to correct her wild, Western ways. She returns in *chania chorris*, "sets of midriff-baring blouses and long full skirts worn under saris," the tops backless, which young South Asian girls often wear sans sari (p. 117). Her parents, once shocked and dismayed by *chania chorris*–like Western counterparts (halter tops and baring blouses), loved the sister's look. "Both Mom and Dad oohed and ahhed, telling her to turn around again, to wear it to an upcoming festival. She pirouetted about flirtatiously. They beamed and clapped. I was dumbfounded, the family friction over my sister's sexuality suddenly and miraculously dissipated" (p. 117). The once unutterable shock at an excessive show of skin is alternately lauded with "oohs" and "aahs," themselves hardly full linguistic articulations. If these sounds were once uttered by the sister's male admirers and duly condemned by her parents, they now exemplify the celebratory status of visible flesh within a new context. At issue is hardly the clothing's scantiness but rather strands of competing cultural, generational, feminist, and national definitions. Kamani's most interesting project, then, delves into nuancing a divide where undress can simultaneously represent "good" and "bad" cultural practices, where cure embodies illness and illness produces cure, where filthy can come clean through dirty practices. But her wresting apart of (healthy) physicality and (dirty) sexuality through class considerations unnaturally undermines the complexity of their confluence.

I will revisit what I consider Kamani's leakiness of binary stratification in chapter 5 as it pertains to women who intentionally ingest tabooed food as a feminist stance against marriage in Kamani's "The Smell," which I then link to women's entanglement in food toxins, men, and meat in Ruth L. Ozeki's *My Year of Meats* (1998). But for now, suffice it to say that Kamani's interest in exploding binary divisions confronts its limits at the feet (and breasts, buttocks, and menstrual blood) of the laboring class. In Kamani's text, the challenge to a model of female disempowerment is itself disempowered, and the reader is left with graphic images whose revelations hardly extend far enough in revealing the woman beneath.

I return to the "thing," or to the female pubic area, discussed at this chapter's beginning, to illuminate the unsaid power of silent servants. In "Waxing the Thing," the unnamed beautician from the rural countryside—"a simple village girl" (Kamani 1995:117)—harbors insight into her economically privileged customers who shamelessly buy into a beauty regimen that consistently exploits women: "They're very clever these rich ladies. But very stupid also. They force their daughters to be beautiful so they can arrange a match with a rich boy, but in the end they are marrying off their girls to boys who are exactly the same as their fathers, who make this and that excuse and don't touch one finger to their wives who are waxed clean and ready from head to toe" (pp. 122–123). Her wealthy clients regard her as an unmarried, "poor village girl"(p. 121), yet she possesses the skills they eagerly seek, and she profits from their obsessions over maintaining a clean and smooth "thing." "I tell you these ladies think they know everything," the narrator confesses, but "I am going to have a love marriage, and have enough money saved so that I can give a good dowry. What husband will say no to that?" (p. 122). She rejects the often loveless coupling arising from arranged marriages. She does so not by verbal rebellion or protest, but by quietly accruing enough money, through her own hard labor, to seek out and "catch" her own husband. While waxing the unutterable "thing," her labor speaks to a silent rebellion, not only against the labor of waxing, but also against what that "dirty" thing has come to signify—money, class privilege, and the politics of cleanliness. Notions of filth are entangled with all women's "things." The labor involved in reimagining them implicates the clean with the dirty and the laboring with the labored on, blurred distinctions from which nothing can come utterly—and unutterably—clean.

Notes

1. A fascinating counterpoint to the political dirtying of Asians and Asian Americans is that of young first- and second-generation Indian and South Asian Americans who adhere to nostalgic constructions of homeland as chaste, according to Sunaina Maira in *Desis in the House: Indian American Youth Culture in New York City* (2002). Their beliefs castigate "mainstream American cultural tropes [as] . . . 'seductive' and 'polluting' influences from which ethnic identity must be protected," whereas "[i]mages of ancestral culture portray traditions as 'pure' and 'innocent'" (p. 78; see Maira's chapter "Chaste Identities: The Eroticization of Identities," Maira 2002:149–187).

2. In his article "Filthy Rites," Stephen Greenblatt states that "the very conception that a culture is alien rests upon the perceived difference of that culture from one's own behavioral codes, and it is precisely at the points of perceived difference that the individual is conditioned, as a founding principle of personal and group identity, to experience *disgust*" (1982:3, emphasis added).

3. Women's uncontainability within heteronormative parameters threaten to flow beyond established and acceptabled (b)orders. Such a view rejects the Cartesian model of a gendered mind/body duality, the latter relying "on essentialism, naturalism and biologism," states Grosz, "[which is] misogynist thought [that] confines women to the biological requirements of reproduction on the assumption that because of particular biological, physiological, and endocrinological transformations, women are somehow *more* biological, *more* corporeal, and *more* natural than men" (1994:14, emphasis in original).

4. Luce Irigaray, in *This Sex which Is Not One* (1985), imagines all the possibilities in which the female lack—that sex which is not one—is more readily a persistent presence, rendering the subversive qualities of the mechanics of female (abject) flow and (filthy) fluid as worthy substances (see her "The 'Mechanics' of Fluids," pp. 106–118). Judith Butler, in *Gender Trouble: Feminism and the Subversion of Identity* (1990), destroys the binary construction of sex into male and female camps and proposes a theory of gender performance that replaces biologically predetermined (fixed) constructions of sex and gender.

5. The definition of "junglee" is taken from the back cover of the paperback version of *Junglee Girl* (Kamani 1995).

6. This is excepting Kamani's story "Just Between Indians," which takes place in New York City.

7. See Arif Dirlik's "Asians on the Rim: Transnational Capital and Local Community in the Making of Contemporary Asian America" (1999:45).

8. Of all bodily fluids within the field of anthropology, "only tears are considered clean" (see Lawrence S. Kubie 1937:394).

9. According to Helmut Bonheim's "The Giant in Literature and Medical Practice" (1994), "symptoms of acromegaly include changes in the growth and quality of hair, the hunching of the back, the swelling of lips and ears, pain in the joints, impaired vision, and bouts of inordinate thirst," none of which Baby possesses.

10. A servant respectfully addresses the woman of the house as *memsahib*; it used to refer to only white women, but this is no longer the case. I thank Asha Sen for this information.

11. "Menstrual taboos are among the most inviolate in many societies," states Janice Delaney, Mary Jane Lupton, and Emily Toth in *The Curse: A Cultural History of Menstruation* (1988), stemming from the "[f]ear of blood, says Freud, who states furthermore that the blood phobia may also 'serve' aesthetic and hygienic purposes" (p. 7).

12. Barbara Stoller Miller (1994) calls the play a "dramatic romance" that "is based on an episode from the epic *Mahabharata* . . . a model of the genre known as *nataka*," or the "heroic romance" in her "Two Classical Indian Plays: Kalidasa's Śakuntala and Śudraka's *Little Clay Cart*" (pp. 201–202).

13. The Sanskrit play also provokes deep emotional reactions within its audience members who are asked to mediate the "critical tension between duty and desire" (Miller 1994:203). If the play is "[s]tructured to give the spectator an experience of extraordinary universality" amid "conflicting social values," then Kamani's story exposes how universal harmony is prevented by the classist views embraced by the *memsahib* and her daughter (p. 203).

14. I thank Jana French for offering up this reference many years before I found its potential usefulness in this chapter.

4

Animals and Systems of Dirt in the Novels of Lois-Ann Yamanaka

From the domesticated to the feral, from the loved to the tortured, from the taxidermal to those inevitably destined for the dinner table, a collection of mangy animals populates the pages of three novels by Lois-Ann Yamanaka: *Wild Meat and the Bully Burgers* (1996), *Blu's Hanging* (1997), and *Heads by Harry* (1999). On the one hand, Yamanaka's depictions conjure up a historical trajectory based in Yellow Peril rhetoric that coupled animals and abject Asian Americans, here Chinese immigrants. According to Nayan Shah, comparisons between Chinese and farm animals, especially rats and pigs, encouraged existing perceptions that these immigrants were inhuman and thus inferior to Whites (2001:27). Rats and pigs in particular have a "place in the racist bestiary because all are associated with residues—food waste, human waste—and in the case of rats there is an association with spaces which border civilized society, particular subterranean spaces like sewers, which also channel residues and from which rats occasionally emerge to transgress the boundaries of society" (Shah quotes David Sibley [Shah 2001:27]). On the other hand, the manner in which Yamanaka sensitively discusses animals in relation to—and not via a conflation of—Hawaiian Locals and their pets defies any easy collapse between an imagined Asian American pathology and bestiality. Animals and their human(e) treatment assist the novels' Local Japanese female protagonists in arriving at sexual and self-realization, processes often inflected and impeded by economic circumstances surrounding their raced and female-gendered status. In my reading, animals announce an economy of dirt and defilement that lends itself to complicated interpretations of the relations between animals and humans.

I begin by referencing the Euro Polynesian wild pig of *Heads by Harry* that I view as a central metaphor of ecological imperialism and land rights and through which I read issues of race, class, and gender. These pigs have been destroying to near extinction several varieties of native Hawaiian plants by using their long, razor-sharp tusks (which can reach phenomenal seven-foot lengths) to rototill the soil. Yamanaka's *Heads* references actual feral pig extermination regulation in Hawai'i Volcanoes National Park, ordinances that allow limited, legal hunting as swine population control and eco-preservation.

Ecologists, animal rights activists, the national parks service, and hunters debate similar ethical, monetary and recreation related questions raised by the "old futs" of Yamanaka's *Heads*, who discuss the pig situation and their livelihoods over cold beers and *pupus* (appetizers). Taxidermist Harry O. states, "By golly, . . . [the pigs are] our recreation, and my bread and butter, and I am against them [whom he calls 'the feds'] killing my fun and my income. Maverick [Harry O.'s neighbor and a park-employed pig hunter] told me they cannot even haul out the pigs for the meat or to mount, nothing. They leave the pigs to waste there. Hey now, that's what I call harming the ecosystem" (Yamanaka 1999:61). "Old fut" Uncle Herb agrees that the inhumanity of killing pigs who breed numerous offspring is not in the suffering inflicted on those left for dead—a position advocated by animal rights activists—but rather, "[I]nhumane is we cannot smoke the meat" (p. 62), especially considering that this Hawaiian variety of feral pig can reach "200-plus pounds of thrashing muscle," certainly a hefty load of wasted pork (Bob McNally 1995:17).[1] Others contribute equally weighty points, such as how organized, "fed"-sponsored pig hunting provides paychecks for young, uneducated men in a community of high unemployment. That the status of the Euro Polynesian pig is more heated than benign, pitting advocates of consumption against ecology-minded groups bent on flora and fauna preservation, drives my questions concerning *what* and *how* filthy animals signify within Yamanaka's Local community caught up in land rights and self-preservation issues.

The pig's conflicted status—as benign or destructive, as food or target practice, as alien or "natural," for human employment (and profit) at the expense of animal suffering—begs difficult questions concerning not only the preservation of "natural" land, but also the process and consequences (for animals and humans) by which it is achieved. Throughout this essay, I refer to the complexity of land (ab)use through the mercenary, yet apropos, term "real estate." The so-called alien Euro Polynesian pig, in its "de-naturalization" of the landscape, crystallizes numerous valid controversies endemic to Hawaii's embattled history of claiming, usurping, domesticating, (re)naming, colonizing, and preserving land. The colonization of Hawai'i has cast into poverty the propertyless who have worked the land and into power those who have acquired it, whether legally or not. Included in this fray are issues related to Native sovereignty and indigenous land rights[2] as well as the stated claims of non-Native Local subjects who are descendents of plantation laborers from China, Japan, Korea, the Philippines, Puerto Rico, Portugal, Norway, Germany, and Russia (Eileen T. Tamura 1994). The term Local refers to a relationship to the Hawaiian land quite different from that of Natives, yet Local constituents are equally fierce in their territorial claims to Hawai'i.[3] Even the wealthier Local Japanese in Yamanaka's work practice discriminatory behavior against their poorer Japanese counterparts, mirroring their own treatment by a larger society that views Locals and Natives as filthier and less civilized citizenry. The complexities of Hawaii's colonization and racial stratification vexes debates that are no longer merely about animal bodies: Which human bodies legally belong on/to the land and why? What types of land use and destruction (invasion) should be permitted and which denied? And who decides the answers, affecting the outcomes, of these vexing questions?

I examine the Euro Polynesian pig as a metaphor for larger issues: its filthy, alien, and destructive presence on native soil; its hybridity; its social acceptability as pet or non-pet; its negotiated value as either sustenance or profit, as useful (as food, for example) or useless (a "natural" park's menace). However, I dismiss any simplistic one-to-one correspondence between humans and animals, into which such an argument could dangerously slip. Through the use of animals in three of Yamanaka's novels, I investigate how forays into the term "natural" have generated erroneous social categories. I intend to expose the linguistic and semantic seams of Yamanaka's use of words and affiliations, referencing dirt, both natural and constructed. By the conclusion of this chapter, I critique Yamanaka's unsettling absence of reference to indigenous people and issues. I expose what her novels overlook, not to answer for Yamanaka, but to provocatively examine how these oversights deeply problematize many of her novels' implications about land and territory and about class, race, and gender as they are bound up in cultural economies of filth.

I first outline the heated controversy over Hawaiian land preservation in its inextricable connection to Native Hawaiian sovereignty claims, arguments that are crucial to understanding the islands' history of annexation and subsequent plantation labor by immigrants, most notably Asian nationals and their descendents. Relatedly, issues of staking out intellectual ground in scholarship by and about Locals, including how the act of naming that ground decidedly shapes it, is echoed in the consternation among Asian American scholars over how to categorize literature authored by Hawaiians and Locals: How is the literature's relationship to the two halves of the term "Asian American" both similar to and different from the mainland's definition of "Asian American" literature? Battles over territorial rights continue to affect how Hawai'i—as territory, as concept, as real, fictional, recreational, and literary space—is used and defined by whom and for what purposes. After constructing this necessary theoretical scaffolding, I draw initial literary examples from *Wild Meat* and *Blu's*, and, in the last third of the essay, focus exclusively on *Heads*.

The idea of conserving precious and beautiful land through the creation of a national parks system seems valid and innocent, important and noble. Yet our nation has practiced an unfortunate history of land colonization that complicates current issues surrounding the practice of what I deem racist real estate, its legitimization and preservation. In 1972, Congress designated territory in Wyoming and Montana as "a public park or pleasuring ground for the benefit and enjoyment of the people," hence the creation of Yellowstone National park (Kurian 1998:417). There is an irony in the congressional establishment of a natural "pleasuring ground" vis-à-vis the extirpation of former Native Americans and their subsequent containment within reservations (a word only one letter short of "preservation"). One wonders whose pleasure and whose public Congress references. Similar terminology is used in the 1916 act establishing Hawai'i National Park, subsequently renamed Hawai'i Volcanoes National Park in 1961, "perpetually dedicated and set apart as a public park or *pleasure ground* for the benefit and enjoyment of the people of the United States" (*The Statutes at Large of the U.S. of America* [1917], emphasis added). In 1917 (the act's official authorization date), the Hawaiian Islands were still an American protectorate and not a legally designated state;[4] thus, one might ask for whom these pleasuring grounds were created and maintained, demanding how we define *the people*—hence *the public*—in the government document's phrase " 'the people' of the United States." Do Natives and Locals fall inside or outside this designation? And what, in fact, is being preserved?

If not committed to preserving certain (Native) people and their culture, then the park preserves the idea of "nature," one method by which to assuage guilt about the devastating removal of "natural" elements, whether people or plants. "The great parks," states Dean MacCannell,

> but especially the National Parks, are symptomatic of the guilt which accompanies the impulse to destroy nature. We destroy nature on an unprecedented scale, then in response to our wrongs, we create parks which re-stage the nature/society opposition. . . . The park is supposed to be a reminder of what nature would be like if nature still existed. As a celebration of nature, the park is the 'good deed' of industrial civilization. It also quietly affirms the power of industrial civilization to stage, situate, limit, and control nature. (1992:115)

If the park's environment is already (re)constructed or (p)re-served in the name of authenticity, then do we call it supernatural? But the larger point is hardly one of semantics. The linguistic play conceals devastating issues of indigenous removal that Yamanaka herself renders invisible in her literary works. She encourages the recognition of Local Japanese human dignity that is ultimately entangled in questions of Native dignity. If the latter is beneficial to, even contingent on, the former, its disappearance affects the value of Native dignity.

Reading Yamanaka's novels through postcolonial theories that un/remap authority once wielded over people and their locales in both literal and figurative ways reveals how their physical and literary terrains are charged with conflict. In Hawai'i, postcolonialism invokes an embattled contact with the West that resulted in colonization, annexation, Local-staged labor disputes, and the immense usurpation of Native images into a multimillion-dollar tourist industry that imagines an "authentic," sexualized, and native identity for economic purposes. In contemporary cultural scholarship of the Pacific Rim, the politics of naming places proliferate with "proper" and "rectified" (or guilt-laden) acts of renaming and replacing territories/islands/states whose appellations have been conflicted for centuries. This is evident as early as Captain John Cook's arrival on the Sandwich Islands; his appellative choice "New Island" reflected the territory's novelty to Cook and crew while ignoring its vibrant existence, for a millennia, before their arrival (Houston Wood 1999:24). More recently, the title of Rob Wilson's *Reimagining the American Pacific* (2000) accurately illustrates the politics of a regional *reimagining* and renaming,[5] while Nicholas Thomas prefers the reinvocation of *Oceania* (1997) in order to forge connections between Hawai'i and Micronesia as places inextricably connected, not abstracted, by "traffic and colonization" (p. 5). "In general," Thomas states, "European and indigenous *imaginings*—of history and place—have intersected, not merged" in what he deems "theaters for imagining" (pp. 5, 4, emphasis added). The process of appellation-as-definition begs questions about the politicization of naming: For whom and for what purpose are the islands named, and to what (devastating) end?

Complicating these already vexing issues is the manner in which Native and many Local subjects consider—and lay claim to—Hawai'i as their homeland. Contemporary Native Hawaiians' embattled push for sovereignty emphasizes the loss of physical place, notwithstanding human dignity, to the United States. To the ring of "Aloha 'Āina" or "love of the land," Natives have been politically mobilized in order to reclaim the "1.2 million acres of Ceded Trust Lands and 190,000 acres of Hawaiian Homes Trust Lands . . . seized during the illegal overthrow of the Hawaiian monarchy by American businessmen in 1893," states Candace Fujikane (1994).[6] As well, they bemoan the loss of culture, spirituality, and community that thrived long before the arrival and eventual dominion of missionaries and sugar plantations. Locals, too, stake fierce claims to the land—each naming it "homeland," says Fujikane—given their own embattled labor-, racial-, and class-inflected histories, battles mirrored in the Local's "multiple and contradictory" definitions. The term arose among plantation workers of predominantly Asian nationalities—but also included those of Portuguese and German descent—who united against plantation owners' nefarious strategy to play one group of ethnic workers against another: employing Filipinos, for example, as strike breakers for protesting Japanese laborers. Despite such evidence of ethnic solidarity, John M. Liu states, "Portuguese were not classified with whites on the plantations. Rather they were treated as a distinct category between Asians and other Caucasians," yet more white than others (1984:207, note 12). If Portuguese and Germans were more acceptably white, and therefore privileged to occupy *luna* (foremen) positions in overseeing Japanese, Chinese, Filipinos, and Koreans, then internal ethnic hierarchies emerged, the internal battles for which white *lunas* strove in order to maintain low wages and guard against prolonged production interruptions. Such conflicts vex the definition of Local, which itself resonates with the politics of who is allowed to *reimagine* real estate, why, and to what end. More recently, Natives and Locals collectively have resisted the encroachment of white (economic) designs—

including the seemingly unstoppable neocolonialism of resort hotels and the rapidly expanding concrete stretches comprising airports and island roads for transporting its seven million annual tourists—but their goals have not always been unified and conflict free.[7] In fact, Locals themselves feel an immense ambivalence in claiming land from which Natives have been displaced, what Fujikane deems the Locals' illegitimate claim to illegitimately seized land.

This has understandably escalated into heated debates about legitimacy, ownership, and (neo)colonization in other territories, namely those of literary production concerning Hawaiian and Local fiction and criticism, creating what Houston Wood calls "geopolitical and geoliterary games" (1999:52). Hence, scholars continue to play out a form of *reimagination*, as invoked by Wilson and Thomas, proposing appellations—with and against existing terminology—that they believe are the most amenable to both the geopolitics of the literature of Hawai'i and within the literary terrain called Asian American studies: Stephen H. Sumida (1992) discusses Hawaii's Asian/Pacific literatures, the slash (/) a recognition of a contest, not a harmony, between the two terms;[8] Candace Fujikane (1994) critiques the term Asian/Pacific American and suggests in its stead Asian/Pacific Islander, which is now the official demographic categorization. Wood criticizes Local authors such as Erick Chock, Darrell Lum, Lois-Ann Yamanaka, and literary critic Sumida—Asian American writers who "supplant," according to Wood, the tradition of "EuroAmerican anti-conquest rhetoric" of Mark Twain, Jack London, and James Michener—for conflating Local and Native Hawaiian experiences that are not synonymous (1999:51). Wood states, in conjunction with my own views, "Such rhetoric linking the Hawaiian people's experience of having their land colonized and their nation overthrown with stories of immigration plantation struggles undermines claims for indigenous rights and reparations" (1999:51).[9] Clearly, Hawaiian land is hardly a paradise, although touted as such by thousands of airlines and tourist brochures. In fact, Jamie James's review of *Heads by Harry* remarks that Lois-Ann Yamanaka "sings of anything but a paradise" (James 1999:90). Fujikane (1994) also states that "popular representations of Hawai'i [construct it] as an apolitical paradise," when, in fact, it is immensely political. Its embattled past cannot be divorced from its Native and Local constituents' present. In Sumida's words, "[I]n Hawaii's island culture *place* is conceived *as history*—that is, as the story enacted on any given site" (1992:216).[10]

Given this brief introduction to Hawaii's land rights issues, cultural practices, and literary history, any attempt to preserve (legitimately or illegitimately) its natural spaces as national parks seems ludicrous. By fashioning a "pleasuring ground" on territory once annexed and now undergoing reclamation from Natives who are certainly displeasured; by protecting "native" flora species from "alien" pig invaders ("alien" in terms of both "Euro" and "Polynesian," as I discuss below); and by preserving "nature" on land no longer heavily occupied by "natives"— the entire concept of a national park seems absurd. Furthermore, recent emphasis on ecological conservation has politically edged out what preservation means in indigenous terms.

Because the Hawaiian Islands are so distant from other large land masses, much of their so-called native ecology depended on plants and animals that traveled well: hearty seeds drifted to the islands via strong winds or were transported through bird stools; insects and animals may have floated in on leaves, twigs, and logs. Pigs, however, which are not hearty log travelers and are certainly unfit for leaf transport, were introduced to the Hawaiian Islands by Polynesians, who contributed a variety of small swine nearly 1,400 years ago and, more recently, by Europeans who added large-sized porkers to the forests (Hardy 1995:5). The eventual interbreeding of the two created the Euro Polynesian feral pig or wild boar, which is *not*, then, in the strictest sense of the word, "native" to the soil. The language circumscribing the pig controversy is inflected with negative terms that scholars have critiqued for their use in describing immigrants, specifically Asian immigrants: aliens, invaders, exotics, and (more widely encompassing all immigrants), foreigners.[11]

Terminology that exposes xenophobia vis-à-vis immigration—prevalent during the Yellow Peril scourge in which Chinese immigrants were alien invaders, foreign pollutants, and undesirable exotics on the mainland—has not been easily abandoned. In fact, because of an unfortunate political efficiency in denoting "bad" versus "good" immigrants and minorities, ecologists' agendas can capitalize on discourses of "bioinvasion" and the dangers of "borderlessness" by judiciously employing notions of "alien" species eradication for the preservation of a "good" and "natural" state.[12] This charged terminology is not "natural" to all biologists in the field; many prefer less negatively inflected terms, using "introduced" instead of "alien" or "foreign," or "adventive" in place of "invasive." For example, plants that are "native" to U.S. midwestern regions, part and parcel of the entire national landscape, may be considered "introduced" into U.S. northeastern territories where extreme climate differences have restricted their growth patterns. It suggests, if only linguistically, that such Northeastern territories are divorced from the national arena to which such plants have already been deemed "native."[13]

This further intensifies the debate over "natural" and "alien." Even though the formal definition of the neutral term "adventist" relates implicitly to similar ideas of co-optation inherent within "invasion" and vice versa, poststructuralists would readily agree that *how* one consciously or unconsciously uses language and images inflects a reading public's perception of the material or idea being addressed.[14] Scientific historian Stephen Jay Gould states, "How easily the fallacious transition between a biological argument and a political campaign." His biological and linguistic foray into "the concept of 'native plants'" explains the "remarkable mixture of sound biology, invalid ideas, false extensions, ethical implications, and political usages both intended and unanticipated" that encompass the term "native," citing—as one such fallacious use—racists' employment of Darwinism as "a rationale for genocide," the Nazis' ideology of Aryan supremacy as a strong case in point (1998:2).[15] In a similar vein, Andrew Ross roundly berates "modern ecological" narratives romanticizing the term "nature," citing back-to-nature campaigns, the marketing of Third World "natural" products, the re-indigenization of formerly colonized spaces as "better than" their predecessors, the move to save "vanishing" cultures, to name a few. He argues that such nature-based language perpetually returns to that of capitalism, creating a "vicious circle" between biology and society (1995:34, 15, 20).[16]

To consciously reject a discourse that refuses participation in furthering a negatively established collection of terms recognizes the ways in which the discourse works.[17] Such a linguistic exercise, especially in cultural studies, could lead one down the dangerous path of biology-as-destiny, or a one-to-one correspondence between biology and issues of race, class, and gender—as elucidated and rejected by Gould—a path I certainly am unwilling to take.[18] But the semantic choices themselves in, say, employing "introduced" over "natural" in biology publications continues to overlook larger issues in Yamanaka of indigenous land usurpation. Hence, while semantic investigations are useful, they, too, can take precedence over more pressing and "real" issues.

Animals are integral to Yamanaka's "real" world, a literature about culturally symbolic filth.[19] Mary Douglas, whose *Purity and Danger* represents, to date, the quintessential anthropological investigation into filth, designates dirt as "matter out of place" (1980:35). Douglas addresses dirt as part and parcel of a system of classification, an avenue by which we organize our bodies, lives, and world, by putting things back into their proper places, whether by arranging ourselves away from filth or by putting it away. "Dirt offends against order. Eliminating it is not a negative movement, but a positive effort to organise the environment. . . . In chasing dirt . . . we are not governed by anxiety to escape disease, but are positively re-ordering our environment, making it conform to an idea" (p. 2). Pollution and "rituals of purity and impurity" underscore a society's necessity to organize experience and offer it meaning (p. 2); "ideas about separating, purifying, demarcating and punishing transgressions have as their main function to impose system on an inherently untidy experience" (p. 4). That which threatens a cultural system, or invokes an impending chaos, may qualify as dirt, more so than any fear of actual ills (germs, disease, infections) associated with a wide range of items generally considered *dirty*.

Douglas's notion of order vis-à-vis purity and impurity deepens our understanding of racial/ethnic xenophobia that borrows from dirt's lexicon in order to define "othered" constituents as disruptions to an already established (Anglo) system. Yet, as some anthropologists have indicated, Douglas conveniently overlooks how cultures legitimize dirt eradication through (not against) associations of dirt with death and disease and not merely through a penchant for order over disorder.[20] Furthermore, associations of dirt have always inhered in the color black, while cleanliness has been (un)equally attributed to white, to purity, and to goodness. Douglas's theory does not explain the culturally constructed concept in which the "darker" half of the black/white binary is always freighted with negative associations that have cropped up in—as well as propped up—discussions of racial/ethnic paradigms. On the one hand, her theory need not account for negative color association in that dirty things such as bodily "orifices and emissions [merely] threaten the neatness of bodily boundaries" (Priest 1993:22). Yet, how does this account for the way in which the nonblack fluids of semen, spit, menstrual blood, breast milk, and urine have acquired a form of culturally coded baggage?

I begin with the filth of Yamanaka's *Wild Meat and the Bully Burgers* (1996), whose title highlights the *wild* inherent within animals, conjuring up connotations of dirt, inappropriateness, and social anxiety over Others' uncontainability. The novel's themes of disenfranchised, and of often self-denigrating Local Japanese characters are echoed in both *Blu's* and *Heads*.[21] As is typical of all three of Yamanaka's novels, they trace Local Japanese female characters' burgeoning sexual awareness that arrives concomitantly with their realization of racial, classed, and gendered boundaries circumscribing their lives in Hilo, Hawai'i. Protagonist Lovey Nariyoshi fumbles through adolescence with her best friend Jerry, whose sexually active elder brother piques their curiosity in ways that render Lovey and Jerry a menace to his burgeoning manhood, or rather, his sense of masculine privilege. Lovey, herself a sibling rival to younger sister Calhoon, is steeped in the world of Barbie and Ken—affordable only when on sale at the local Woolworth's, what the children deem a "cheap" store for second-class shoppers—which reflects an arena of white privilege she desires but cannot attain.

Rather than categorize Yamanaka's novels as coming-of-age stories, although they certainly can be, I prefer to regard them as coming-to-consciousness stories. The latter may inherently encompass the former, but coming to consciousness more accurately illuminates the particularly racial and gendered terrain in which the protagonists navigate and not merely the maturation issues (including sexual issues) inherent in the term coming-of-age. Finally, all of Yamanaka's female protagonists yearn for their fathers' respect, incur their displeasure, and eventually heal the father-daughter rift, the common skeletal thread to her narratives. Mothers in both *Wild* and *Heads* are less prominent and therefore less influential, a stark change for Asian American literature long wedded to exploring mother-daughter relationships.

As the title *Wild Meat and the Bully Burgers* suggests, the production of animals into food obliquely references the messy, bloody, bullyish process of slaughtering animals for nourishment. Food is intensely stratified across class lines, wherein eating "wild" animals such as the calf referred to in Yamanaka's "bully burgers" may be deemed less dignified and refined than eating prime cuts of domesticated animals like cows. Ponder, as well, why white meat on a bird is usually prized, and subsequently priced, over dark meat. However, with the recent rise of culinary adventurism among wealthier American diners, "wild" meat has been gracing the dinner tables of the elite at prices incommensurate with former attitudes castigating dirty pigs or wild fowl as unsuitable for consumption. It is either humorous or ironic that diners eating high-priced, "exotic" *pork* as a measure of class distinction conveniently forget that those who consume wild *pig* on a regular basis may be just the people from whom an upper-class desire some distinction in food, manner, kind, and custom. Defilement becomes refinement, depending on which side of the dinner table one eats from.

In *Wild* (Yamanaka 1996), Lovey Nariyoshi embodies a learned self-defilement in Hilo's racially and ethnically diverse neighborhood and school district. In her mixed community, *haole* (technically "foreigner" in Hawai'i Creole English, but in Yamanaka often coded as "Caucasian") residents elevate themselves above Locals in a falsely acquired sense of priority and hierarchy over the "darker" and less monied inhabitants of the island, including those of Japanese, Chinese, Filipino, and even Portuguese descent.[22] Moreover, Lovey's wealthy Local Japanese neighbors distance themselves from contact with their poorer Japanese counterparts, like the Nariyoshis. In her own self-rejection, parallel to Pecola Breedlove's desire to possess Anglo features in Toni Morrison's *The Bluest Eye* (1993), Lovey yearns for a Shirley Temple look, "with [her] perfect blond ringlets and pink cheeks and pout lips, bright eyes and a happy ending." For "Blond hair . . . [is] . . . [g]ood," Lovey imagines, and "Black hair. Evil" (Yamanaka 1996:3, 28). In constructions of clean/dirty, natural/unnatural, beautiful/ugly, and rich/poor, Lovey allies herself with each binary's negative half. In her self-contempt, she attempts to conceal, if not purge, those aspects of her everyday existence that she has been taught to regard as uncivilized, unacceptable, dirty, or polluted, most particularly those elements that arise when filthy and disorganized nature intrudes on a supposedly clean, ordered domestic space. For instance, her father pierces the geckos that crawl across the TV screen with a sewing needle taped to the end of his chopstick, a rudimentary form of pest control; her mother's garden variety of pest removal involves dropping slugs into a Clorox-filled can. Lovey plucks blood-filled ticks from the family dogs, throwing them into a bucket of turpentine; she squeezes the yellow centers from the blackheads that pepper her mother's back or removes her mother's silver hairs, laying them side by side, the white "waxy bulbs" aligned on a dark pillow case (1996:35–36).

Her wealthier peers, on the other hand, conceal the natural, polluting elements of skin blemishes and white hair, of body and toilet odors, of pet and garden pests through expensive products, entangling income with socially constructed degrees of cleanliness and filth. The Anglo Beckenhausers exemplify a necessity to whitewash and sanitize their existence, especially of ethnic acquaintances like Lovey; with the Beckenhauser's caveat in mind, Lovey and Vicky Beckenhauser play in Vicky's closet, secreting Lovey's presence from parental eyes. Patricia Yaeger, in her *Dirt and Desire* (2000), writes that "pollution is also a politically disreputable category that allows ascendant peoples to put those who are less powerful in their place [here, the closet]. That is, dirt becomes the arbiter of cultural categories that are both offensive and arbitrary" (pp. 66–67).[23] Because Vicky's white existence establishes difference through filth and disgust to/for Others, and not vice versa, Lovey possesses an intense self-shame: she is ashamed of her

> pidgin English. Ashamed of my mother and father, the food we eat, chicken luau with can spinach and tripe stew [tripe being a particularly apt example of what many might deem unacceptable food]. The place we live, down the house lots in the Hicks Homes. . . . The car we drive, my father's brown Land Rover without the back window. The clothes we wear. . . . Ashamed of my aunties and uncles. . . . Ashamed too of all my cousins, the way they talk and act dumb. . . . And my grandma. Her whole house smells like mothballs. . . . And nobody looks or talks like a haole. Or eats like a haole. . . . Sometimes I secretly wish to be haole. (Yamanaka 1996:9–10)

Lovey compares her own shabby domestic space with that of the Beckenhauser's *"Perfect Haole House"*: the bathroom sports a Dixie dispenser eliminating the need to personalize a recyclable cup, as done with a magic marker in her own family; beds are covered with "pink ruffles and white eyelet bedspreads," not homemade quilts that are pieced together from worn-out clothing by industrious relatives; Beckenhauser mothers and daughters wear identical nightgowns during the holidays rather than a father's elongated T-shirt, as does Lovey; coffee tables boast a fanned array of magazines unlike her own family's propensity to "stuff the *TV Guide* into the crack of the La-Z-Boy" (Yamanaka 1996:20–21). While the Dixie cups illuminate class difference, they also render the Nariyoshi's paper cup recycling unsanitary. Economic differences become fodder for falsely construed judgments about health and welfare, equating low-income living to unsanitary domesticity. Endemic to this system is the interrelationship between self-loathing and economics.

Lovey is keenly aware of those name-brand products that her family cannot afford: Lysol, Coca-Cola and 7-Up, Pez candy, a Zenith TV and a Magnavox hi-fi, a Cougar, Torino, or Duster, Goody barrettes, Dr. Scholl's, and Karo corn syrup. In that acknowledgment, she questions the cruel irony in naming Japanese American boys after cigarette brands: Winston Wang, Carleton See, Kent Wong, Tareyton Tong. In hoping to buy fame and fortune for their children—attempting to capitalize on recognized brands—the parents who choose such names inadvertently equate their children with dirt/ash and the disease and death that cigarette smoking can cause.

The filth and stench embodied by many of Yamanaka's animals reflect just the socially constructed aspects that her female characters reject about themselves, contrasting a derogatory and socially constructed darkness against their Anglo neighbors' so-called clean and pristine whiteness. The Nariyoshis are the quintessential pigs, so to speak, even though pigs themselves are often noted for their cleanliness. And those who find themselves at the bottom of a racial-ethnic hierarchy attempt to reconstruct a superiority by antagonizing weaker others, like animals, illuminating how self-rejection inflicts a cycle of learned pain and suffering on others. Yamanaka creates angry and frustrated characters whose violence against animals exemplifies their own frustration as disenfranchised citizens. Lovey's father in *Wild* reminds her, "so the *hoale* owner, he treat you like one dog, I promise, even his own dog eat and sleep better than us" (Yamanaka 1996:145). Consider *Wild*'s Local Japanese character Larry: he jams firecrackers into frogs' anuses, flinging their shredded carcasses into the trees, their limp and smelly skins reminders of his pathetic power. His misdirected anger rises not only from his intense feelings of disempowerment, but also from his own immaturity and the natural curiosity of both Lovey and his younger brother Jerry who expose and embarrass his private life of sex and drugs. And in *Blu's*, the Local Filipino Reyes family and the Local Japanese Blu torture cats as they themselves are "tortured" by insensitive and racist teachers, by the absence of positive parental guidance, by the perverted actions of their neighbors.

The treatment of animals in Yamanaka's novels *could* establish a convenient link between a petkeeper's conduct toward pets and his or her morality, a link outlined by critics such as Harriet Ritvo and Kathleen Kete.[24] While there is no doubt that those characters who torture and mistreat helpless animals are morally unattractive, I am hesitant to create a strict one-to-one correspondence between human moral behavior and animal treatment, not only for the racist quagmire it creates between the novel's "good" and "bad" raced pet owners, but also because Yamanaka's characters are much more complicated than such a narrow reading suggests.[25] That is, although Yamanaka's protagonists either love their pets or feed them glass mixed with beef, to anthropomorphize animals who then test characters' morality in Hawaii's racist environs is much too pedestrian a reading for Yamanaka's complicated novels, even if such a reading could be sustained.[26] Rather, if Yamanaka's animals are dirty—pets of mangy, feral, lice- and tick-infested status, or taxidermal carcasses that are disemboweled and completely larvae-eaten to the bone—how might they be accounted for in Douglas's system of dirt? And should they be? Do the possibilities and limitations of Douglas's scaffolding demand revision when coupled with racial paradigms? Yaeger (2000) similarly asks, "What do we do with bodies and experiences that fall *outside these* [Douglas's] *categories?* . . . Is there a pollution outside pollution, a remainder beyond this remainder, a politics of dirt that falls outside such structuralist transparencies, outside the libels of status?" (p. 66, emphasis in original).[27]

Humans do, indeed, (ab)use animals. Yet we must account for how animals provide food; and how *Heads by Harry* character Harry O. depends on shooting and preserving animals in his taxidermy business if he intends to feed, clothe, and send his three children to school; and how some animals, including dogs and bunnies, are bred for money. These constitute the practical, natural economy of Yamanaka's literary terrain, despite animal activists' resistance to the term "natural" in this context. My task is not to debate the activists, but to illustrate that Yamanaka's young, female protagonists acknowledge how animals are incorporated into their daily existence and why. Animals existed long before humans as well as alongside humans, both components of the natural world. But with the specter of colonialism and domination arises the so-called domestication of wild animals, encouraging cogitation over notions of superiority versus inferiority, of civilized versus savage, of freedom versus confinement.

Many of us pride ourselves in a hierarchical superiority over animals, whether rightly or wrongly, in our human ability to reason and to feel emotion over animals' suspected stupidity and emotional aridity.[28] In fact, zoos once "reenacted and celebrated the imposition of human structure on the threatening chaos of nature" through overt domestication of these seemingly less valuable creatures (Ritvo 1987:218). Pets, for example, may remind us daily of our seeming superiority when the "lower" species come to depend on us for food and shelter in their domesticated inability to provide for themselves. In other words, we have cultured the (uncivilized) nature out of them, marking *culture* a positive and superior category over *nature*.[29]

Rather than anthropomorphize a pet, *Heads*'s (Yamanaka 1999) taxidermist Harry O. understands what Richard Klein warns concerning blurring "the distinction between humans and animals, which in turn may lead, and often has led, to the worst forms of biologism, racism or naturalism" (Klein 1995:23).[30] Humans certainly benefit from animal domestication: in cattle raising we benefit through the maintenance of breeds that yield much milk, and through the agribusiness notion of "manufacturing" new breeds that fatten quickly at the trough or produce beautifully marbled meat for the market; the reproduction of show dogs and cats (as well as cattle, pigs, llamas, goats, and all manner of farm animals may be included here) for their temperament or their prize-winning beauty.[31] In all such cases, breeding results in profit, consumption, or both. The words *breeding* and *consumption* are inflected with negative connotations within Yamanaka's work. These processes often result in horrifying conditions of confinement for those animals bred for the table; and inbred animals may be wracked by crippling, painful, or life-threatening genetic defects in the desire to create prize winners.[32] However, indigenous voices, those of Native

Hawaiians, on animal use and treatment, are glaringly missing from her pages. Perhaps if such a view had been acknowledged, a different system may have emerged. Thus, a wresting apart of the "natural" affinity between humans and animals, on many levels, has occurred, so much so that Yamanaka's work itself attempts to renaturalize the so-called natural, with all of its attendant complications of semantics and their politically charged effects.

Such a colonization of animals is practiced by Mrs. Ikeda, a breeder of cocker spaniels in *Blu's* (Yamanaka 1997), in which the three central characters are grieving their mother's recent death. The children literally embody their sorrows: five-year-old Maisie refuses to speak; Blu consumes copious quantities of fatty foods; the eldest sibling, twelve-year-old Ivah, is burdened with the task of premature motherhood; while their father, Poppy, sinks his insurmountable grief into marijuana and becomes increasingly more irate and impatient with his children. Mrs. Ikeda's dank and dim basement is floor-to-ceiling stacked with cages of breeding spaniels, their whelps earmarked for profit. Ivah and her siblings receive a small stipend for cleaning the cages and for exercising the dogs: one outing per week, per dog. They reinvest their earnings on the dogs even though the reader is aware, from *Blu's* first chapter, that the children crave a financial standing to eradicate a staid, unhealthy diet of white bread spread with mayonnaise and cumin: "You know what I would wish if I could have one wish in the whole wide world?" muses Ivah, "I wish my house was underneath Kaunakakai Groceteria. . . . Then I can choose *anything* I want to eat when I get hungry, when all you, Maisie, Poppy, and I have to eat in the house is mayonnaise bread, peanut butter and jelly, or dry saimin" (Yamanaka 1997:9, emphasis in original). Psychologically and emotionally unable to care for themselves, they steep themselves in animal concern.

One cannot deny Yamanaka's implicit moral comment about Mrs. Ikeda's barbaric practices for sheer profit; nor can one overlook the explicit goodness exhibited by the three children who grieve for the suffering, captive dogs, showering them with love, with treats purchased from the money earned on the job, and with "proper" burials as they perish, one by one, from illnesses, neglect, and mistreatment. In the most pedestrian interpretation, the children are metaphorically caged, relegated as inferior by the likes of Mrs. Ikeda, and mistreated by their white, superior-minded teachers. The latter are eager to categorize their pidgin-speaking Local students as mentally incapacitated to prove their own faulty theories of Anglo superiority. They dash the students' hopes of achieving anything beyond (or because of) their poverty-stricken lifestyles. This reading is obliquely reflected by the novel's central mystery—of the complexities and connections uneasily forged between health and race relations—of the imprisonment of the children's parents in the infamous leper colony of Molokai.[33] Poppy hides the scars of his past, the silvery marks on his hands, and remains taciturn about the experience, mystifying it until a confession to Ivah: his wife Eleanor, ever fearful of a relapse and thus a return to yet another form of social stigmatization, continues medicating herself beyond necessity, resulting in the liver failure that eventually kills her.

The literal pathology of those afflicted with leprosy, renamed Hanson's disease to erase the linguistic stigma of the term leprosy, is the book's outward manifestation of the family's socially constructed racial pathology.[34] What kills Eleanor is an overdose of the cure and not the disease itself. Her self-imposed sanctions anticipating societal judgment and treatment direct her actions and hence her fate. On the one hand, her death is a metaphor implicating minorities' anticipated (deadly) actions to expected social reactions. On the other, it is also a convenient method by which the majority blames victims for their own demise.

Mrs. Ikeda's dog breeding practices reveal insights into the children's maturation process. The children understand that animals are used, and often abused, for economic gain or for consumption. They must accept, reluctantly through firsthand experience, how today's pet can become tomorrow's dinner, how a human-nurtured wild animal defies domestication, and how animal abuse can relate to human abuse. Mrs. Ikeda derives profit from her practices, no matter how horrific one may find them. Along with other breeders, she might justify her behavior through arguments about caged animals' naturalization of and concomitant accommodation to habitat.[35] In Mrs. Ikeda's view, the confined dogs, because they know only a caged existence, accept these conditions as normal. But the children empathize with the spaniels' whimpers as agonized protests against dirty, infected bodies: sores riddling their skin, fur caked with dried feces and urine, limbs atrophying from lack of exercise.

Despite Mrs. Ikeda's justification, and despite an understanding of the monetary value of dog breeding, Yamanaka resists the idea that nature, here animals, can and should be contained. Rather, she accepts that animals provide food and other forms of produce from which humans may benefit as long as actions surrounding their care, and ultimately their deaths, render as little suffering as possible.[36] The maturation of *Heads'* protagonist, Toni Yagyuu, for example, is mirrored by the novel's opening scene involving a pig: the shooting of a sow with newly farrowed young subtly alludes to Toni's eventual out-of-wedlock pregnancy. That is, the book begins and concludes with both infancy and maternity-as-maturity occupying opposing positions within the maturation trajectory, beginning with the sow's death and concluding with the birth of Toni's child. The piglets are rounded up as bait for training hunting *bulls*, as Yamanaka calls such dogs, while the sow's meaty carcass is dragged out of the forest for food. Harry allows Toni to domesticate (or mother) one of the piglets whom she names Fern, referring to the quintessential children's book on pigs, E. B. White's *Charlotte's Web* (1952). This association is important. In both books, young girls develop an emotional attachment and affection for their pigs. In White's children's literature, the pig survives a potential trip to the market as meat slated for consumption. Toni's Fern, however, is eventually mauled to death by a dog on her uncle's farm, where the immense and voracious pig has been relegated to contentedly live her life. As such, Yamanaka clarifies that wild animals cannot be domesticated. Indeed, even her uncle's so-called domesticated dog reverts to its wild and animal nature, proving that humans cannot cultivate it out of them.

Growing up in Yamanaka's fictional world demands recognition, especially from children, that animals function in incomprehensible ways. For instance, the Dutch bunnies that Lovey breeds for money sometimes eat their young, a concept that Lovey accepts but with fear and trepidation. She also learns that bunnies have natural predators when she discovers them dismembered, most likely by a pack of wild dogs. Even in children's literature animal domestication is never happily realized. "But there is never a happy ending in stories with a child and a wild animal. E. B. White knew," writes Yamanaka (1997:8).

If Fern's mature years bring death, Yamanaka's female characters eventually accept other equally uncomfortable aspects of the "natural" world. In *Wild*'s chapter "Dead Animals Spoil the Scenery," Lovey repeats her father's philosophy about the unequal relationship between humans and animals: "Humans more important," he quips when he strikes a cat with his car and continues driving nonchalantly (Yamanaka 1996:151). Yet despite this seemingly careless attitude, the Nariyoshi family cannot stomach eating the "bully burgers" of the novel's title, made from a calf called Bully whom the children regard as a pet long before it graces their dinner table (p. 82). Or consider Nanny and Billy the Kid, two mountain goats that Lovey's father rescues from maternal abandonment. Lovey cuddles with Nanny, nestling with her in a sleeping bag, and is heartbroken over her pitiful bleating when the Nariyoshis are forced to leave the mature animal at a petting zoo, surrounded by a bevy of rams who mount her, one after the other. Lovey understands the necessary and natural process of reproduction, but cringes at the violence by which it is executed. Billy the Kid, on the other hand, becomes uncontrollably wild, causing Lovey's father to "shoot it up the ass," all the better for taxidermal mounting. In all cases—Toni's pig Fern, and Lovey's Bully, Nanny, and Billy—the animals are necessarily returned to their wild natures or become victims of those wild animals whose natural instincts dictate their behavior. Maturity and sexuality go hand in hand.

Toni, who prefers this shortened form of the very feminine Antoinette, is her father Harry O.'s favorite child, but her immature decisions, guiding her toward drugs and sex and away from her father's lessons in self-pride, emotionally alienate the two. When Toni is young, Harry O. hones her hunting techniques and teaches her the process of taxidermy in all of its stench and gore. He boosts her confidence and encircles her in fatherly affection, while creating for himself a female substitute for the son he claims he never had. For much to Harry O.'s chagrin, Toni's elder brother Sheldon is gay and prefers the more feminine appellation "Shelly." If Toni is the family tomboy and Shelly is Harry O.'s disappointment, then her younger sister Bernice, nicknamed Bunny, is proudly Harry O.'s quintessential girl: she worries about her hair, her makeup, her nails, and her school popularity; along with Shelly, she enrolls in a local sewing course, the two of them creating enough clothing in order to proudly wear one new outfit every day of the week without repetition.

Toni's insecurity enmeshes her in sibling rivalry. Attractive Bunny may not be smart, but her femininity wins her father's approval and her good looks many a boyfriend. Shelly may displease his father, but at least he possesses strong self-conviction—happily defending his homosexuality—despite paternal disapproval. Toni, on the other hand, feels unattractive, dumb, and hardly knows who she is and what she likes, except that attending college would make her father proud. She proves psychologically unable to apply herself intellectually at the university, propelling her toward drugs (not books) and a keen interest in sex, all the while questioning whose goals her university attendance fulfills. Losing Harry O.'s respect wounds her deeply, and like Lovey from *Wild* and Ivah from *Blu's*, she must rectify her actions in a manner that demands difficult choices as she moves toward re-earning paternal respect as well as garnering self-respect and self-preservation in a racist, sexist, and often economically depressed environment.

Yamanaka's work underscores the violence of self-preservation when characters are circumscribed by racial tensions among prejudiced *haole*. Taxidermy provides a cogent metaphor for such self-preservation in that hunting prizes are immortalized in positions that most attractively showcase their pre-death glory. On a figurative level, the inhabitants of Toni's mixed-race, lower-middle-class neighborhood are themselves solidly immortalized in the lifestyles and habits of a sometimes sordid existence that is never free of subtle reminders of their race and class limitations, and for Toni, gender restrictions. While Harry O. and Toni can adeptly mold and embellish a pheasant into a proud and regal bird after its untimely death, a social-racial trace prohibits Harry O.'s three children from easily manipulating their exterior selves in an effort to boost an interior self-confidence. Like the animal skins with which she works, Toni's life—from girl to woman—is turned inside out as she experiments in the filth of taxidermy, the dirt of drugs, and the violence (violation) often accompanying her burgeoning sexuality.

Hanging prized and preserved hunting trophies on the wall is a form of animal domestication through which Harry O. and Toni develop a loving relationship. Pets represent another form of domestication, reflected in Toni's treatment of the piglet Fern, that plays on human attraction to animals "with juvenile features," or physical aspects that remind us of babies. They elicit "affection and nurturance" in adult humans, says Stephen Jay Gould in his article tracing Disney's methodical infantilization of Mickey Mouse's facial features (1979:34).[37] Toni's actions vis-à-vis Fern bear this out: "I had her [Fern] paper-trained in no time. I bathed her in the tub with Suave strawberry shampoo. . . . I fed [her] with an EvenFlo bottle" (Yamanaka 1999:8). Neoteny, or the "[p]rogressive juvenilzation as an evolutionary phenomenon" in animals, is related to human growth in which infantile "cuteness" appears in the possession of a large head contrasting a smaller body, a "bulbous cranium" and large eyes (in proportion to the head), as well as "pudgier legs and feet" (Gould 1979:32). If we develop affection toward cute human babies in order to ensure their (and ultimately our own) survival as humans, this is then cathected to those animals who possess babyish features, and thus, says Gould, we are "fooled" by nature into "experiential attachment" (1979:34). "We are drawn to them," he states. "[W]e cultivate them as pets, we stop and admire them in the wild—while we reject their small-eyed, long-snouted relatives who might make more affectionate companions or objects of admiration" (p. 34).

Gould's conclusions expose the natural affinity of humans and animals in Yamanaka's *Heads* (1999) at the same time that they comment on characters' maturation, or lack thereof. On one of many Yagyuu-Santos hunting trips, for example, a wild boar mauls Maverick Santos's beloved hunting bull. Toni is attracted to Maverick, son of Lionel Santos, the Yagyuu's neighbor operating a marquee across the street. Maverick, who subtly returns her interest, is a handsome boy teetering on the edge of manhood, experimenting with his sexuality and his masculine privilege, which often arises through inappropriate gestures and language and through aloofness. For the two-hour trip out of the woods, Maverick hauls the seventy-five-pound pet on his shoulders. The dying bull heavy-handedly symbolizes the necessity to grow up that is weighing on Maverick's shoulders: to focus on finding a job after high school and to retire his drug habits. Only pages earlier, Maverick confesses to Toni, "I don't know what I going to do after I grad" (Yamanaka 1999:47). At the same time, the hunting ordeal reminds the reader that his exterior bravado and rude language cannot quell his inclination toward immaturity as an adolescent on the cusp of adulthood. Maverick cries in anguish, "Daddy, my dog," hauling the dog like a man while the boy inside can hardly carry such devastating, emotional weight (p. 48).[38]

Yamanaka illustrates the process of maturation through animal references—whether Toni's essentialized maternal feelings toward Fern or Maverick's anxiety over the bull and his own maturity—so much so that Harry O. allows Toni a pet (Fern) whose features render it "cute" at the same time that a fellow hunter can skin the piglet's mother before she is dead. Even "after a couple of stabs in her throat to stop her noise. . . . Her sounds don't stop until he skins a portion of her hide off the flesh" (Yamanaka 1999:8). The non-neotenic, fully mature sow is more easily slaughtered than the piglets once suckling at her teats—the former is food, the latter pets. However, once the maturing Fern loses much of her babyish charm, facially and in her ungainly heft, she is transferred out of the Yagyuu home, the same familial extradition meeting Lovey's Nanny in *Wild* upon the goat's sexual maturation. Interestingly, when the family's sexually mature pet is relinquished, Toni is in the midst of her own sexual experimentation, emphasizing how Yamanaka uses animals to refer to human maturation. This distances her from Harry O., who reluctantly retires visions of a childish, pliable Toni. He must learn, however difficult it is, to accept the maturing daughter whose opinions and actions run increasingly counter to his own, whose mistakes affect her education, her relationships, and eventually her life when she becomes pregnant.

Wyatt Santos epitomizes that growing up is frustrating and confusing. His attraction to Toni—in competition with that of his more handsome, more popular, and elder brother Maverick—is not altogether rejected. But much to Toni's consternation, Wyatt's behavior expresses his extreme immaturity and his nascent, often clumsy and offensive sense of how to act properly among adults, specifically young women. He passes gas, burps, and spits in Toni's company: "Wyatt . . . burped and farted a lot" (Yamanaka 1999:14); "he propped himself up with three pillows, burped and farted, and turned on the TV" (pp. 14, 287–288). In their analysis of secular (and not ritual) pollution, Peter Clark and Anthony Davis (1989) argue that social conditions defining what is and is not considered defilement are foundations for culturally constructed identity formations in all cultures.[39] Because we are living beings socialized into a system dictating categories of purity and impurity, the "integrity of one's self-image" is easily destroyed by the "uninvited intrusion" of things considered defiling; or, because we inhabit living bodies, anything that indicates a state of death or decay is considered highly polluting because it suggests humans' natural (and resisted) trajectory toward death and decay (Clark and Davis 1989:657). The fact that "obscene" derives from the Latin "dirty" or "filthy" renders obscene any "dirty" language in its explicit reference to defilement. Recognition of and concomitant control of foul behavior (by restraining oneself from burping, spitting, or passing gas in public) is part of maturation. Infants and toddlers, for example, do not find feces, urine, intestinal gas, or other bodily emissions disgusting in the least. Children will play with their own feces or used diapers, they will swish their hands in an un-flushed toilet if allowed, and find no fecal smell repugnant, no matter how strongly so to an adult. This indicates the culturally constructed nature of what is considered dirty or defiled, what is considered unpleasant smelling or fragrant.[40] Such recognition and compliance separates us from animals, which have no diffi-culty defecating, urinating, or vomiting in public. In fouling himself in public, then, Wyatt exhibits a profound immaturity.

If culture remains a necessary tool by which power relations are sustained, whether through notions of defilement or through other vehicles, then this particular tool offers avenues by which dominant races, genders, and classes can persist in methods of subordination. In "Filthy Rites," Greenblatt (1982) states that in-dividuals are "conditioned" to experience "disgust" at the pre-cise point where another's cultural codes of behavior are perceived as different from our own (p. 3). Wyatt, at least uncon-sciously aware of his culturally coded existence, takes advantage of his defiling behavior in gender-dominant ways, especially if, as Clark and Davis state, "dirt and defilement only exists [sic] when there is a significant other (or even an insignificant other) to behold it" (1989:658).[41] If his passing gas and burping are de-filing to others, they "dirty" Toni who must endure his smells and noises while forced into his company on mutual Yagyuu-Santos hunting trips, leisure activities, and, eventually, working environments when Toni is briefly employed at Hawai'i Volca-noes National Park as its first female pig hunter.

If "places are defined, maintained and altered through the impact of unequal power relations," according to Judith Okely,[42] then Toni's initial motivation toward her pig hunting job (which brings her income and perhaps a reevaluation by her disap-pointed father) is besmirched by her hunting companions' foul language. She is teamed up with the Wyatt brothers, two Local Portuguese men (Ringo and Pocho) and one Local Japanese man (JoJo). The young men objectify gender and animals, or gender *as* animal, subordinating them both in order to exert a pitiful power over something—anything—in their own disenfranchise-ment. Like Wyatt, they resent the park's racial hierarchy in which an educated white man controls the team's hiring and firing; the young men themselves are high school educated and dependent on jobs like hunting pigs that require no college degree. These frustrated men, some at the height of their sexuality, direct their frustrations at women, "animals" who occupy a lower rung in their social ladder. "You never had none of this Portagee sausage yet," hunter Ringo Ferreira says to Toni, "squeezing his balls tight in his huge hand. 'You *never* go back to your little link once you taste this sucka . . . He fat. He fat. And fuckin' juicy'" (Yamanaka 1999:192, emphasis in original). According to Gershon Legman's *Rationale of the Dirty Joke* (1975), jokes are "a response to or an expression of social and sexual anxieties they [the tellers] are otherwise unable to absorb or express" (p. 20). He explains that if "the person 'denuded' by the joke is really the teller himself, or herself," then "The 'only' joke you know how to tell, is you" (p. 16). Legman's list of anxiety-producing subjects includes sexuality, hostility, and women, topics with which Ringo is familiar. Ringo-as-joker unveils his own "prevailing anxieties" in a public forum (Legman 1975:17)—or an exorcising—of subjects that "nauseate or frighten" him (p. 19); that is, he might, in fact, possess a small "link" in the whole scheme of "sausage" sizes. In his disenfranchised status, Ringo expresses intense anxiety about his masculinity and his race, couched in hostility against "weaker" women rather than in racism's and classism's institutionalized systems. It is a perverted (meaning both a skewed and sexualized) form of self-reassurance that denigrates another in the face of intense self-insecurity. And that Ringo performs his dirty joke in the company of his hunting peers and against Toni's gender confirms Legman's hypothesis that jokes are an *"exchange of hostilities disguised as an exchange of amenities"* (p. 24, emphasis in original). Ringo believes that his male peers, supposedly "in" on the joke, accord themselves with his sexist attitude.

Sexuality is not inherently dirty; however, according to social etiquette, sex-related topics are best left for private conversation. Consider terms used to describe pornographic materials—smut, filth, obscenity—that easily derogate sex to uncleanliness. This is corroborated in a survey by Clark and Davis in which participants exhibit nausea toward objects and instances referring to fluids that are naturally related to sex: such as blood (that of bloody napkins and tampons) and semen (improperly disposed condoms). To practice a discreet (or polite) sexuality and to pursue one's pornographic interests privately marks the mature manner of handling such subjects. But in an overt, sexual advertisement of his immaturity, Wyatt names his dogs "Debbie" "Does" "Dallas" and "Deep" and "Throat." When he verbally cries their names, shouting "Debbie Does Dallas" or "Deep Throat," he announces an offensive joke publicly (Yamanaka 1999:100). While one might condemn Wyatt's dirty joke for exposing a socially sanctioned sexism, one might also be tempted to sanction the attendant public exposure of the taboo.

For Yamanaka's protagonists, reaching maturity is thoughtfully realizing how the treatment and use of animals relates to the manner in which women's bodies are (and are not) acknowledged. In calling Toni a cunt, a pussy, or a bitch, all words used against her by the "boiz," as Ringo calls himself and the male members of the hunting gang, she is objectified, animalized, robbed of agency.[43] Wyatt falls easily into Ringo's sexist rhetoric: "Women, they just like pigs. You hunt um. You sniff um. You poke um. You leave um" (Yamanaka 1999:68). Or, he suggests, women are pigs. But according to Toni, so are men. The metaphor circles endlessly, attributing a different derogatory value to *pig* according to characters' gendered opinions: women are pigs in Yamanaka because, to put it crudely, they are easily screwed and screwed over; men are pigs in their crudeness, their cruelty, their sexual lust.[44] Toni becomes cognizant of an uncomfortable equation between her verbally brutalized body at the mercy of her hunting peers and the squealing, thrashing pig at the hunter's knife. But she finally, even maturely, realizes that it could be any female body that they address: "Every day it got clearer to me that it wasn't about me. I was a body there. They talked big and bigger for each other. It could be any hole, any crevice, any slit. I was just a conversation piece" (p. 193). As the only female hunter among the men, she is their convenient scapegoat.

Toni arrives at a markedly more positive acceptance of her body when lost in the park with Billy Harper. Billy is a *hapa haole* or half-white/half–South Asian boy, whom Toni's family briefly adopts during a difficult time in Billy's life, and whom Toni loves far beyond her brief infatuation with Maverick. But his sixteen years to her twenty-two prohibits her from acting on her sexual attraction. During their park employment together, they shoot a pig in the snout, but fail to kill it. Its spared life is an oblique reference to Billy's gentle personality in the novel's larger scope of rough and rude men; he is unable to slay the pig, unlike the Santos brothers and the other Local Portuguese men who shoot and stab with precision. Billy's character raises troubling questions about stereotypes of race and masculinity in Yamanaka's novels. One may wonder, via such racial preferencing, if she intends to equate crude behavior to nature or to nuture. In rendering Anglo/South Asian Billy gentle, over his cruder Local Portuguese counterparts, what does Yamanaka imply (if anything) about Billy's whiteness or about his South Asianness? Does my reading invoke a nefarious form of book policing, of rooting out imagined forms of ethnic insensitivity according to politicized notions of what constitutes literary racism and what does not? Toni muses, "I realized that each tree and stone, each plant life, wind, and animal possessed an equality of significance in this place [in the park]. Billy and I were two small foreigners on this landscape. Yet we had presumed our dominion and shot the pig" (Yamanaka 1999:177). She intellectualizes her own insignificance vis-à-vis the pig, the land, their unwelcome intrusion and self-appointed dominion that attest to an understanding of place-in-the-world far beyond the profit derived from pigs and land. That evening, Billy touches her tenderly, heeding her desires to just lie and not "do." "From Billy I learned that love is easy—to truly *like* a man, remarkable. . . . and Billy's face leaning into mine, his hands on my body, such wonder in touch" (p. 184).

If the Local Portuguese and Local Japanese inhabitants are hierarchized below their Anglo bosses and neighbors, then *hapa haole* Billy possesses race privileges that provoke the Santos brothers' envy. Wyatt detests Billy not only for advantages accorded to *hapa haole* (or the privileged status appended to Billy's Anglo half), but also for those reasons that Toni adores him: "He hated Billy's ease in his own body the same way he hated it in Maverick. He hated Billy Harper's father. He hated *haoles* in general. He hated Billy's relationship to our family. He hated Billy and me sitting in the movies" (Yamanaka 1999:172). Billy's position as *hapa haole* allows an ease within his raced body denied to Wyatt. In fact, Billy temporarily moves from Hawai'i to Alaska and back, by novel's end, movement not always available to his Local, grounded counterparts. And if Wyatt and his peers toss invectives at Toni as conversation, Billy talks with her, not at or down to her. Wyatt is envious of the more intellectual conversations he imagines between Billy and Tony, and this prompts his disrespect toward Toni's body in inverse proportion to Billy's respect for it.

Toni's realizations about Billy's more respectful behavior, however, do not accord themselves with her more self-destructive actions. As she observes Wyatt "tak[ing] savage bites" from his meal, "his legs spread," Toni admits, "I was repulsed by him, but also drawn to his seductive anger, a kind of sickening, naked attraction" (Yamanaka 1999:33). In recognizing the barrier of Billy's youth and intimidated by Maverick's attraction to her, Toni eventually settles for Wyatt's crude affections, his stereotypical masculinity vis-à-vis Billy's so-called gentle femininity. In fact, both of the Santos brothers' given names—Maverick and Wyatt—conjure up masculine notions of the Wild West, of "cowboys and Indians," and of Manifest Destiny, of quick and often violent usurpation of space.[45] Andrew Ross delineates connections between "codes of maverick male autonomy" and "territorial aggrandisement" (1990:88). The relationship between American cowboys and Yamanaka's characters is ironic because the Hawaiian land on which they live is hardly theirs to claim and possess as once-colonized and then annexed territory. Furthermore, Maverick and Wyatt's appropriation of an appropriation resonates with the wresting of masculinity mythology by Whites from non-white men that has bolstered the former and emasculated the later.[46] In bullying Toni, the young men attempt to reclaim a culturally constructed emasculation. Ross also explains that in "the heyday of the independent maverick gunfighter in *Gunsmoke*, *Wyatt Earp*, and *Colt 45*," the cowboys shunned domesticity at the same time that they strove to protect it, which plays out in the Santos brothers' verbal repetition, to Toni's mother Mary Alice, that they will protect her children from the taunts of other kids in the schoolyard. At the same time, however, they inundate Toni with verbal abuse and later "shoot her up" with their sperm. Maverick and Bunny become involved sexually as well, not to mention her brother Shelly's sexual desires for Maverick.

But Maverick's masculine bravado crumbles in the face of white power, solidifying a racial hierarchy to which Local is insignificant. After Toni is incapable of sustaining another day of verbal-sexual abuse among her hunting counterparts, she quits and threatens to report the sordid, foul-mouthed lot of them (excepting Maverick and Wyatt out of family obligation), to Billy's father, their white boss, who would most likely fire them. Maverick implores Toni to carefully reconsider the dire consequences of what he deems a potential bad mouthing: "Pocho get three kids, you know, and they living in the basement of his mother-in-law's house. . . . And Ringo's old lady expecting her second kid, and the first one had bad asthma, you know, and needed one special breathing machine. And JoJo one of your father's oldest customers, all his sons and son-in-laws, his brothers and uncles them" (Yamanaka 1999:215). In other words, Toni's limited empowerment in the form of a powerful invective against them is enmeshed in a potential outcome that her conscience cannot accept. She reluctantly heeds Maverick's advice, her actions aptly exemplifying a coming to conscience of the limitations and confinement of not merely Locals, but specifically Local women like herself. Finally, the "boiz," who regard their own behavior as nothing more than good-natured joking, will forever be ignorant of her sacrifice for their families' economic protection. In quitting, Toni loses personal dignity, potential income, and incurs Harry O.'s renewed disappointment at her so-called failure. Such a reading illuminates the subtle ways in which the emasculated young men empower themselves through and by pigs and women.

Toni's burgeoning self-identity plays out through musings over her own body, a self-loathing exacerbated by insecurities vis-à-vis her siblings. Shelly revels in a body that performs a gender socially at odds with his sex; totally unshaken by societal criticism, he flaunts his body using so-called feminine gestures, much to Harry O.'s disappointment amid continued hopes for his son's heterosexuality. Toni harshly judges her awkward body against Bunny's whose name resonates with the sexually playful Playboy Bunny "pets," and this reinforces a distinction between "bestiality and incest" (Marc Shell 1986:124). Yamanaka's Bunny embellishes her well-endowed corporeality, "[l]ong, tanned legs, and ass cheeks hanging out from ultra-tiny Dove shorts and shirts . . . cut right below her voluptuous honeydew tits" (Yamanaka 1999:108). Frustrated, Toni eventually steeps herself in filth. Sharing an apartment with Shelly and Bunny near the University of Hawai'i, where the three are enrolled, Toni wastes her afternoons in marijuana-induced highs, cocaine stupors, or endless dorm parties; when she's not passed out on weekends, she runs the bar/disco circuit with her siblings, always drinking. Says a visiting Maverick of the neglected apartment, "Your carpet blacker than the road" (Yamanaka 1999:112). After flunking out of the university and being fired from her summer job as Hilo Hattie's *mu'umu'u* factory hostess, she is employed in the hunting position that "made me sick" (p. 171). What sickens her is not only her hunting peers' crude behavior, nor the gore involved in killing and preserving animals, to which she is accustomed. For as a child, she impresses her father by observing, without vomiting, the filthy process in which maggots clean up her father's animal skulls for mounting: "The smiling pig grimaced with its moss-rotting, blackened molars, tusks dripping yellow water, and its long pink jawbone still covered with strands of meat. Maggots poured their fattened bodies out of holes in the skull, falling in clumps on top of each other into the water" (p. 57). Rather, Toni is most deeply disgusted with her own behavior and shortcomings as they are mirrored in Wyatt's. The burping, farting, foul-mouthed Wyatt eventually fails high school because he cannot read; Toni, too, eventually fails all of her university classes. Both characters offend those they love: Wyatt, attracted to Toni, exhibits affection by drunkenly groping her in a darkened movie theater. Belittling herself as too physically unattractive for the likes of Maverick, Toni refuses his subtle advances. Her refusal to sleep with Billy and, finally, her pregnancy after sleeping with both Santos brothers—suggesting that the seemingly weak sperm of *two* very masculine Santos brothers are necessary in the conception of *one* child—compels the emotionally devastated Billy to move away. Toni thinks she can rise above the sexist, gas-passing Wyatt. But she does not know how. Like Wyatt, Toni not only acknowledges her socialization into a pernicious racial and gendered hierarchy, but she adopts it as her own. Toni and Wyatt are seemingly rendered helpless in their own bodies.

Yet the final third of Yamanaka's *Heads* makes frequent reference to Toni's growing acknowledgment of her corporeal value far beyond the routine (ab)use relegated to a pig. She re-enrolls in a community college in order to study wildlife biology. Her proud father appoints her his new Heads by Harry taxidermy partner. Reaccepted into her father's fold, and working alongside business partners Maverick and Wyatt, Toni's maturation process is melded to that of the (economic) business of animals. Her success occurs through a line of consumer items produced through animal consumption: "Wyatt, Maverick, and I made pig feet, goat feet, deer feet, and buffalo feet ashtrays. I made deer thermometers. . . . We made reindeer footrests. . . . I made peacock fans with handwoven lauhala handles" (229); "We had aunties coming in for loose feathers and T-shirts . . . all original designs by Wyatt. Painters and teachers purchased the photos. High school boys bought shark teeth and boar tusks on black leather cord necklaces. My mother's petroglyphs and macramé fungus necklaces went over big . . . a couple of reindeer sold every Christmas as Rudolphs. . . . We sold a lot of leg lamps on tri-foot stands" (Yamanaka 1999:233). She concentrates on production, a future of monetary solvency, as if subconsciously preparing for the labors of her own (maternal) reproduction. In fact, she admits her pregnancy in the shop while preserving a woman's pet dog, whose neoteny renders it a "baby" in the woman's loving eyes. Her father has always refused pet preservation; and Wyatt reminds her of Harry O.'s shop rules: "Nah, we no do pets. That's our number one policy. He not going look like your dog was in real life, and you going blame us, when us not God" (Yamanaka 1999:262). Toni, noticing that the woman "get all sentimental. . . . She hugged that dead dog like was one . . . one . . . one—" baby, accepts the job because it references her own maternal feelings toward her unborn child. Shortly after the woman's departure, Toni tells Shelly of her pregnancy (p. 263).

By the novel's conclusion, the entire family is reunited through commerce: Toni is responsibly employed in Heads by Harry; Bunny and Shelly are chief owners and hairdressers in the adjacent Heads by Bunny. Wyatt, in his own brief burgeoning maturity, takes paternal responsibility for Toni's child, helping Toni with all of the infant's late-night feedings during the first three months of the baby's life: "It was Wyatt who helped me adjust Harper's [the baby's] body. . . . 'Football style . . . That's what the book said. . . . Twenty minutes per [breast]. Move your arm. Lean back little bit'" (Yamanaka 1999:287). Billy, too, returns "in a man's body. His legs were no longer lanky and awkward; his chest was full, his face still smooth" (p. 304). This time, Toni chooses her men more wisely. In having named her daughter Harper Santos Yagyuu she acknowledges her love for Billy Harper and lovingly accepts her own raced body, for the child's name proudly announces the racial mixing her daughter embodies: "Hapa," as Wyatt calls her in his pidgin, reflects the Hawaiian term *hapa* used to indicate a person of mixed race. Toni says, "When I returned to the shop and looked at all of them through the glass window, the darkness around me hallowed and still, I saw Billy talking story with my father, Wyatt sharing a cigarette with my mother, and the rest of my Mamo Street family mingling in a known constancy of bodies and place" (p. 311). So the novel concludes with a comfort in body and place, including Harry O.'s invitation that Toni join the family gathered outside, saying, "We all saved a place for you," the book's concluding words (p. 311). The shop is "home" to the gruesome practice of taxidermy. But this art of preservation is reflected in the characters' own self-preservation as they recognize their own, and others' (including animals') worth and dignity as bodies sharing space and place.

Toni finally understands that the irreverence for pigs' bodies that once sickened her is bound up in self-reflection; that the nausea she felt when Wyatt and Maverick drowned feral cats as bodies for mounting practice and the sexist comments of her male peers parallel the mistreatment of her own body. "In the luminosity of the window, I saw the eyes of the birds and animals around me, their bodies frozen, their beaks open, their eyes flashing, wings spread, glossy skins, polished teeth, the trellises of antler and horn. I saw myself in the reflection" (Yamanaka 1999:311). Toni can accept the gruesome task of taxidermy, but she refuses to accept any blatant, unnecessary suffering inflicted on animals or people even as she maturely acknowledges that the unfortunate "nature" of some human relations may not be so easily amended.

Wild similarly concludes with Lovey's excursion to a homeland, here her father's birthplace, returning with a fistful of sweet-smelling dirt, one avenue by which her father (recently visually impaired) can "see" the home to which he yearns to return. *Blu's* concludes with hope that grieving Poppy will rectify misdirected anger at his children, aided by his wife's ghost who is mythically embodied by the family dog. In fact, in time of great need, Ivah envisions her dead mother by rubbing her pet dog's tears into her eyes, thereby making mythical and practical use of a supposedly dirty animal fluid.

But despite these positive-leaning conclusions, even illuminations, of the novels and their "clean" uses of "dirty" products, the novels' underlying premise smacks of paternal dictates in that all of the female protagonists please their fathers in conventionally female ways: curbing their sexuality, downplaying overt resistance to female and racial boundaries, and returning home to a patriarchal fold. The idea of home as a paternal, safe space in Yamanaka is further complicated by the novels' glaringly absent indigenous voice. That is, if the novels highlight Local Japanese and Local Portuguese plights, they simultaneously overlook crucial indigenous issues, whether concerning land rights or sovereignty movements. As such, the 1998 controversy amid constituents of the Association for Asian American Studies who debated whether *Blu's* Filipino or Filipina representations were disparaging or whether they represented part of Yamanaka's personal experiences from whence she draws her lived (or real) and literary materials demands reassessment. In talk about censure of ethnic authors' depiction of ethnic groups other than their own—a dangerous censure teetering on the expense of artistic expression at the behest of restrictive definitions concerning what counts as ethnic sensitivity[47]—the debate has overlooked this silenced group of Native Hawaiians on whose land all others frame their debates, whether Locals or Whites, scholars or tourists. What occurs is nothing less than Native Hawaiians' double erasure. Native and Local must be inextricably linked in Yamanaka's work on race, nature, land, and profit, and in overlooking the former, can one take seriously claims of the latter? In the confined space of a conclusion, I cannot pursue these important considerations. Rather, I expose them as venues for cogitation and future research, both for myself and for others.

Notes

1. For others who discuss the wild boar as a game sport animal for "ecotourists" or as new culinary adventures in (lean) meat, see Quentin Hardy's "In Hawaii, the Wild Boar Hunt Ends with a Knife in Its Heart" (1995) and William Grimes's "Where the Deer and the Antelope Braise" (1998).

2. I thank Siobhan Senier for pressing me to reconsider my interpretations about land in light of Yamanaka's intriguing absence of indigenous views and claims. The absence of Native ideas on dirt and defilement points to how culturally dominant views, often through colonization, come to be accepted as the norm (personal correspondence, September 21, 2001). Recently, Viet Thanh Nguyen in his *Race and Resistance* (2002) came to similar conclusions.

3. For more on Local identity, see Jonathan Okamura (1994). In spelling "Hawai'i" throughout, I use the 'okina, but I will Anglicize the possessive (Hawaii's) and adjectival (Hawaiian) forms. However, some authors quoted do not use the 'okina, and I have honored that.

4. For the history and for current politics concerning Hawaii's land use rights, see Candace Fujikane (1994).

5. Wilson also mentions appellations such as Micronesia, Melanesia, and Polynesia, pointing out the Greek roots of "micro" (small), "poly" (many), and "mela" (black) (2000:75–76). Wilson's "Pacific" work includes forays into the literature of the Pacific Islands, New Zealand, and Australia. Gananath Obeyesekere's debunking of the apotheosis of Captain John Cook, in his *The Apotheosis of Captain Cook: European Mythmaking in the Pacific* (1997), falls squarely into this category of *re-imagination* in his doubt that "the natives created [Cook as] their European god [a standard narrative]; the Europeans created him for them" (p. 3).

6. Because I refer to the online version of her article, which is unpaginated, in-text references to this work will not be followed by any page numbers.

7. See Fujikane (1994). For example, while activist Haunani-Kay Trask posits the seeds of the current Hawaiian Movement in the Kalama Valley Protest of 1971, when Natives and Locals united in order to resist tourist development, Trask herself denies that Locals can feel the same emotional and spiritual connection to the land as do Natives:

Native Hawaiians, like most Native people, have a special relationship to our *one hānau* or birthsands. Land is our mother whom we must nurture and cultivate, and who in turn will feed and protect us. . . . Immigrants to Hawai'i, including both *haole* (white) and Asians, cannot truly understand this cultural value of *mālama 'āina* even when they feel some affection for Hawai'i. Two thousand years of practicing a careful husbandry of the land and regarding it as a mother can never be and should never be claimed by recent arrivals to any Native shores. Such a claim amounts to an arrogation of Native status. (Trask 1993:247–248)

8. See Sumida's reading of Samuel Manaiakalani Kamakau's *Ruling Chiefs of Hawai'i* (compiled in 1866) in which Captain Cook's 1778 arrival is driven not by an assumed Western history, but by Kamakau's iteration of "naming of chiefs and their respective realms," a decidedly "native Hawaiian point of view" (1992:223).

9. Wood accentuates "the differentials in access to power, in land ownership, in ability to publish and to be heard," which are "almost as great in the islands today between Japanese Americans and most Native Hawaiians as they were between Twain, London, and Von Tempski, and the Kanaka Maoli they presumed to represent" (1999:52). As an example, he points out that the U.S. government had paid a "token" $20,000 to "each person of Japanese descent who had been illegally in-

terned during World War II," yet similar reparation for the overthrow of the Hawaiian monarchy has never been seriously considered. Wood attributes this to the power that Japanese Americans hold in local and national politics (in the scope of "geopolitical" and "geoliterary games" to which Wood refers) as opposed to the disempowered Native Hawaiians (1999:52).

10. For a literary excursion into the meanings of place and land in "three third-generation writers from Hawai'i," including Yamanaka, see Rocío G. Davis (2001:47).

11. For more on animals and imperialism, especially on pigs, see Alfred W. Crosby's chapter "Animals" in his *Ecological Imperialism: The Biological Expansion of Europe, 900–1900* (1986). I also suggest Jared Diamond (1997).

12. In the biosciences library, for example, I selected from among a collection of similar titles Chris Bright's *Life out of Bounds: Bioinvasion in a Borderless World* (1998), which capitalizes on the discourse of the "natural" versus the alien. While cultural studies invoke positive images of the postmodern subject in a borderless world, the term "borderless" for Bright becomes an ominous warning of the "global threat of extinction" (1998:21). Also see Brosing S. Lemonick's report of how "exotic plants and animals are ruining the nation's wilderness" in "Invasion of the Habitat Snatchers" (1990); George Wuerthner's "Alien Invasion" (1996); and James T. Carlton's "Marine Bioinvasion: The Alteration of Marine Ecosystems by Nonindigenous Species" (1996).

13. This terminology is gleaned from a phone conversation with Garrett Crow, chair of the plant biology department at the University of New Hampshire (July 11, 2001). Also consider Stephen J. Gould's reexamination of the term "natural" as it is used in biosciences, to which I will return later in this essay. He concludes that what is deemed natural is not necessarily the same as native, or born to a particular place. If Native Hawaiians are not technically "native" to the land, they are seen as staking a false claim to it. Such an interpretation would, unfortunately, justify the usurpation of Hawaiian lands by Europeans, who would then become "natural" residents of Hawaiian land.

14. While one could cite numerous examples, I have in mind Paula Triechler's *How to Have Theory in an Epidemic: Cultural Chronicles of AIDS* (1999).

15. The term "native" has two formal denotations in *The Compact Edition of the Oxford English Dictionary* (1987): the first denotes the idea of being "born in bondage," used in 1450 (later in 1535), encompass-

ing the more familiar designation of people born " 'in a place' one connected with a place by birth." The second denotation states, "[b]elonging to, or connected with; a person or thing by nature or natural constitution."

16. In my research, what is "natural" and how one arrives at that definition is an extremely contested and pressing contemporary topic. Ross states, "As capital goes through its latest cycle of binge and purge, scarcity, ecostyle [his emphasis on the abuses of the term "natural"], has become one of the new discourses of regulation, directed with the force of religious guilt at the level of the individual conscience. The result is an acquittal, on the one hand, of corporate responsibility, and an evasion, on the other, of the hedonism that environmentalist politics so desperately needs for it to be populist and libertarian" (1995:17). The idea of the "natural," for Ross, is unnaturally constructed, skewing our vision of precontact, indigenous societies, social justice, and environmental preservation. Also see MacCannell's *Empty Meeting Grounds*, where what he calls performative primitivism, ex-primitivism, and constructed identity (1992:26) (how the so-called natives of touristic shows "go-native-for-tourists" [p. 159]) blatantly reveal that the "term 'primitive' is increasingly only a response to a mythic necessity to keep the idea of the primitive alive in the modern works and consciousness," mostly for economic reasons (p. 34).

In her article on Holt's *Waimea Summer*, Najita quotes Greg Dening, from *Islands and Beaches: Discourses on a Silent Land: Marquesas 1774–1880*. In speaking of "the ethnographic present," one existing before Western contact, he says that "[It] is a moment that existed in the past . . . there is no 'ethnographic present' of traditional societies which is not post-intrusion" (2001:172). Also see John Urry's *The Tourist Gaze: Leisure and Travel in Contemporary Societies* (1990), whose work seems a precursor to both Ross's and MacCannell's studies, for Urry is interested in the touristic gaze on place and vice versa.

17. *The Compact Edition of the Oxford English Dictionary* refers to both humans and to plant and animal species as "native" from as early as the fifteenth century; the term acquires a negative connotation in the 1800s, when "odious natives" are contrasted with "much superior" neighbors.

18. For example, Gould defines "native" plant species as follows:

[those] that happened to find their way (or evolve *in situ*), [and] not the best conceivable for a spot. Proof that current incumbency

as 'native' does not imply superiority against potential competitors exists in abundance among hundreds of imported interlopers that have displaced natives throughout the world: eucalyptus in California, kudzu in the American southeast, rabbits and other placental mammals in Australia, and humans just about everywhere. "Natives" are only those organisms that first happened to gain and keep a footing. (1998:8)

If one were *not* to heed his argument about the liberal (and what he terms fallacious) use of biological terms and conditions for cultural studies, then somebody could fashion arguments denying the "native" claim in Native American, or the "native" status of Polynesians in Hawai'i, thereby debunking their claims to land and against colonization. Such a political use is not my intention.

19. My definition of culturally symbolic filth is partially informed by Robert Joseph Priest's "Defilement, Purity, and Trangressive Power: The Symbolism of Filth in Aguaruna Jivaro" (1993:567).

20. In his study of the Aguaruna, Priest notes the link between dirt/ filth and fear of death and defilement, which leads him to state, "[O]ne reads Douglas in vain if one is looking for evidence that people fear death, non-being" (1993:41). Finding that "it is here that Douglas . . . first goes astray," Priest intends to advance his own anthropological findings about the Aguaruna's "moral discourse" that "utilizes a language of filth with which to express moral values" and deliberates about how other usages in cultures worldwide would revise Douglas's theories (Priest 1993:42, 511). Peter Clark and Anthony Davis (1989) also question Douglas's equation between dirt with disorder, quoting Marvin Harris on the subject: "Even Douglas might not be willing to accept disorder as the sole or principal component of dirt if she was obliged to tidy up a lawn strewn with gold watches and diamond rings" (p. 652).

Georges Vigarello, in his *Concepts of Cleanliness Changing Attitudes in France since the Middle Ages* (1988), studies the rise and fall and rise again of baths, bathing, and washing in France to reveal that the goal of hygiene embedded in the concept of "cleaning" was stressed only as early as the late nineteenth century, and that ill-conceived myths of how skin, internal organs, and the body in general reacted negatively to water (seeming to provoke disease and langor) resulted in early washing guidelines antithetical to our present notions of washing for cleaning/hygienic purposes. No comparable study exists about changing forms of contemporary American cleanliness, despite potential for a fascinating cultural studies approach to a 1990s manufacturing frenzy of clear (or so-called pure) products and the overwhelming abundance of antibacterial products (now considered unhealthy in their elimination of "good" pathogens). For related reading, see Suellen Hoy's *Chasing Dirt: The American Pursuit of Cleanliness* (1995); Nancy Tomes's *The Gospel of Germs: Men, Women, and the Microbe in American Life* (1998); and Frank Muir's *An Irreverent and Thoroughly Incomplete Social History of Almost Everything* (1976).

21. I thank Sau-ling Wong for encouraging me not to dismiss *Wild Meat* as simply a precursory novel to Yamanaka's subsequent *Blu's Hanging* and *Heads by Harry*, but rather to notice its proliferation of dirt and contamination (private correspondence, October 1999).

22. For a discussion of plantation "caste-ism," see Lauri Sagle (1994).

23. Yaeger quotes Peter Stallybrass and Allon White—"what is socially peripheral is frequently symbolically central" (2000:67)—to prove her point that those in superior positions depend on those they categorize as inferior for their higher place.

24. The anthropomorphizing of animals as well as their embodiment as placeholders for more civil human action arises throughout Yamanaka and resonates with other critics' material on the matter. According to Harriet Ritvo in her study of animal treatment in England's Victorian Age, "Critics viewed cruelty to animals as both an index of depravity and a predictor of further moral degeneration. . . . The Victorian critique of 'inhumanity' . . . confounded two missions: to rescue animal victims and to suppress dangerous elements of human society" (1987:130). Also see her chapter "The Emergence of Modern Pet-Keeping" (Ritvo 1988). Kathleen Kete's *The Beast in the Boudoir: Petkeeping in Nineteenth-Century Paris* (1994) outlines the connection between bourgeois sentiment (class and culture) and animals in the emergence of modernity: the rise of animal protection services, for example, heralded the desire to clean up the violence of working-class Parisians only to discover that the persistent practice of vivisection by "respected" doctors—despite a protracted campaign led by the *Societe protectrice des animaux*—implicated more than just the *sous-peuple* or under people in committing acts of "masculine violence" (Kete 1994:6, 21). Or, that the introduction of petkeeping—the initiation of the beast into the boudoir—signaled a human need for emotional fidelity, an emotion sorely absent among humankind.

Peter Stoneley's "Sentimental Emasculations: *Uncle Tom's Cabin* and *Black Beauty*" (1999) is an extremely provocative article on the evocation of and social necessity to repress sexual desire via black male bodies (blackness and beastliness) in what Stoneley considers the "two most famous nineteenth-century women writers to deal with black bodies": Harriet Beecher Stowe and Anna Sewall, the latter the author of *Black Beauty* (Stoneley 1999:57). Also see Stoneley (1998), where the political regimes of colonialism and Hitler's fascism inform "different orders of racial subjugation" (p. 253). Jennifer Mason (2000) addresses the entangled nature of equestrian training, developing female intellect, and middle-class moral rectitude in the protagonist Ellen of Susan Warner's novel *The Wide, Wide World*. Other sources on pets and pet keeping include Keith Thomas (1983) and Hester Hastings (1936).

25. I am more comfortable reading Yamanaka's animals through a model established by Kathleen Kete in *The Beast in the Boudoir* (1994) in which she illuminates human fantasies projected onto pets, particularly dogs, of the bourgeois imagination: "Petkeeping imagined a better, more manageable version of the world. It described the promise and sometimes displaced the terrors of class" (p. 2).

26. In the contested region of Hawai'i, amid a colonial past, neocolonial labor relations, and ethnic conflicts, such a moral reading is dangerous, for if perpetrators are Filipino or Filipina characters (as in *Blu's*) who shove firecrackers into cats' anuses or feed them glass mixed with ground beef, then the argument gestures toward a racist reading. Because Yamanaka's books have already been scrutinized and chastized for what many view as a racist treatment of Filipinos and Filipinas, this is just the messy path I hope to avoid. One can conjure up morality issues, but one must do so with Hawaii's historical and ethnic contexts in mind.

27. Yaeger's task lies in African Americanizing southern literature—steeped in "flesh that has been ruptured or riven by violence" (2000:xiii)—for it has been viewed traditionally and narrowly through the image of the southern belle (p. xii). Yaeger says,

> If literature by southern women thrives on dirt and fetishism, it is because dirt, filth, contamination, and decay become sites for condensing the social complexities that emerge from any encounter with abjection, with people—and this includes 'white trash,' African Americans, and women in general, characters who experiment with disorder. . . .
>
> The border separating filth from cleanliness operates with near-tactile authority: it becomes a rigid demarcating system separating inside from outside, high from low, man from woman, lady from prostitute, white from black. (p. 264)

28. See Susan McCarthy and Jeffrey Moussaieff Masson (1995).

29. See Stephen Budiansky's *The Covenant of the Wild: Why Animals Chose Domestication* (1999). The book's subtitle expresses Budiansky's argument that the human connection to nature is through, and not against or over, the natural, anthropological, and evolutionary evidence that some animals have come to happily depend upon humans: "human society and human behavior formed an environmental template that—*intentionally* or not—acted as a selective force in the evolution of to-be-domesticated animals," an opinion rendering the "domestication of animals . . . a natural product of evolution" (p. x, emphasis in original, xix). In defending himself against animal rights activists, he offers examples, through archaeological findings, stating that some animals (including cattle, horses, and sheep) would have become extinct without domestication while others, like dogs and cats, found supreme advantages of living with humans and thus "chose" domestication, as his book's subtitle suggests. He confronts issues addressed by animal activists, providing explanations that I find lacking in substantiation.

30. "Whenever the radical heterogeneity between human and animals is erased, the door is open to brutally eugenicist arguments advanced under the guise of biological necessity or the authenticity of nature," says Klein (1995:23). He references Kathleen Kete's *The Beast in the Boudoir*, which traces a history of the dog in France from the nineteenth century to the dog's treatment in Paris: "You may bring a dog into any French restaurant," Klein quotes Kete, "[But] you may never bring a baby" (Klein 1995:19). Klein intones that there exists something uneasy about such a phenomenon, yet also cites how Americans are able to buy their pets designer clothing, "poultry-flavoured toothpaste" and "sparkling water," place them on doggie diets, pay for their hip replacements and chemotherapy treatments, and purchase expensive plots in a pet cemetery (p. 19).

31. For discussions of pedigree and Hawaiian racial genealogy in bull breeding and slaughter, see Najita (2001), specifically pages 195–197.

32. James Serpell (1995) mentions the painful, physical consequences of bulldog breeding: "Their squashed up faces lead to respiratory problems and dental difficulties. The wrinkles and folds of skin around their faces which give them such comical and endearing expressions harbour bacteria which often give rise to serious infections" (p. 84).

33. In *The Chicago Gangster Theory of Life*, Andrew Ross (1995) cites

an unpublished study by Barbara Yngvesson (wrongly affiliated with the University of New Hampshire; rather, she is professor of anthropology at Hampshire College in Massachusetts) and Christine Harrington (New York University) on how Kalaupapa, the former leper colony, has become a National Historic Park and hence "a burgeoning tourist destination." The two scholars "show how this exercise in 'alternative tourism' has provoked competing claims (from the National Park Service, the Hawaiian Home Lands Commission and the patients themselves) about the discourse of *preservation*" (Ross 1995:284, note 117, emphasis in original).

34. The image of the caged dogs gestures toward readings on race and hybridity. Those who condemn interbreeding fear the results of hybridity, a muddying of a so-called pure white race prevalent in the "one drop" rhetoric of white supremacy in the nineteenth and early twentieth centuries. Such prohibitions were echoed in miscegenation laws against and interdictions to cross-racial intimacy, as in banning cross-racial kissing in Hollywood films. They mimic the desire to master (colonize) less civilized, or more natural, citizens through the regulation of racial and cultural breeding. While this racist ideology has passed, a persistent management of interethnic breeding, to put it crudely, recurs, not only in the continued (albeit subtle) social segregation of ethnicized urban locales, but also via the media. Lauren Berlant finds such a powerful gesture in *Time* magazine's 1989 issue featuring a seeming celebration of America's mixed race children in a digital creation of "The New Face of America" (Berlant 1997:175–220).

35. Mrs. Ikeda's thinking is hardly unique. Her justification can be supported by the likes of Stephen Budiansky, who argues against animal rights activists in his book *The Covenant of the Wild: Why Animals Chose Domestication* (1999). He states that dogs raised in cages do not exhibit the same negative stress responses to their confinement as so-called free range dogs (i.e., they accept and incorporate what is familiar in the absence of anything else) (p. xiv). He continues his argument by quoting David Rindo, who suggests that while humans can "select [what aspects of a plant or a dog they intend to enhance or diminish through breeding, they] cannot dictate the variation from which . . . [one] must select" (p. 32). In other words, breeding practices are limited by and to the dogs' genetic codes themselves, despite human arrogance to believe otherwise. He seems to suggest that this fact places humans' propensity toward god-like creations into perspective, a rebuttal to animal rights activists who see otherwise.

36. In this rubric of justification, one can state that because humans

are omnivores, "Cruelty in the sense of indifference to the pain and needs of another being is a product of necessity," states Yi-Fu Tuan in *Dominance and Affection: The Making of Pets* (1984:89). However, animal rights activists would disagree, claiming our ability to produce enough protein-rich foods to satisfy our nutritional needs without relying on animal meat.

37. "We cannot help regarding the camel as aloof and unfriendly because it mimics, quite unwittingly and for other reasons, the 'gesture of haughty rejection' common to so many human cultures," says Gould (1979:34). Gould does not answer questions concerning why such a response exists: is it "innate and inherited directly from our ancestral primates"? Or, is "it learned from our immediate experience with babies and grafted upon an evolutionary predisposition for attaching ties of affection to certain signals"? (1979:34). See Budiansky's discussion of neoteny in his chapter "Youthful Designs," where he proposes that humans have selected, unconsciously, these appealing traits during the process of animal domestication, thereby encouraging their selection (1999:108).

38. Although the three Santos men use the term "Daddy" regularly, including the eldest son Butchie, the fact that the emotionally distraught Maverick cries out for his "daddy" is unusual, given a former show of bravado.

39. This is echoed by Stephen Greenblatt (1982):

Proper control of each of these products [bodily products such as "urine, feces, mucus, saliva, and wind"], along with the acquisition of the prevailing table manners and modes of speech, mark the entrance into civility, an entrance that distinguishes not only the child from the adult, but the members of a privileged group from the vulgar, the upper classes from the lower, the courtly from the rustic, the civilized from the savage. (p. 2)

40. Clark and Davis state that "Young children have no sense of defilement. Both coprophilia and urolagania are exceedingly common, with young children handling excreta much as they would any other object in their environment" (1989:657–658).

41. They state, "Culture becomes a vehicle for the maintenance and reproduction of dominant-subordinate relations in so far as it extends, through enculturation and identity construction processes, differential sensibilities and vulnerabilities in relation to defiling situations and substances. Such differentials provide the dominant with a means to distinguish itself from the subordinate while also providing the domi-

nant with a device to control and manage dominant-subordinate relations" (Clark and Davis 1989:651).

42. Okely is quoted in Linda McDowell (1999:5).

43. According to Carol J. Adams in her book *The Sexual Politics of Meat* (1990), animals, like women, are objectified as "it" or as "things"; for example, we disassociate *meat* from *pig* when it morphs into *pork* at our dinner tables, when *cow* becomes *beef* or *steak* at the grocery store, when a *lamb's leg* becomes the more palatable *leg of lamb*, the careful linguistic construction distancing the lamb from its own bodily possession (pp. 64, 67). Also see Adams and Josephine Donovan (1994).

44. What makes it more offensive to call a person a "pig" or a "dog" as opposed to a "bear" or a "squirrel"? Edmund Leach attempts to answer this question in "Anthropological Aspects of Language: Animal Categories and Verbal Abuse" (1964), where he outlines a theory in which verbal taboos using animal-inspired invectives are directly related to incest taboos and the edibility and inedibility of certain animals. John Halverson's reply (1976), however, destroys many of the foundations on which Leach builds his hypothesis.

45. According to *The Compact Edition of the Oxford English Dictionary*, Maverick's name means "a calf or yearling found without an owner's brand" and is eventually defined as somebody who is "roving and casual." Maverick drifts from woman to woman. He seems destined to become the property of she who will take him into her bed, ultimately a disempowering position for a man exhibiting the kind of masculine egotism he does throughout the novel. He is rejected both by Toni, whose affections return to Billy, and by Bunny, who marries a local haole deputy prosecutor by novel's end. In fact, both Santos brothers, despite their masculine positioning, conclude the novel single, deflating their former sexual success with women.

46. Ross is not unaware of the "debt of the Southwestern cowboy mythology to the Mexican *vaquero* culture of cattlemen . . . along with the culturally specific macho codes of the *rancheros*" (1990:88).

47. See Nguyen's (2002) discussion on the Yamanaka debate which, he argues, reveals that in the field of Asian American studies "when prejudice is intraethnic rather than racial, the ability of Asian America to articulate a cohesive identity is fractured," not so unhealthy for the field, according to Nguyen. See his astute discussion of Yamanaka on these points in his subsection "The Limits of Asian America" (pp. 157–166).

5

Inside the Meat Machine: Food, Filth, and (In)Fertility in Ruth Ozeki's *My Year of Meats*

While Yamanaka concerns herself with a domestic, cultural anxiety over the relationship between humans and animals, and while Kamani attempts to subvert derogatory definitions of South Asian women's bodily health and worth, in *My Year of Meats* Ruth L. Ozeki (1998) considers the consequences of human ingestion of animal flesh, its subsequent pathological effects, and the transnational circulation of such food toxins. The novel's focus on food pollution encompasses the permutation of human and national borders by filth that affects the novel's displaced and rejected characters, mostly women and minorities. When the two female protagonists realize that a culturally sanctioned alliance between meat and men marginalizes women and poor minorities, their findings beg a host of questions about the many unsavory affiliations among seemingly disparate arenas. What do meat and prostitution have in common? What unites race and gastronomy, women and food? Why might fattening cattle affect human fertility? *My Year* is about what, in fact, human and animal bodies *in*corporate and how eating and sexuality decidedly intersect as natural and "instinctual appetites" (Roger Abrahams 1984:24), where prohibitions against transgressive orality provide opportunities for, or caveats against, sexual relations.[1]

I begin by returning briefly to Ginu Kamani whose short story "The Smell" references gastronomic transgression of

Hindu food taboos as a form of justified bodily pollution if it defers, even abolishes, the possibility of marriage. "[G]irls who don't eat meat *always* get married," mutters character Rani as she surreptitiously introduces beef to friend Nila's plate (Kamani 1995:187). The outraged Nila exclaims, "'When did I eat meat! I'm not like you, dirty girl. I'm a hundred percent vegetarian'" (p. 186). While Nila retches into her hand, Rani recalls her cousin Sonia's constant vomiting hours before her arranged marriage instigated by a meat-eating groom whose beefy stench clinches Sonia's refusal to tie the knot. "I was thrilled!" Rani cries out, "My cousin was refusing marriage! Finally, we would have a real rebel in the house" (p. 193). Within an hour, however, Sonia's parents locate an alternate, truly vegetarian groom. "Now Sonia and her husband live somewhere far away. . . . But I hear every now and then that even with a vegetarian husband, Sonia vomits every day. She smells meat everywhere, all the time. Her husband beats her daily because she won't let him touch her. . . . no one is allowed to say anything about Sonia" (Kamani 1995:193–194). In "The Smell," collaborative work between meat and marriage establishes a proper young South Asian woman's appropriate, disgusted reaction to meat, but little commensurate direction about marriage except that a woman must dutifully submit to conjugal relations, no matter how much her husband makes her vomit. What is filthy, Kamani suggests, is less the introduction of beef into these "pure" female bodies than the introduction of men to their purity, allowing the characters to adopt a feminist stance against a religion inimical to them. Women, sexism, marriage, transgression, and Hindu food taboos are thus strangely and inextricably linked.

Maggie Kilgour reminds us that "[c]onsumption and consummation are the same word" in French (1990:7). If "[l]ike eating, intercourse makes two bodies one" (p. 7), then Rani expresses prurient delight in sneaking bites of meat, an act that reaffirms her individuated personal and sexual selfhood through rebellion and confirms her aversion to men. But in Ozeki's novel, sneaking meat supports brutal acts of sex and sexism as well as the nefarious meat industry, endorsed by transnational capitalism upheld in Ozeki by predominantly men. I address the interrelation of *in*gestion and *in*tercourse in Ozeki, both of which begin with a prefix of corporeal *in*vitation but conclude with the devastating consequences of corporeal and corporate/capital abuse, eventually meted out on women and the poor.

The novel's plot revolves around Jane Takagi-Little and Akiko Ueno, whose introduction arises through beef. Born in Quam, Minnesota, Jane is the product of a Japanese mother and an Anglo American father. While residing in New York City, she is appointed coordinator for *My American Wife!*, a televised documentary series promoting American beef to Japan-based consumers through the televised depiction of a 1950s fantasy family world reminiscent of *Father Knows Best* or *Leave It to Beaver*. The series' Tokyo-based producer is Akiko's husband, Joichi Ueno, who demands that his wife rate the shows for "Deliciousness of Meat" and "Educational Value, Authenticity, [and] Wholesomeness" of the programs' families (Ozeki 1998:21); spousal disagreements over the series' reality factor—especially considering that "the commercials were to bleed into the documentaries, and documentaries were to function as commercials" (p. 41)—provoke him to verbally, physically, and sexually abuse his wife, more so when he is frequently drunk. Akiko is expected to dutifully prepare the featured meals to "put some meat on her bones" and provide a family heir, preferably a male one.

Meanwhile, Jane is diagnosed with a damaged fallopian tube—she will never provide biological progeny. And beef, she discovers, is the culprit: while pregnant with Jane, her mother was prescribed vitamins containing growth hormones that were initially developed to fatten cattle quickly at the trough. Thought to prevent women from miscarrying, they were later linked to in utero birth defects. Through Jane's and Akiko's struggles with beef, meat production foreshadows a figurative consumption of women who battle both men and infertility.

The chapter's organizing principle is the dichotomy inside/outside given its salience to the permeability of bodily borders (*in*gesting what is *ex*ternal) and given its indispensability for discussing the novel's many related binaries, including but not limited to white/Other, purity/pollution, production/consumption, true/false, natural/artificial, and fertile/infertile. In a host of critical work, from anthropology to psychoanalysis, from food culture to poststructuralism, "inside" is privileged above "outside" because it allows us the illusion of bodily and intellectual control; if we cannot manage what occurs outside of our bodily borders, at least we can negotiate what flows in and out of them. In religious food taboos, for example, the sullying of one's "clean" corporeal interiority (as a pure spiritual place) occurs through the ingestion of tabooed or unclean alimentary matter. But what is dirty is both complicated and politicized when considering that the Hindu taboo against fowl can be explained as "a negative reaction to their [chicken and egg] use by Moslems, or . . . in a desire to distinguish between their [Hindus' clean] way of life and that of tribal peoples who use fowl in ceremonial propitiation" (Frederick J. Simoons 1994:150). Feminist and psychoanalytic critics refer to "dangerous" and "polluted" corporeal social transgressions that disturb any strict division between the two halves of the socially constructed binaries. Homosexuality, for example, vexes the so-called separation of male and female. According to Judith Butler, the porosity and *not* the solidity of sex and gender constructions threaten the seemingly impermeable, unchangeable, and comfortably homogeneous social orders under which all bodies are forced to "harmoniously" operate (1990:132).

In anthropology, "[A]nything which either symbolically or in reality emerges from the body [such as spit, semen, menstrual blood, breast milk, to name a few], or which has been sullied by contact with a body aperture" is dirty, says Lawrence S. Kubie, even if its former existence within the body is deemed proper, clean (1937:391). Take the moisture in one's mouth—the normal, cleansing, digestive bodily product called saliva—which is benign (and alternately clean, useful, pure, sanitary) as long as it remains inside its proper oral cavity. Once ejected, it becomes filthy and impure, as in the invective, "I spit upon you," or the grimaces evoked when a parent "cleans" a child's face with a mouth-moistened handkerchief (p. 391).

Similar pure/impure designations surround hair and fingernails, considered neutral as they grow within their proper places (on the head, at the ends of fingers). But hair is immediately rendered disgusting as unattached strands on the bathroom floor, and fingernails are dirty as stray, half-moon nail clippings embedded in the carpet or discovered under sofa cushions.[2] More important and more interesting, then, is the tenuous space located within the slash (/), an in-between-ness that "does not respect borders, positions, rules."[3] Mediated by a slash that both unites and separates, the two halves are not mutually exclusive but rather their interdependence invites ambiguity and vulnerability of the two terms' accepted denotations. In a direct reference to Mary Douglas's theory of dirt as "matter out of place," Judith Butler states, "Douglas suggests that all social systems are vulnerable at their margins, and that all margins are accordingly considered dangerous. If the body is synecdochal for the social system *per se* or a site in which open systems converge, then any kind of unregulated permeability constitutes a site of pollution and endangerment" (Butler 1990:132). Butler concludes accordingly:

> What constitutes through division the "inner" and "outer" worlds of the subject is a border and boundary tenuously maintained for the purposes of social regulation and control. The boundary between the inner and the outer is confounded by those excremental passages in which the inner effectively becomes outer, and this excreting function becomes, as it were, the model by which other forms of identity-differentiation are accomplished. In effect, this is the mode by which Others become shit. (pp. 133–134)[4]

The inside/outside dichotomy is therefore nothing but a "crude system of values" according to Kilgour, a rather simplistic hierarchy wherein a good *inside* is too easily privileged above a bad *outside* (p. 4).[5]

That which must be symbolically evicted beyond (bodily, identificatory) borders retains negative metaphoric associations (Other, abject, the maternal, shit), implying that if one intends to retain accepted social systems, the inside must be maintained as a space of the good, the clean, and the pure, while the outside must represent a repository of the bad, the dirty, and the impure.[6] Yet this other's (this rejected's) former existence as part and parcel of an inside interrogates and prohibits any restrictive division between what is self and what is not, between in and out, and between pure and polluted.[7] In rejecting what we loathe, revile, and ultimately fear, we castigate those aspects of ourselves—from which we erroneously think we can so easily separate—that we find mirrored in others. The fact of mutual in-exclusivity becomes both problem and cause for the characters in Ozeki's novel on many fronts: for those who fight to keep what is contaminated outside the clean interior of the body; for those who claim to know truth over fiction; and for those who delude themselves into possessing control over what crosses and what remains confined within bodily and national borders. Definitions of clean and dirty, of truth, national good, and healthy food are not definitive, confounding any character's attempts to ingest, literally and figuratively, what is good for him or her.

Food's status as either disgusting or delectable has always pivoted in the space of the slash (/), based on human classification by one (dominant) subset of people for their own finicky and fluctuating tastes in a manner that shapes its meanings for other groups of people. I return to the wild boar from chapter 4. It was once considered a food of marginal edibility, deemed palatable for only poor individuals who can hunt and prepare the meat at little cost. But recently the wild boar has been elevated to a sought-after, exotic delicacy, gracing the tables of expensive restaurants for wealthy individuals who prefer that others kill and prepare their meated meals—for a very high price.

Along similar lines, what is coded as "wild," "gamey," and hence "distasteful" or "unrefined" is rarely found at the local meat counter, neatly wrapped in cellophane; rather, such game is shot in the wild and consumed by a population deemed to possess a less sophisticated palate until the food in question becomes the delicacy of the day. Consider, for example, the repugnance by which many Americans in the late 1970s viewed the skunk-, porcupine-, woodpecker-, egret-, and eagle-eating habits of Hmong refugees—an eating pattern structured by wartime necessity.[8] Many Americans continue to be disgusted by the "frog-eating Frenchman and the dog-eating Chinese";[9] and the inedibility of Japanese sushi was loudly proclaimed until its introduction as an expensive delicacy.

In a broader context, food has (ill-)served as a cultural signifier. When speaking of race relations, food often embodies the palatable side of an "other," a side that many Americans find easier to digest than these so-called others' religious, familial, and social practices.[10] Imbibing what others eat is to embody a cultural difference—to ingest that other—in its most simplistic sense, sating the necessity to exert a more concerted effort toward knowing a particular group of people outside of frequenting a Chinese, Mexican, or Indian restaurant for one's weekly fill of culture.[11]

Furthermore, beef to vegetarians and animal activists represents unnecessary cruelty to animals and has sparked debates over animal rights in research laboratories.[12] Meat's gruesome production, vividly discussed in Upton Sinclair's *The Jungle* (1946) and illustrated in Ozeki's slaughterhouse scenes, reveals larger issues surrounding the rise of unions and prohibitions against child labor as well as more recent laws concerning safe and sanitary working conditions and the standardization of hygienic food processing.[13] The place of food preparation, likewise, has traditionally been a female gendered one, on which Joichi happily capitalizes in his televised images of domesticated women. Yet tradition also notes that the rise of the predominantly male realm of haute cuisine conveniently "borrowed" recipes from its female originators.[14] The "low" of cooking becomes the "high" of cuisine—paralleling how the "low" of pig metamorphoses into the "high" of exotic pork—once it is divorced from women, yet the trace of domestic, female contribution defies any such stark distinction.[15]

If "gamey" sells, "exotic" becomes a convenient advertising euphemism for foods previously considered inedible, elaborating on alimentary categorizations and hierarchizations. Character Joichi's proclamation that "Beef is best" over all other meat poses an interesting foray into food taboos and the changing Japanese diet (Ozeki 1998:12). Joichi, who advocates meat's superiority over the so-called lesser grains of bread and rice, ignores the history of Japan's hesitant acceptance of beef in his television marketing campaigns.[16] That is, consumption of beef was initially forbidden by sixth-century Japanese Buddhism to exhibit mercy toward all living creatures. Much later, the Japanese regarded the product, quite derogatorily, as Western and therefore barbaric. Yet with the rise of modernization and Westernization, and the American occupation of (and influence within) Japan after World War II, the Japanese accepted, even revered, beef. In fact, a dish dubbed "a civilized bowl of rice" contained beef or pork slices, states Emiko Ohnuki-Tierney (1997:166–167). However, the Japanese Eta, the "slaughterhouse caste" who handle cattle butchering and hide tanning, are still castigated as untouchables, the reviled, and the socially abjected, relegating beef production—as socially stigmatizing—considerably less civilized than the act of beef eating itself (Simoons 1994:210). Despite beef's current growing popularity among Japanese youth, meat still takes a backseat to the Japanese staple, rice (Ohnuki-Tierney 1997:168). The stubborn and ignorant Joichi intends, through the aggressive television series *My American Wife!*, to forcefully incorporate beef into the lives and bodies of Japanese citizens.[17]

In the heavily meat-eating West, however, rice is tantamount to bread: the latter may be privileged as a national staple, but it lacks the prestige afforded to beef. Carol J. Adams (1990) reports how, historically, "intellectually superior" people (men in general and white men in particular) have been urged to eat meat (p. 31). Adams considers expressions coupling strength and virility with that of beef, such as "beefing something up" or "getting to the meat of the matter" (p. 36). It is no wonder that in many stateside locations, the luxury of consuming a piece of bloody meat is prized far above consuming a loaf of bread (albeit many vegetarians would disagree).

As an apropos visceral foray into the organizing principle of inside/outside and its relation to meat within *My Year*, I draw from the social and racial classification surrounding chitterlings, eaten predominantly by Blacks in the South. In equating race and gastronomy, I am interested in how otherness becomes symbolic of our rejected selves, and how, in equating the abjected *inside* to its *outside*, binary categories are wholly destabilized. Chitlins, as they have been colloquialized, are hog bowels. According to Doris Witt, they are the corporeal location in which "food becomes excrement, and accordingly through which hog and not-hog are negotiated, [thus] hog bowels point to the fragility of the boundary that divides food from non-food, self from not-self" (1998:267). In imbibing that visceral portion of the pig that is simultaneously hog and not-hog, chitterlings are a food that "question borders" in the whole scheme of "dietary regulations" and prohibitions (Oliver 1992:73). The act of consuming chitterlings vacillates between acceptable and disgusting, food pleasure and food pollution, in its tenuous and ambiguous definition as food or as not-food. Hence, bowels that are properly situated within hog intestines—a corporeal space where food is digested, some may even say cleansed of impurities and either absorbed or expelled—are viewed improperly as consumptible/edible once they exit the pig's corp(se) and are used for non-hog purposes: human nutrition. Animal filth, for some, is not destined for human consumption.

The consumption of chitterlings, according to Witt, disorders the seemingly well-defined borders between inside (clean) and outside (dirty), interrogating Douglas's categorization of systematizing (cleaning up) certain matter. If Douglas advocates that "clean" arises from the act of putting filth in its place, where is the disorder in consuming soul food? Is it embedded in the eater of chitterlings, asks Witt, in the act of eating chitterlings, or in the chitterlings themselves (1998:265)? Ambiguity exists not only in locating the exact source of the filthiness in hog bowels, but a frail border is subsequently established between when hog bowels are food and when they are not—the point at which they might clearly be both clean and dirty.[18]

More importantly, Witt's argument foregrounds issues of race through gastronomy, exploring the connection between "the subjective fascination with 'filth' . . . and the social stigmatization of certain peoples and practices as 'dirty' and 'filthy'" (1998:268). In explaining the 1960s popular emergence, subsequent vilification, and eventual white co-optation of African American soul food, to which chitterlings belongs, she highlights not only the contested nature "over the appropriate food practices of blackness" (p. 259) but also other less generous "fascinations" (p. 259) with African American culture and representations of "black femaleness and filth" (p. 261). Rather than representing an "interracial gastronomy," chitterlings reestablish "enduring stereotypes of [filthy] blackness" (pp. 258, 267). The inside/outside paradigm that chitterlings erodes in its location within the slash (/) is therefore an appropriate paradigmatic erosion for Ozeki's novel—questioning what is healthy meat and who is considered Other—and provides nothing less than a messy narrative serving up no easily digested food for thought.[19]

—⁓—

The liminal space of the slash arises in Jane's visible hybridity. Not quite Anglo and not quite Japanese, she is a physical, intensely public reminder of the ways in which hybrid bodies represent bifurcated, multiply constituted, and thus visibly notable disruptions to homogenous systems whose smooth operations rely on the suppression of such difference. It is no wonder, then, that Jane is considered an outsider in both the United States and Japan. In the latter nation, she exacerbates her inability to fit through a self-conscious exhibition of freakishness that publicly accentuates her otherness: "I cut my hair short, dyed chunks of it green, and spoke in men's Japanese" (Ozeki 1998:9). As a self-promoting "[p]olysexual, polyracial, [and] perverse" anomaly (p. 9) in a nation that adheres to the motto "The nail that sticks up gets hammered down," Jane intensifies her visible differentiation, exaggerating her space of liminality in order to liberate the public from inhibitions against staring—she hands them license to gawk.

Back in the States, she hardly melts into its multicultural pot; she aptly describes, through spatial terms, both her visible hybridity and its intersection with her work on a television program that sells American beef to Japanese consumers: "Being racially 'half'—neither here nor there—I was uniquely suited to the niche I was to occupy in the television industry . . . as a go-between, a cultural pimp, selling off the vast illusion of America to a cramped population" in Japan (Ozeki 1998:9). Thus, Ozeki makes good textual use of Jane's Japanese-Anglo identity by marrying bi-racialism to issues concerning capital, consumerism, and commercialization: "Halved as I am, I was born doubled. . . . My talent for speaking out of both sides of my mouth was already honed. On one hand I really did believe that you could use wives to sell meat in the service of a greater Truth. On the other hand, I was broke after my divorce and desperate for a job" (p. 176). Jane's actions and decisions in her new position promoting meat via television seem as conflicted as the confusion instigated by her visible, racial identity. However, as the novel progresses, America is eventually privileged over Japan—or West is hierarchized over East—a gesture by which Ozeki retreats from the intensity of racial liminality in order to force a choice of one affiliation over another, of consumer capital over issues of racial identity.

Joichi Ueno's character corroborates my theory of Ozeki's textual move that inadvertently pathologizes her Japanese characters. Joichi is a Japanese national possessing a puzzling fascination with whitewashed American images, so much so that his views are a degradation of his own nationality, his own masculinity, and of Japanese women. Joichi demands that the Anglo American women featured in his directorial project *My American Wife!* be palatable to his Japanese, female audience according to his own fantasies: they must possess "Attractiveness . . . warm personalit[ies]," "Attractive, docile husband[s]," "Attractive, obedient children," and "Attractive friends & neighbors" (Ozeki 1998:11–12). Such constructions reduce American women to stereotypes of domesticity and certain gradations of condescending femininity at the same time that they assume Japanese women's inability to separate fact from fiction. Furthermore, he demands that *My American Wife!* contain no "synergistic association with deformities. Like race. Or poverty" (p. 57). He bristles at filming what he deems second-class families whose mixed-race children represent impediments to his attempt to portray a pure America. Considering not only that American laws against miscegenation included prohibitions against Anglos marrying Japanese, but also that Japanese American internment was an extreme racist response to an alien and threatening constituency, his racist outlook begs questions of his own self-placement, of his own self-hierarchization, and of his self-appointed affinity to a kind of "honorary" whiteness in all of its racist trappings. Joichi's behavior suggests a longing to be white, affirmatively coding the West (affiliated with whiteness and the dominant population) and negatively marking the East in ways echoed throughout the novel: Jane, for example, is once employed in Tokyo but produces her most successful documentary work in the States; when Tokyo-bound Akiko eventually leaves her brutish husband, she heads for New York City. America and not Japan becomes *the* idealized location where women, specifically, can live their dreams. West is "in"; East is "out."

According to Jane, white is "out" and minority is "in." Despite Jane's underlying resistance to accepted notions of racial and gendered othering and despite her condemnation of falsified connotations of "natural" and wholesome meat, Jane's propensity to showcase a form of troubling immigrant nostalgia eventually guides her actions, as if biology were somehow destiny. This seeming textual schizophrenia is Ozeki's criticism of both Joichi's whitewashed views of America and Jane's presentations of happy multiculturalism. Consider the debut episode of *My American Wife!* under Joichi's direction. The spot's host Suzy Flowers leads the audience on a tour of home and family before showcasing a quick 'n' easy Coca-Cola rump roast. Jane wearies of such similar episodes, sporting Japlish-sounding titles such as "My Hobby," "Lady Gossip," or "Pretty Home,"[20] and featuring overly domesticated homemakers like Suzy, wedded to their staid families and sterile existences.[21] As she gains more production responsibility, Jane embarks on cinematic forays into other so-called less appropriate angles of America. Her directorial debut features the Mexican American Martinez family whose specialty is beefy burritos. Much to Joichi's chagrin, beef becomes secondary to Alberto Martinez's narrative explaining how he lost his hand in a farming accident, and how he eventually fulfilled his wife's dream of producing an American son, Bobby. Jane remarks, "Bert [Alberto] paid for her dream with his hand," subtly evoking the violence by which immigrants become "American" (Ozeki 1998:58). Bobby, dressed in baggy pants and his father's felt hat, happily poses in the parting shot with his "4-H project piglet" he has ironically named "Supper" (Ozeki 1998:61). Joichi berates Jane's multiethnic choices and her featured meats, eventually including lamb, supplied by a rival Australian export company, or pork, which he regards as a second-class meat.

In Jane's view, meat is less the problem than capitalism itself. While Coca-Cola and BEEF-EX (the United States' Beef Export and Trade Syndicate) are monetarily rewarded after the Suzy Flowers episode via the rapid depletion of their products from grocery shelves and freezers, Suzy discovers (in midfilming) her husband's affair with a cocktail waitress. Beef consumption requires wholesale visual consumption of such tranquil domestic television images wherein Japanese housewives conveniently get a taste of America. In turn, the industry consumes its least suspecting victims, like Suzy. Yet Jane's counter to Joichi's whitewashed images slips into a form of veiled minority condescension in which she can cheerfully tout the loss of one's hand in the making of an American, a so-called celebratory immigrant narrative. The text's irony lies between rejecting Joichi's ridiculous allusions to a so-called American dream and accepting Jane's nonhegemonic revisions that are heavily invested in America's romance with difference, of which the nation's primary acceptance has arisen through ethnic food. Because such a flattening and homogenizing of difference veers little from Joichi's approach, Jane can be equally accused of cleansing her images. What both characters have imbibed about ethnic others borders, to varying degrees, on racist, sexist shit, which they recycle in equally falsified television representations.

The notion of recycling shit is an important metaphor for the books' television and meat industries, both mired in the space of the slash (/). Jane's filming forays to the Dunn & Son beef ranch and slaughterhouse, for example, edifies her about the nefarious process (for both animals and humans) by which "factory farms" fatten livestock more quickly and easily at the feeding troughs, eliminating large tracts of grazing land and saving ranchers thousands of dollars on feed. She learns that John Dunn and his son Gale use a legal, manufactured feed additive, or an "exotic feed," that might consist of any of the following: "recycled cardboard and newspaper . . . by-products from potato chips, breweries, liquor distilleries, sawdust, wood chips. We even got by-products from the slaughterhouse—recycling cattle right back into cattle" (Ozeki 1998:258). Gale informs her that the latest development in quick-bulk feed at lower costs employs plastic pellets, which expand on ingestion and can be collected "right out of the cow's rumen at the slaughterhouse" for the creation of "new pellets. . . . Feed the animals shit, and it gets rid of waste at the same time!" Gale exclaims with enthusiasm (Ozeki 1998:259–260). What is technically considered garbage/excrement and wholly inedible becomes, literally, a recycled, "clean" product for eventual human consumption. In fact, England's Bovine Spongiform Encephalopathy (BSE), or mad cow disease, originates similarly through "the feeding of the remains of one species to another," thereby "transforming . . . herbivores into carnivores"[22] and repeating the sickening cycle of consumption and pathology—of mixing inside and outside—that self-criticizes the contradictions of the good/bad dichotomy.[23]

Jane's investigations reveal a seamier side to what is touted as healthy beef, questioning not only meat's wholesome and natural goodness, but also the merits of its production practices.[24] Cattle on such farms are given injections of what Gale calls "a prophylactic dose of Aureomycin and then [we] implant 'em with Syvonex as a growth supplement," an artificial method to speedily fatten cattle at the trough, a process by which the beef is harmfully tainted for human consumption (Ozeki 1998:257).[25] Gale, who handles the drugs on a regular basis, exhibits signs of hormone overdose: his voice is becoming unusually high. As well, his five-year-old half-sister Rosie, who visits the hormone-saturated feedlots daily, shows signs of thelarche (premature maturation in the form of developing breasts, pubic hair, and the commencement of her period). This corroborates Jane's research on similar beef-related circumstances, like the FDA's discoveries in 1959 of how synthetic hormone diethylstilbestrol (or DES) showed "signs of feminization" in "low-income families in the South . . . after [they ate] cheap chicken parts and wastes from processing plants." While the embedded hormones result in "plump [chicken] breasts and succulent meats" for America's dinner tables, they also produce pathologies, most often in the poor (minorities and Anglos alike) who ingest those less expensive cuts in which growth hormones are more highly concentrated (Ozeki 1998:124). According to a puzzling film shoot featuring the African American Dawes family, many poor Blacks like Purcell Dawes often purchase less expensive chicken parts (such as necks and chitterlings). Their repeated consumption over prolonged periods results in visible breast development and audible voice changes from the inadvertent ingestion of hormones. Purcell hails from Harmony, Mississippi, ironically named in light of the tragic disharmony between human corporeal development and hormone-infected meat; hence, the notion of conspicuous consumption takes on an entirely new meaning in the visible, corporeal-altering effects of tainted meat. Health and wealth, suggests Ozeki, are often reserved for those who set the criterion for acceptable consumption, not for those consumed in the process.[26]

According to her research, after Europe banned U.S. beef imports in 1989 for their unnacceptably high hormone levels, a new trade agreement was brokered in 1990 between the United States and Japan. That is, DES was eventually banned from use in poultry, but still approved for use in cattle. At one time, Jane discovers, it was approved as a vitamin for pregnant women, even being advertised in the prestigious medical *Journal of Obstetrics and Gynecology*. Despite initial warnings, the drug-as-vitamin sold rampantly, boasting "an estimated five million" prescriptions. But in 1971, a group of Boston-based physicians terminated its use after discovering that young women whose mothers took DES often developed forms of uterine cancer as well as "irregular menstrual cycles, difficult pregnancies, and structural mutations of the vagina, uterus, and cervix" (Ozeki 1998:126). The male progeny of DES-prescribed women battled congenital disorders that increased their own "risk of testicular cancer and infertility" (p. 126).[27]

Consumption and fertility are twinned, Jane discovers. In fact, a recent St. Paul, Minnesota, newspaper article praising organic food over its manufactured counterparts intentionally frames consumption via consummation: "With antibiotics, pesticides and a slew of hormone disrupters affecting our food, I have to wonder if I should be nibbling corn on the cob through a condom. What if you could ask your food how many partners it's had? Has it engaged in risky pollination? When was the last time it was tested? Did it use drugs?"[28] Jane discovers that despite a DES ban, the continued though illegal use of DES in feedlot animals (a usage as high as 95 percent) regularly finds its way onto America's dinner tables and into American bodies. Given the 1991 production of *My American Wife!*, Jane can only surmise that the United States had exported its defectively dangerous product to the overseas market in Japan and promoted its superior qualities.[29] Alimentary products (ingestion/rejection) correspond to reproductive activity (fertility/infertility) in the novel's heavy emphasis on eating, sex, natalism, and race.

Issues of consumerism for transnational corporations like BEEF-EX, and their pawns like Joichi, capitalize on generic (easily digestible) images of women and minorities. Equally, Ozeki's textual use of Jane's racial hybridity intertwines the text's complicated questions of racial identity with notions of consumerism. Jane's biracial otherness codifies socially sanctioned stereotyping: Joichi prohibits "racial deformities," a coded term for prohibiting all raced characters from the television series in their so-called impalatability to Japanese viewers/consumers. As well, Jane's visible difference promotes a type of ethnogastronomic stereotyping within her work environment, establishing a food hierarchy tangential to a racial hierarchy. A white slaughterhouse employee, for example, derogatorily asks Jane if Japanese like her eat cows' "assholes and everything," equating her nationality with polluted eating habits, an insult veiled in a seemingly innocent inquiry (Ozeki 1998:266). The cowboy's question is ironic given that a delicacy among some Americans is the euphemistically named "oysters," or bulls' testicles, so named to mask what some may consider their inedible origins (Ozeki 1998:208). But nobody elevates the oyster-eating habits of some Americans to a national, gustatory phenomenon as does this Dunn & Son ranch hand, unconditionally coupling all Japanese and Japanese Americans with tripe consumption. Furthermore, the ranch hand may sneer derisively yet little does he know that the hormones he has been injecting into Dunn cattle will eventually find their way to his dinner plate. The constant pursuit of more rapid ways to manufacture cows into steaks is self-pathologizing. Quick profit does not always make corporeal sense. The novel raises questions about the interconnection between racial embodiment and capital when raced consumers like Purcell Dawes become the affected excrement—the shit—in the process of production.

Already a hybrid product, Jane eventually becomes a meat process victim when she discovers how that which is considered filthy and outside the body's boundaries is eventually introduced into the body via meat, often with devastating consequences for women. Jane feels victimized by the meat industry for her infertility, her eventual "miraculous" pregnancy, and her unfortunate miscarriage. Her damaged fallopian tubes, for example, are attributed to her mother's DES hormone-related use during pregnancy when the drug was touted as preventing miscarriages, to which her mother had a propensity. After frequent unprotected sex with her lover Sloan, however, she becomes pregnant. As she agonizes over whether to keep the child, she is involved in a slaughterhouse accident when a freshly killed carcass moving along a conveyor belt topples her, renders her unconscious, and supposedly causes a miscarriage. The pathologist's report confirms, however, that the fetus had died a week before the accident, the slaughterhouse accident therefore contributing nothing toward terminating her pregnancy. Jane can hardly agree. As a matter of fact, beef and the beef-related filming of *My American Wife!* has everything to do with her twisted fallopian tubes, her initial difficulty in conceiving, the death of the fetus, and the improbability of ever conceiving again.

Coupled with the blood of the slaughterhouse, the fetus represents the tenuous border straddled by both birth and tainted meat, illustrated in Jane's dream occurring only days before the accident:

That night I dreamed it was time to give birth. . . . so I went out behind the milking barn where I used to play on my

grandpa's farm . . . and I pulled up my dress . . . it started to
emerge, limb by limb. . . . It was wet, a misshapen tangle, but
I could see a delicate hoof, a twisted tail, the oversize skull, still
fetal blue, with a dead milky eye staring up at me, alive with
maggots. (Ozeki 1998:276–277)

The bloody baby/calf narrativizes elements of food, female, and
cultural prohibitions. Blood, for instance, is essential to life but
reviled once it leaves the body. In the slaughterhouse, Jane
watches blood spurt from the neck of a freshly stunned cow that
is figuratively and literally hanging (on meat hooks) between life
and death. "Foods that call into question separation, or identity,
[are] . . . impure or unclean," states Kelly Oliver, "For example,
the blood of animals is not to be eaten because blood is the life
of an animal and to eat both the dead flesh and its life is to mix
two elements from different orders, flesh and blood, death and
life" (1992:73). Ozeki introduces maggots to the image, creatures
that derive life from the ambiguously defined being/carcass
now unfit for human consumption but fit for the nutritional
needs of maggots. When does the *cow* become the linguistically
palatable *beef* or *steak* for human consumption? At what juncture
in the slaughtering process does *animal* become *edible* and when
does that time frame expire?[30] Jane's dream adumbrates the
manner in which the novel's strict binaries are eventually eroded
within the slash (/) of ambiguity.

If consumption and consummation are inextricably intertwined, as in births and slaughterhouses and pregnancy and
beef ingestion, then so, too, are food hierarchies and women,
meat and men. While Akiko battles against beef consumption,
Joichi relishes meat as much he "enjoys" women, not only bounc-
ing "big-breasted American women" on his lap, but also concluding his *My American Wife*–inspired dinners in forced, brutal
sex with Akiko (Ozeki 1998:42). His program choices reflect his
frustrated efforts to manage his sexual identity, or rather, to
manage his identity through his sexuality.[31] His desire to film
only attractive women—indicative of some deep-seated sense of
his own physical and even emotional ugliness—is plainly indicative of sexist views that coincide with his own insatiable and

sadistic lust: the more he degrades women, the more he desires them.

Even more so, the show's penetration into private, domestic spaces (like the marital distress of Suzy Flowers) that is offered up for public consumption allows sexually unsatisfied viewers like Joichi to play with their food. It is not surprising that *My American Wife!* must "culminate in the celebration of a featured meat, climaxing in its glorious consumption," Joichi states. "It's the meat (not the Mrs.) who's the star of our show!" (Ozeki 1998:8). "Of course, the 'Wife of the Week' is important too. She must be attractive, appetizing, and all-American. She is the Meat Made Manifest: ample, robust, yet never tough or hard to digest" (p. 8).[32] Joichi heeds his own advice, literally climaxing into the "Mrs." at each *My American Wife!*–inspired bout of his consumption as consummation. A well-done rump roast can therefore invite foreplay. The televised meat itself glistens moist and pink like the pages of soft-core pornography, offering up forbidden pleasure that is intricately connected to "female servitude and objectification" while at the same time its presentation represses any of the background "processes of production." Thus personified, such "food pornography" cries out, "Eat me! Eat me!"[33] It is no wonder that "[t]he modern Japanese housewife finds the human interaction necessary to purchase meat distasteful. . . . [That they] find it embarrassing to say the names of the meat cuts out loud," reports a Super Marushin Grocery store market survey in Ozeki's novel. To utter "rump roast" or "chicken breast" to the male butcher and in the company of other highly self-conscious female consumers represents a blatant linguistic coupling of food and sex.[34] The survey indicates that many women prefer purchasing meat via vending machines in the same manner that condoms and pornographic magazines (or other illicit materials) can be inauspiciously gotten in Japan. Jane finds the idea of "dehumanized meat quite interesting" in its connotations for the dehumanization of the novel's women (Ozeki 1998:88). She similarly discusses the constraints of a punishing filming schedule in which "[y]ou are doing a wife or two a week. While you are shooting them, they are your entire world and you live in the warm, beating heart of their domestic narratives, but as soon as you drive way from the house . . . then it is over" (pp. 35–36). The violence in "the shoot" and in a love 'em and leave 'em attitude resonate with Joichi's own lascivious attitudes toward women—Texas lap dancer Dawn "straddled his tenderloin and offered up her round rump for his inspection"—and in his spousal abuse (p. 43). That Jane's work on meat-related films advocates the same crass sexist attitude embraced by Joichi indicts capital consumption along sexist lines.

Food preparation can be food pornography, reverberating uncomfortably with how images of women are airbrushed and glossed, plucked and prepped for male gazing. Akiko's character subtly parallels that of the manufactured image of *My American Wife!* Suzy Flowers whose on-screen romance is an off-screen disaster, whose Quick 'n' Easy Rump Roast bubbles hot and savory on the screen only after hours of patting and drying, primping and reshooting the slowly graying lump of meat. The novel questions whether it is the meat or the woman who is quick and easy. Ozeki illustrates this merging of alimentary and sexual appetites during the Uenos' first few years of marriage, when conceiving is a low priority. At this juncture, Akiko once presses a "Mandom SuperPlus [condom wrapper] . . . carefully between the pages of the cooking magazine she'd been studying," indicating how she is inextricably linked to Joichi's "sexual appetite" in her everyday cooking routine (p. 45).[35] After several years of marriage, when Joichi desires a child, he is wholly convinced that Akiko's conception relies on heavily meating her meals, tethering meat to fertility at the same time that Jane links meat to her resulting infertility. Joichi confines Akiko to the meated recipes of his liking, allowing *My American Wife!* to limit her to repressive cooking patterns that are wedded to his imposing ideology. Cooking, which is a traditionally feminine task, is tied to fertility in Joichi's desire to fatten his wife for reproduction. His contributions to a masculine and lineage-directed notion of reproduction is embodied by a yearning for a male heir over a female one, yet reproduction here remains a female process in that Akiko's continued inability to conceive is blamed on *her* bodily shortcomings and not on *his* possible infertility. He desires what she cannot deliver. But beefing up provokes resistance (coded as male) in Akiko, and not acquiescence (coded as female), as if beef's nutritional "value" represents just the masculine connotations it has acquired.

Male and female connection and identity are linked to "passage of bodily boundaries," says Carole M. Counihan (1999). Food, sex, and reproduction presage not only gender roles and relations, but also allude to "self-control" or lack thereof (p. 61).[36] When Joichi announces that they should work toward conception, not only has Akiko long lost a taste for food and sex, but her periods have ceased from chronic bulimia: "like an animal alive . . . [meat] would climb its way back up her gullet, until it burst from the back of her throat. . . . She could not keep any life down inside her," whether beast or baby (Ozeki 1998:37–38). Self-control over food and dieting marks the anorexic, who regards abstinence as the proper method by which to remain good and clean, whereas indulgence (ingestion) is filthy. Akiko is sickened by the ingestion of meat and by Joichi's forced intercourse following each meated meal, intertwining pathology and sexual aversion. Her own daily retching is akin to Rani's cousin Sonia's in Kamani's "The Smell," where one questions if Sonia vomits from the smell of her husband's meated meals or from his sexual invasions, for the two are linked within the story. Read crudely, Joichi's "meat" enters Akiko uninvited, nauseates her, and requires a violent, corporeal emission. "Fear of, disgust with, and refusal of sexual connection are common themes in the worldview of anorexics."[37] If oral ingestion is connected to sexual penetration—"a lifelong connection between oral pleasure and sexual pleasure"—one may question if Akiko's distaste for food and sex results from her own psychological imbalance (Counihan 1999:63). Or is it Joichi's imbalance, whose lust for beef and women is of equal urgency? When is too little pleasure pathological? When is too much pleasure problematic? In the limited bodily control Akiko still possesses, she attempts to seal off her orifices, both mouth and vagina, provoking Joichi to brutally rape her, first anally, then vaginally. Several days afterward, Akiko investigates her painful anal wound (shaped like a "bleeding eye") in a small hand mirror, after which she makes a concerted decision to leave Joichi and to question her sexual preference for women (Ozeki 1998:251).[38] To refuse meat, in Ozeki's novel, is to reject men.

The majority of men in Ozeki's text who do eat and promote meat are patently unattractive, physically and morally, while those who eventually express contrition over the consequences of their actions are described as naive or are infantalized. Take physical descriptions of Joichi whose interior, bodily workings become exterior and filthy emissions, metaphors for his morally polluted behavior: "Ueno was a large, soft-bodied man, with smooth, damp skin and a stunningly profound halitosis, indicative of serious digestive problems, that rose, vaporlike, from the twists of his bowels" (Ozeki 1998:42). A womanizer with "carrion breath," his carnivorous habits have rendered him animallike in his spousal abuse and his attempted rape of Jane after a company-sponsored dinner. Her sexual services are an expected return for Joichi's alimentary provisions.[39] Thus, while actual cows/animals are linguistically transformed into terms such as beef and meat for consumption, Joichi's ingestion of such products render his humanity animalistic. If Akiko is once viewed as the edible "Mrs."—the meat made incarnate—it is finally the abusive and reprehensible Joichi who devolves into a cur, a pig, a dog, to employ animals as insults in a manner that expresses our culture's inimical relationship to creatures who remain outside of human civility.[40] "[I]n coming days," states Karen Davis, "we may marvel at the strange phenomenon of constituting ourselves by the intimate act of eating beings we despise."[41] In many ways, Joichi's consumption of woman as meat renders him a barbarian, a cannibal, wherein the eating of human flesh is the ultimate taboo. The novel thus endlessly circulates mediated images in which animals are meat, in which meat represents men, in which men become what they eat—animals.

Ozeki effectively deflates Joichi's character by allowing Jane to dub him John Wayno (as "Ueno" is pronounced), linking Joichi to the racist and sexist characters often portrayed by television icon John Wayne.[42] Consider, as well, male character Gale Dunn, cast with animal-like features: his "reddened wattles bunched up" around his collar as he twitches uncomfortably in his suit; his nervous blue eyes resemble those of a "newly farrowed sow" (Ozeki 1998:255). The discovery that he fondles his stepsister Rosie creates a sexual sadist from this seemingly harmless man. Furthermore, his father John Dunn is a lecherous man whose feedlot hands are racist and sexist men, such as slaughterhouse employee Wilson whose office walls sport "a large poster of a young blond Amazon in jungle bikini, who overlooked the meat-cutting operations below" (p. 280). Jane addresses her Japanese crew (who are without first names throughout the book) as "boys" and never as men. Jane's lover Sloan Rankin—whose name resonates with the *rank*ness of rotting meat—is, not ironically, a man cadaverously thin, "an exquisite corpse," who sporadically appears in and out of Jane's hotel bedrooms (p. 55). Because his apartment has no soft angles, Jane equates it to an abattoir, suggesting that it is she who has come to be slaughtered.[43]

The men of Ozeki's novel rely on sublimated (unleashed) sexual appetites. They hunger for bodily satisfaction, their desires sated by both meat and women. Their immoral behavior—whether entangled in marketing *My American Wife!*, in engineering cattle growth through nefarious chemicals, or simply embedded in ignorance—becomes a form of moral pollution that damages themselves. Even though Oh and Suzuki remain the least offensive male characters in that they no longer entertain themselves, at novel's end, by shooting out the crotches of poster "girls" with an air gun; and even though they heroically salvage indicting Dunn & Son slaughterhouse footage from Joichi's destructive wrath, they are nevertheless minor characters whose eventual goodwill cannot erase the novel's weightier collection of physically and morally unattractive men. It is no wonder, then, that no viable heterosexual relationship exists by the novel's conclusion, highlighting instead the loving bond created between the mixed-race, vegetarian, lesbian couple Lara and Dyann.

Kamani's "The Smell" (1995) equally criticizes the marriage of men and meat, and what that implies for women in matrimony, for Rani will happily eat, smell, and touch meat in order to resist a future match.

I draw the mutton smell into my nose with long breaths that fill me up. I exhale reluctantly. I arrange a line of the spicy ground meat along my finger so that it resembles a moist dark caterpillar. I lick at it slowly. . . . *When I grow up, I will never vomit. When I grow up, I will never marry. When I grow up I will smell the meat on men and the smell will keep me hungry.* (1995:194–195, emphasis in original)

Her status as a single woman will have less to do with the "smell" of the tabooed meat emanating from her body than with her choice to remain single, to reject men in order that she may revel in the forbidden taste of meat as well as in the sexually liberating status of being a single woman. Therefore, when Rani says that "[E]*ating meat is not good for women,*" do we believe her (1995:194, emphasis in original)? As a woman who relishes the delicious meat she craves, she announces the opposite of what she practices, intending to subvert a system that privileges patriarchy.

In Ozeki's novel, eating meat is certainly "not good for women," but despite that fact, meat eating women are married and spilling over with children in the text's heavy emphasis on natalism.[44] The status of women as alternately revered and reviled—forms of gendered love and gendered hate—illuminates men's awe and envy at women's reproductive capabilities in an ironic division between the "good" woman and the abjected maternal. In literature one finds evidence of fascination and frustration over men's desire to recreate the natural arena of birth through limited, artificial means—to abject what they cannot reproduce at the same time that they embrace their own (faulty and tainted) creations—as in Mary Shelley's *Frankenstein* and Nathaniel Hawthorne's "The Birth Mark," and their disastrous conclusions. In Ozeki, the close association between men and meat production, between food and sex, begs the question, "Is meat the male equivalent of birth?"[45] Or, in a novel about dichotomies, how is the taming of nature simultaneously coded as an abjection of women? And how does the manufacture of meat by men renaturalize culture? The production of meat on factory farms implies the creation and growth of living beings, here cattle, that resonates obliquely with birth metaphors. But the final polluted product establishes a caveat against unnatural creation and against its ingestion. Food and filth, through birth metaphors, are reassociated; "good" culture cannot replace an abjected nature. As such, Rosie Dunn, afflicted with thelarche via airborne chemicals in her hormone-infected feedlot-as-playground, is a Frankensteinian "offspring of meat and genetics."[46] Even Bunny, Rosie's mother, represents a male-inspired remake: she once performed as an exotic dancer until her ample bosom attracted John Dunn's attention and eventual monetary protection; he rescues her from her seedy nightlife through marriage, hence making her respectable. Her refashioning rests on a natural, female "monstrosity" that is (or must be) domesticated in the service of both motherhood and in restoring John's manhood, for in his confinement to a wheelchair, he is emasculated. "You think I don't realize I look like a goddamn cartoon character with these inflated boobies and this big old butt?" she interrogates Jane's filming crew. "These babies are Nature's Bounty. . . . No artificial growth enhancement here" (Ozeki 1998:253). But clearly, both Bunny and Rosie are "products of male desire."[47] Just as the novel circulates representations of representations, men's interests in Ozeki's novel revolve around reproductions of reproductions. They attempt to replicate what they abject in women by fabricating birth. The results are a moral pollution embedded in seemingly edible foods.

In *My Year*, nothing is freed from criticism, not factory farming, nor Joichi's behavior, nor Jane's reincarnations of her boss's Americanized images. Everything is subject to being turned inside out, resonating with other of the novel's binaries that are eventually interrogated and dismantled. Like Joichi who swallows images of a 1950s *Leave It to Beaver* family without careful mastication; or like Jane whose happy multiculturalism in all its glossing of racial hardship remains unpalatable, what we uncritically ingest taints us, both literally and figuratively. At the heart of the novel's many dichotomies lies a national obsession with the "West," its masculine connotations, its culture over nature, its "goodness." This reverberates in Jane's contemplation over the documented case of Yoshihiro Hattori and Rodney Dwayne Peairs, the former a Japanese exchange student who was "accidentally" shot by Peairs in Louisana. "Hattori was killed because Peairs had a gun, and because Hattori looked different. Peairs had a gun because here in America we fancy that ours is still a frontier culture, where our homes must be defended by deadly force from people who look different" (Ozeki 1998:89). Jane cannot help but wryly point out that Peairs, affiliated with the Ku Klux Klan, was a meat packer at a "Winn Dixie supermarket," equating meat, men, and racism in ways that echo Joichi's and BEEF-EX's ideology concerning "proper" meat production (Ozeki 1998:88). "Guns, race, meat, and Manifest Destiny all collided in a single explosion of violent, dehumanized activity." Violence, says Jane, is one of those American narratives that makes us a "grisly nation" (p. 89). Is the meat industry, Jane wonders, not similarly grisly in the transformation of a bloody, embattled process to its neat, clean packaging at the grocery store? Such a question strikes at the heart of Ozeki's novel as she addresses the mediated nature of products and persons alike through the rubric of consumption: patterns of ingestion, attendant consumer culture, and the work of this culture on the American Dream. If the literal process of meat production is "grisly" and "embattled," as Ozeki suggests, so, too, is that of an acceptance of others, which has always been marked with a regeneration of violence.[48]

Jane's final documentary reporting on the "truths" of factory farming is itself a mediation of cultured images construed according to her particular agenda. In such a manner, the novel implicitly addresses the acts of duplicity inherent in both linguistically and visually establishing inside/outside, edible/inedible, truth/fiction, and natural/artificial. The artificial and the natural are not irreconcilable opposites, and the reviled can be revised, according to Ozeki, by nefarious male hands. "[T]ruth wasn't stranger than fiction," Jane discovers by novel's end, "it *was* fiction" (1998:360, emphasis in original). That (re)production is revisited only to be (re)contaminated turns the entire idea of female abjection and racial rejection inside out. What occurs is nothing less then a recycling of shit, a desperate attempt to naturalize culture and to culture the natural through definitions steeped in the ambiguity—in the slash (/)—between the two. What we ingest may result in our own unintended consumption.

Notes

1. Maggie Kilgour says, "a less totalizing but still bodily image for incorporation is that of sexual intercourse, which is often represented as a kind of eating" (1990:7). Ron Scapp and Brian Seitz, in the introduction to their edited collection *Eating Culture*, mention the transformation of eating places to meeting places in the 1970s: "Eating and sex combined in novel new ways, fusing desires into a new atmosphere, as well as a new market, a new kind of 'meat market.'" (1998:9). And Roger Abrahams says, "At the deepest levels of our talk of others, our language provides us with attributions of their animal character that turns on their inability to 'talk right,' to 'eat right,' or to enter into approved sexual relations" (1984:22). According to Carole M. Counihan, "Food and sex are metaphorically overlapping. Eating may represent copulation, and food may represent sexuality" (1999:9). Consider that *The Joy of Sex: A Gourmet Guide to Lovemaking* was a best-seller in the 1970s according to Janice Delaney, Mary Jane Lupton, and Emily Toth (1988:18).

2. Mary Douglas outlines unwritten rules of etiquette involving utensils, specifically their uses and prohibitions regarding the mouth. "Meals properly require the use of at least one mouth-entering utensil per head, whereas drinks are limited to mouth-touching ones. A spoon on a saucer is for stirring, not sucking" (1999:236).

3. Kristeva says this of the abject in her *Powers of Horror* (1982:4).

4. I found this useful passage quoted in Doris Witt (1998:261).

5. Kilgour states that "body politics, whose coherence and unity can be asserted through the analogy with the body corporeal, tend to view what exists beyond themselves as evil, . . . to be different, separate, and unassimilated" because we reject what we fear (1990:4). Kilgour's work has been instrumental to my own thoughts about inside/outside in Ozeki, and many of my ideas in this chapter are indebted to her fascinating work.

6. Equally, Kristeva's abject is that which has been "jettisoned" out of boundaries, most specifically those boundaries sustaining prohibitions by which society is ordered. Yet because what is abject is "on the border" itself—it is "ambiguous," "in-between," "composite," says Kelly Oliver, quoting Kristeva—"it threatens identity" and "distinctions themselves" (Oliver 1992:70, 71). Like Douglas's system of purity, Kristeva's is less a "lack of cleanliness or health that causes abjection but what disturbs identity, system, order," says Kristeva (1982:4). The maternal body represents the ultimate abject—in its embodiment of

potential (oedipal) incest—or the body of authority that could prevent indivisiblity and thus necessary subjectivity and identity. Oliver's work in both *Reading Kristeva* and "Nourishing the Speaking Subject," the latter of which "reveals some aspects of the relationship between food and women and their oppression" (1992:68), has informed my reading and understanding of Kristeva.

7. Kilgour glosses Derrida, who views this particular dichotomy as a foundational binary, and she eventually references Freud, whose theory of (sexual) obsessions with orifices retains important implications for the dichotomous inside/outside:

> Expressed in the language of the oldest, that is, of the oral, instinctual impulses, the alternative runs thus: "I should like to eat that, or I should like to spit it out"; or, carried a stage further: "I should like to take this into me and keep that out of me." That is to say: it is to be either *inside* me or *outside* me. . . . The original pleasure-ego tries to introject into itself everything that is good and to reject everything that is bad. From its point of view, what is bad, what is alien to the ego, and what is external are, to begin with, identical. (1990:4)

8. Anne Fadiman explains how many Hmong refugees were chastised and ridiculed for hunting and eating "skunks, porcupines, woodpeckers, robins, egrets, sparrows, and bald eagles," animals they may have eaten in Laos or had been forced to consume during their escape from the murderous, communist Pathet Lao" (1997:188). Also see Sau-ling Wong (1993) on "images of unpalatable food and strenuous eating," as well as "sacrificial eating," and "quasi-cannibalistic familial eating" (p. 24, 40, 34).

9. Abrahams 1984:22. "[I]t is somewhat clearer why such animals as possum, coon, or squirrel might be regarded as strange ones to eat, and why those who eat them are regarded as cultural vagrants, or backward people. . . . [because] coons and possums raid our garbage," says Abrahams (p. 33).

10. "In American popular culture we are engaged in a romance with ethnic foods," says Abrahams (1984:20). See Sau-Ling Wong's chapter "Big Eaters, Treat Lovers, 'Food Prostitutes,' 'Food Pornographers,' and Doughnut Makers" for a thorough explanation of what food means in Asian American literature (Wong 1993:18–76).

11. According to bell hooks, "The overriding fear is that cultural, ethnic, and racial differences will be continually commodified and offered up as new dishes to enhance the white palate—that the Other will be eaten, consumed, and forgotten" (1998:200).

12. For a counterargument to Carol J. Adams's discussion of vegetarianism, see Kathryn Paxton George's *Animal, Vegetable, or Woman?* (2000). She takes issue with Adams and other pro-vegan advocates such as Peter Singer, Deane Curtin, and Tom Regan. Their assumptions about the moral value of being vegan, she says, are based on "male psychological ideal[s]" and conveniently ignore the unique nutritional needs of women (especially pregnant women) and children (George 2000:3). She proposes a "feminist aesthetic semivegetarianism" as a more egalitarian (and moral) dietary imperative in "its consideration of all members of the moral community" (2000:10). In short, "moral vegetarianism is inconsistent with feminism" for George (2000:16).

13. I thank Carole Doreski for reminding me to mention *The Jungle* (August 1, 2000, private correspondence).

14. See Jack Goody's *Cooking, Cuisine and Class* (1982:193). While the kitchen has served as the "birthplace of many technical operations" once strictly relegated to women, when these processes left the house, they were usurped by men (p. 193).

15. With the question "Unpretentious or uncouth?" Pierre Bourdieu, in *Distinction: A Social Critique of the Judgment of Taste* (1984), contrasts the "table manners" of the working class with the bourgeoisie.

16. Unlike its lesser status in the East, explains Massimo Montanari (1994), meat has always enjoyed a favorable position in the West. Historically, meat (pork and lard in particular) was prioritized over bread in Western European countries as a "valued element of human nutrition" (p. 13). The aristocracy viewed meat as "a symbol of power, a tool for generating vigour, physical energy and the ability to do combat, qualities that constituted the primary legitimation of power. On the other hand, rejecting meat constituted a sign of humility and of marginalization . . . from the society of the strong" (pp. 14–15). Montanari traces the decline of meat consumption among the poor during population increases, restrictions against animals in cities, and the usurpation of agricultural land for other purposes (pp. 104–105). This did little to hierarchize bread and grains above meat; rather, it reemphasized the assumed superiority of the aristocracy over those classes that were unable to afford meat. Vast improvements in feedlot practices, packaging, and transportation technologies, according to Montanari, prompted an increase in beef consumption despite "the first English vegetarian society" in 1847 that rallied against eating meat in a "new humanitarian concern" for animals (pp. 145, 153–154).

17. For current information about Japan's import/export beef market, I also consulted James R. Simpson, Yoichi Kojima, et al. (1996), William A. Kerr, Kurt K. Klein, et al. (1994), and Carol Andreas (1994).

18. Lawrence S. Kubie (1937) expresses amazement at inconsistent definitions of filth, wherein mother's milk is sanitary and nourishing only when inside a mother's or a baby's body, but it becomes disgusting on its exit. He cites the personal knowledge of "two young interns in paediatrics who promptly vomited on discovering that they unwittingly had drunk human milk from the supply in the hospital ice-box" (p. 394, note 2).

19. Take the mysterious "natural flavoring" used in McDonald's french fries, documents Eric Schlosser, flavoring that is derived from "animal products." So those who assume that McDonald's fries are good, "clean" vegetarian fare confront the shocking news of their affiliation with meat (2001:128).

20. "Japlish" describes the syntactic and grammatical errors that arise when one translates Japanese phrases directly into English, attempting to convey not only the meaning of the translated word or phrase, but the Japanese sentiment or idea as well: "We at Tokyo Office wish you all have nice holiday season. Now . . . we ask your hard work in making exciting *My American Wife!* Let's persevere with new Program series!" (Ozeki 1998:11). Such "speak" is frequently found on Japanese stationery, T-shirts, shopping bags, lunch sacks, baseball caps, and food packaging.

21. Such values have been propagated by television through comedies such as *Father Knows Best*, in which American families were predominantly white as well as middle class and in which gendered roles confined mother to the domestic realm and father to employment beyond that realm. A genealogy of representations of the Other is recorded in such television shows as *Good Times, The Jeffersons, Diff'rent Strokes, Happy Days, The Cosby Show, All-American Girl, The Fresh Prince of Bel-Air, The Golden Girls, Roseanne,* and *In Living Color,* to name only a few. Articles and books discussing issues of race, class, and gender in contemporary TV sitcoms are too numerous to list. I will mention here only those that I consulted for this chapter: Herman Gray's *Watching Race: Television and the Struggle for "Blackness"* (1995); Darrell Y. Hamamoto's *Monitored Peril: Asian Americans and the Politics of TV Representation* (1994); Tania Modleski's *Studies in Entertainment: Critical Approaches to Mass Culture* (1986); Darby Li Po Price's "'All American Girl' and the American Dream" (1994); June M. Frazer and Timothy C. Frazer's "'Father Knows Best' and 'The Cosby Show': Nostalgia and the Sitcom Tradition" (1993); John D. H. Downing's "'The Cosby Show' and American Racial Discourse" (1988).

22. See Rod Brookes and Beverley Holbrook (1998:177).

23. In the disease, reproducing proteins called prions attack healthy proteins and slowly damage neural tissue. Frighteningly, prions cannot be eliminated even after reducing consumable meat to ash. This information was reported in PBS *Nova*'s "The Brain Eater."

24. See Diamond (1997) for a fascinating discussion on the introduction of germs via cattle to the New World. His ideas contribute to this sense of endlessly circulating pathologies that Ozeki's novel invites: immunized cattle become reinfected on factory farms, eventually finding their way, as tainted meat, onto our dinner plates.

25. Ozeki cites Sue Coe's *Dead Meat* (1995) for information about cattle feed additives. Coe, an illustrator and essayist, has visited numerous slaughterhouses in the United States and England. Because cameras and other filming devices are prohibited in abattoirs, denying what Coe regards as public access to the horrors of meat production, she illustrates and publishes accounts of the animal suffering she finds, making her work accessible to those who are interested. However, if cameras are prohibited in an abattoir, then it seems highly contrived that Jane and her crew, laden with visual and audio recording devices, could have gained entry into the slaughterhouse so easily.

26. In order to understand some of the complexities of the beef industry—from the views of both consumer advocates and cattle ranchers—I consulted Kathleen Jo Ryan and Elmer Kelton's *Texas Cattle Barons* (1999) and Kathleen Jo Ryan's *Deep in the Heart of Texas* (1999); for meatpackers' views, see Carol Andreas's *Meatpackers and Beef Barons* (1994) and Rick Halpern's *Down on the Killing Floor* (1997); and for cattle women's views, see Elizabeth Maret, *Women of the Range: Women's Roles in the Texas Beef Cattle Industry* (1993). See also the website offered by the San Luis Obispo County Cattle Women at http://www.-catlewomen-slo.org/. I thank Carole Doreski for this Web address.

27. Ozeki includes a short bibliography citing her sources on DES and its cancer-causing properties as well as provides addresses for the DES Cancer Network and DES Action U.S.A.

28. See Hee Won (2001:5).

29. This exemplifies what Palumbo-Liu says about the unpredictability of what meanings are appended to cultural capital in transit and how its cultural values fluctuate (1993:27).

30. Once slaughtered, a formerly living animal is linguistically recreated in order to conceal its former existence as a life form: "animal," "cow," or "chicken," denoting living beings, literally and linguistically become "food-producing unit[s]" or "edible parts," all suggesting *things*, states Adams. These "protein harvesters" are then butchered or

fragmented on the assembly line, packaged for shipment, and most importantly, renamed "to obscure the fact that these were once animals" (Adams 1998:47). They become beef, pork, and sausage for inevitable consumption.

31. I borrow this idea from Abrahams: "Culinary as well as sexual choice enters into our campaigns to manage our own identities by optimizing our stylistic choices constantly" (1984:25).

32. Joichi's televised women metamorphose into meat incarnate, readily digestible; this parallels the view of Carol J. Adams, who states that women, like butchered animals, are "packaged" for consumption, or objectified (a form of anesthetization) in preparation "to be made consumable in a patriarchal world" (1998:55). Adams records that rape victims often claim feeling "like a piece of meat," prompting her to question the connection "between being entered against one's will and being eaten" (1998:54). She points to a particular rape and murder case in which pieces of a woman's body were discovered simmering in several pots on the stove and in the oven. Moreover, three women who were chained in the basement had been forced to eat the dead woman's arms and legs (1998:40).

33. From Deborah R. Geis (1998:217, 218), who borrows the term "food pornography" from Rosalind Coward's *Female Desires: How They Are Sought, Bought and Packaged* (1985) and the phrase "Eat me! Eat me!" from Jeremy MacClancy's *Consuming Culture: Why You Eat What You Eat* (1993). In Asian American studies, food pornography is "making a living by exploiting the 'exotic' aspects of one's ethnic foodways," says Sau-ling Wong. It constitutes a "promotion . . . of one's ethnic identity" (1993:55). While Joichi prostitutes images of perfect American wives to Japan, Jane replies through her advertisement of ethnic Americans and their food.

34. Mary Douglas maps a food hierarchy—sweet and salty, liquid and solid, cold and hot—in which the latter term of the binary opposition is ranked above the former. Lighter appetizers and soups suggest a sexual progression toward the weightier and crowning (orgasmic) height of the meal—the *main* course—its *meat*. As the meal progresses, gravies become more viscous and thus richer as semi-liquid puddings are replaced by cakes topped with hardened (once-liquid) icing (1974:87). In such a value judgment on food, one can see how a supper of soup (particularly cold soup) would be deemed a lighter or more feminine fare than that of a hot slab of beef. In fact, women's luncheons more readily conjure up images of salads with light dressings, light sandwiches with the heavy crusts removed, and vegetarian fare. It

would be interesting to investigate the wet/dry dichotomy of this food scaffolding in relation to sex/gender through Luce Irigaray's "Fluid Mechanics" from *This Sex which Is Not One* (1985).

35. Jessamyn Neuhaus renames cookbooks of the 1920s and 1930s "marital sex manuals," exemplified by titles such as *The Seducer's Cookbook*, *The How to Keep Him (After You've Caught Him) Cookbook*, and chapters like "Beau-Catchers and Husband Keepers" (2001:96, 95). However, I keep in mind that Akiko is a Japanese woman living in Tokyo to which these ideas may not apply.

36. Jane Gallop, in an edited collection *Our Monica, Ourselves: The Clinton Affair and the National Interest*, claims that while the right "is still really moralistic about sex," the left is equally so about food, establishing a "new style of moralism about control. . . . Well-educated liberal people are supposed to be in control of the amount of body fat they have." Quoted in a review article: "Trash Tropes and Queer Theory: Decoding the Lewinsky Scandal" (*New York Times* 2001, p. 7).

37. See Delaney, Lupton, and Toth's *The Curse* (105).

38. Akiko and her nurse Tomoko share a kiss. "Are you a lesbian?" Akiko asks her. "I don't know . . . I've never thought about it," she answers. "I have," says Akiko, "but I don't know either" (Ozeki 1998:318–319).

39. Of restaurant meals shared in the company of men and women, Rosalind Coward says, "Services are bought for a fee. In routine sexual relations, [female sexual] services are expected in return for [male alimentary] provision" (1985:110).

40. For more on this, see Adams (1998).

41. Adams quotes Karen Davis (Adams 1998:72). Abrahams (1984) mentions that bad table manners elicit comments such as "You eat like a pig!" or "Don't chew your food like a cow!" or "Don't wolf your food!" (p. 28).

42. Wayne killed Indians in the movies, while Wayno/Ueno regards Blacks, Mexicans, and children of mixed racial heritage as un-American. Wayne's sexist character, often a bachelor riding alone into the sunset, seeks women only for enjoyment, while Wayno/Ueno finds gratification in "animal-like" spousal abuse. Wayne exudes a reputation of rough bravado and attractive indifference; in contrast, Wayno/Ueno is characterized as an ineffectual cowboy, a Japlish-speaking, feminized Asian whose only power resides in subordinating his wife to his sexual demands.

43. Unlike Jane, who desires intimacy, Sloan searches for a "perfectly safe" partner: "He wanted a simple answer to a nagging ques-

tion, like scratching an itch," Jane says. "I wanted something else. . . . I wanted more" (Ozeki 1998:161). His initial reaction to her surprising pregnancy (given that she has been medically confirmed as infertile) is to abort the baby, which has less to do with the added responsibility of being a father than with his anger at Jane's inability to keep her promise about being perfectly safe without birth control. Sloan's tears render little sympathy when he weeps over the miscarried fetus later in the novel. That the status of their relationship is decidedly ambiguous at the conclusion underscores the novel's wary stance toward men and the impossibility of a harmonious and workable heterosexual relationship.

44. What follows is a list of the novel's families and their children: the Beaudroux—who boast two biological and ten adopted children, some of whom are Amerasian war orphans with cleft palates or emotional problems and others who are South American children missing fingers or exhibiting psychosomatic abnormalities—occupy a renovated Southern plantation, with one of their more sulky teenagers moving into the slave quarters; the Mexican immigrant family the Martinezes are endowed with long-awaited American son Bobby; the Bukowskis are the parents of daughter Christina; the Thayers have two children; the Purcells six; even the lesbian couple of Dyann and Lara have two adopted daughters. I thank Pamela Thoma for pointing out the book's promotion of natalism.

45. I borrow this quote from Randy Moser, a graduate student in my spring 2001 Literature and the Body course, whose class presentation revolved around numerous astute questions on Ozeki's *My Year* concerning women, motherhood, maternity, natalism, men, birth , and the slaughterhouse (May 1, 2001).

46. Moser, personal correspondence.

47. Moser, personal correspondence. Listed are only a few of Moser's many intelligent questions that are obliquely related to my own ideas: "Are big-breasted women coded as unnatural?" What is the real [natural] man in the novel?" "How is motherhood constructed as a biological truth?" "Consider also the suggestion of incest [Gale fondles half-sister Rosie] and how that corresponds to the 'unnatural' birth of meat (and Rose)." "Why does Jane lose her baby at the moment she enters into this masculine uterus [the slaughterhouse]? Women assemble parts together as human beings inside themselves, men cut the body apart [in beef production]."

48. I am referencing hero mythmaking from Richard Slotkin's *Regeneration through Violence: The Mythology of the American Frontier, 1600– 1860* (1973).

6

Conclusion: Filth and Asian American Literary Criticism

It is valuable to investigate what many deem superfluous. Filth, as such seemingly extraneous matter, offers a way of thinking through literature in a sustained manner, encouraging potentially transgressive reading practices and reconceptualizing conventional narratives, both fictional and critical/theoretical, of ethnic identity. To recognize subjectivity and agency in formerly abjected female characters, both *in spite of* and *through* filth, illuminates the slipperiness of definitions of dirt that can both debilitate and empower, pathologize and purify, victimize and liberate. Conclusions of such a nature release individual embodiment from certain binaries—what Nayan Shah (2001) might call "contagious divides"—that order and drive national knowledge. Extra-textually, forays into dirt can simultaneously support and vex interdisciplinary conversations in the field of Asian American studies: dirt interrogates racial pathology and definitions of white trash or gender trash; it yokes anthropologists' interests in cultural symbolism to linguists' attention to foul language or to the nuances of things naturally clean or dirty; and it works toward denationalizing Asian American studies through discursive allusions to filth and to their rethinking, evident in imported sweat shop labor, deracination, mobile food toxins, and ecologically damaging dumping grounds (Choy 2003; Parreñas 2001; Schlosser 2001; Bullard 2000; Diamond 1997; Enloe 1990).

The politics of categorizing Asian American literature reflects just the themes that the novels of my study address: rejection and acceptance. For in spite of Asian American literature's interdisciplinarity and transnationalism—as evidenced in the works of Kamani (1995) and Ozeki (1998) or addressed by scholars such as Shirley Geok-lin Lim (2000), Rob Wilson (2000), Arif Dirlik (1999), Evelyn Hu-DeHart (1999), Sheng-mei Ma (1998), to name a few—Asian American studies often has overlooked or bypassed, if subtly, fiction that focuses more heavily on plots, characters, and issues surrounding the Asian half of the term Asian American literature. Scholars in the field have remarked how Asian American literature unevenly borrows from and contributes to both sides of its appellation, and they have discussed its impact on the field.[1] As such, Kamani's collection *Junglee Girl* (1995) *as* Asian American literature is an interesting case to investigate. The collection's stories are not located on U.S. soil (except for one) but in Bombay, unlike the rest of the novels under investigation in *Filthy Fictions*. Her designation as an Asian American author asks us to reconsider what is deemed Asian American literature, why, and how we critique it; and her work prompts questions about how the field is configured and how it changes. Do Kamani's Bombay-based plots and characters reflect American or South Asian influences or their mélange? How are we to determine these designations, and is this determination important?

How one answers these questions lends itself well to current debates that condemn an Asian American criticism focused almost exclusively on fiction dealing with American, domestic concerns for one that considers those works emphasizing characters' Asian-based experiences and influences (Koshy 2000; Hu-DeHart 1999; Ma 1998; Mazumdar 1991; also see Wong's [1995] "Denationalization" for a counterargument). David Palumbo-Liu (1993), borrowing from Pierre Bourdieu, argues that cultural objects, and I would add cultural practices, "are appropriated to fulfil [sic] different interests" and that "the operations of cultural capital as cultural objects are uprooted from their 'field of origin' and reconfigured in a 'field of destination'" (1993: 9, 11). If I use this compelling view in my own analyses, then particular,

national constructions of representations of women's impropriety or their invalidity are reworked in the field of destination,
creating new, national meanings that are themselves mired in
transnational reconfigurations. If cultural objects (including cultural narratives and representations) are appropriated by cre-
ators and users, it becomes unclear what cultural fact might be
borrowed from which nation, which fiction might be created at
what location, and what is Eastern and what is Western, allowing works like Kamani's that straddle international borders to
trouble the parameters of Asian American critique and designations over what constitutes Asian American literature.

It is with much irony that just as scholars in Asian American
studies are skeptical of a restrictive adherence to the American
side of Asian American literature by extending criticism beyond
this homeland approach, Kamani's (1995) collection of quirky
stories has found only a small readership and enjoyed no sustained critique in academic journals. If Kamani's female characters are rejected for their sexual or class-based improprieties, no
matter how imagined they may be, her book itself has been little
recognized in Asian American studies. Perhaps she has been
overlooked for the same reasons that her characters face rejection: for their overt sexuality. States Rachel C. Lee, "Too often,
concerns over narratives of gender and sexual awakening are accused of undermining the 'serious' work that Asian American
texts are expected to perform" (1999:140). In fact, none of the
novels I examine garnered much scholarly attention at publication, except for Ozeki's (1998) *My Year of Meats* (now being produced as a film starring, ironically, Gwyneth Paltrow as the
Anglo-Japanese Jane)[2] and Yamanaka's (1997) *Blu's Hanging*,
which attracted mostly negative attention when the Association
for Asian American Studies revoked its literary award for *Blu's* in
1998. Critics opposed Yamanaka's depictions of overly sexualized,
and thus stereotypical, Local Filipino and Filipina characters. The
controversy sparked debate over the rights and "rules" of how
minority authors should depict other minorities, rather than over
Yamanaka's literary accomplishments. Despite the nearly non-
existent body of critical work about such fiction, especially
Kamani's fiction, it now becomes extremely (even necessarily)

important in the delimiting of the literature and its criticism. The often futile attempts of Asian American studies to authenticate what social or cultural textual references are borrowed, nationally and globally as outlined above, and to what impact and importance that authentification has, often renders "Asian" and "American" designations indiscernible.

A concentration on textual dirt also liberates us from a certain type of reading in which one views only how the dominant population circumscribes and limits Asian American women. My aim in several sections of the book has been to uncover how Asian American characters themselves participate in pathologizing and dirtying others, and how some authors and characters reinvent the specter of filth in creative, subversive ways. This reading strategy encourages a necessary recognition of the instability of definitions and uses of dirt: Are Asian Americans authors or critics adhering to a dominant ideology or are they creating narratives of dirt based on other cultural practices and premises that might both merge with and diverge from the majority? How does the recognition of Asian American participation in the perpetuation of dirt affect Asian American critique?

I have tried to illustrate the concept of dirt in its displacement of Asian American women and in its concomitant subversion of definitions that circumscribe their bodiliness. New readings of filth in Asian American and other ethnic fiction will open novel avenues of critique that take us beyond anxieties over dirty matter and concomitant bodily inscription.

Notes

1. See Rocío G. Davis and Sämi Ludwig's (2002) *Asian American Literature in the International Context: Readings in Fiction, Poetry, and Performance.*

2. Ruth Ozeki discussed this with me (personal correspondence, October 2001).

References

Abrahams, Roger. "Equal Opportunity Eating: A Structural Excursus on Things of the Mouth." *Ethnic and Regional Foodways in the United States: The Performance of Group Identity*. Ed. Linda Keller Brown and Kay Mussell. Knoxville: University of Tennessee Press, 1984. 19–36.

Adams, Carol J. "Eating Animals." *Eating Culture*. Ed. Ron Scapp and Brian Seitz. Albany: State University of New York Press, 1998. 60–75.

———. *The Sexual Politics of Meat: A Feminist-Vegetarian Critical Theory*. New York: Continuum, 1990.

Adams, Carol J., and Josephine Donovan, eds. *Animals and Women: Feminist Theoretical Explorations*. Durham, N.C.: Duke University Press, 1995.

Andreas, Carol. *Meatpackers and Beef Barons: Company Town in a Global Economy*. Niwot: University Press of Colorado, 1994.

Anzaldua, Gloria, ed. *Making Face, Making Soul/Haciendo Caras: Creative and Critical Perspectives by Women of Color*. San Francisco: Aunt Lute Foundation Books, 1990.

Bahri, Deepika. "Disembodying the Corpus: Postcolonial Pathology in Tsitsi Dangarembga's *Nervous Condition*." *Postmodern Culture: An Electronic Journal of Interdisciplinary Studies* 5.1 (1994): 1–59.

Balibar, Etienne. "Is There a 'Neo-Racism'?" *Race, Nation, Class: Ambiguous Identities*. Etienne Balibar and Immanuel Wallerstein. Trans. Chris Turner. New York: Verso, 1991. 17–28.

Berlant, Lauren. *The Queen of America Goes to Washington City: Essays on Sex and Citizenship*. Durham, N.C.: Duke University Press, 1997.

Bonacich, Edna. "Asian Labor in the Development of California and Hawaii." *Labor Immigration under Capitalism: Asian Workers in the United States before World War II*. Ed. Lucie Cheng and Edna Bonacich. Berkeley: University of California Press, 1984. 130–185.

Bonheim, Helmut. "The Giant in Literature and in Medical Practice." *Literature and Medicine* 13.2 (fall 1994): 243–254.

Bourdieu, Pierre. *Distinction: A Social Critique of the Judgment of Taste.* Trans. Richard Nice. Cambridge, Mass.: Harvard University Press, 1984.

Bow, Leslie. *Betrayal and Other Acts of Subversion: Feminism, Sexual Politics, Asian American Women's Literature.* Princeton, N.J.: Princeton University Press, 2001.

"The Brain Eater." *Nova.* PBS. WMEB, Maine. Tuesday, October 3, 2000.

Bright, Chris. *Life out of Bounds: Bioinvasion in a Borderless World.* New York: W. W. Norton, 1998.

Brogan, Kathleen. *Cultural Haunting: Ghosts and Ethnicity in Recent American Literature.* Charlottesville: University Press of Virginia, 1998.

Brookes, Rod, and Beverley Holbrook. "'Mad Cows and Englishmen': Gender Implications of News Reporting on the British Beef Crisis." *News, Gender and Power.* Ed. Cynthia Carter et al. New York: Routledge, 1998. 174–185.

Budiansky, Stephen. *The Covenant of the Wild: Why Animals Chose Domestication.* New Haven, Conn.: Yale University Press, [1992] 1999.

Buell, Frederick. "Nationalist Postnationalism: Globalist Discourse in Contemporary American Culture." *American Quarterly* 50.3 (September 1998): 548–591.

Bullard, Robert D. *Dumping in Dixie: Race, Class, and Environmental Quality.* 3d ed. Boulder: University of Colorado Press, 2000.

Bulosan, Carlos. *America Is in the Heart: A Personal History.* New York: Harcourt, Brace, and Company, 1946.

Burke, Timothy. *Lifebuoy Men, Lux Women: Commodification, Consumption, and Cleanliness in Modern Zimbabwe.* Durham, N.C.: Duke University Press, 1996.

Butler, Judith. *Bodies That Matter: On the Discursive Limits of "Sex."* New York: Routledge, 1993.

———. *Gender Trouble: Feminism and the Subversion of Identity.* New York: Routledge, 1990.

Carlton, James T. "Marine Bioinvasion: The Alteration of Marine Ecosystems by Nonindigenous Species." *Oceanography* 9.1 (1996): 36–43.

Cha, Theresa Hak Kyung. *Dictée.* Berkeley, Calif.: Third Woman Press, 1995.

Cheng, Anne Anlin. *The Melancholy of Race: Psychoanalysis, Assimilation, and Hidden Grief.* New York: Oxford University Press, 2000.

Chiu, Monica. "Motion, Memory, and Conflict in Chuang Hua's Modernist *Crossings.*" *MELUS* 24.4 (winter 1999): 107–123.

Chow, Rey. *Ethics after Idealism: Theory-Culture-Ethnicity-Reading*. Bloomington: Indiana University Press, 1998.

Choy, Catherine Ceniza. *Empire of Care: Nursing and Migration in Filipino American History*. Durham, N.C.: Duke University Press, 2003.

Chu, Louis. *Eat a Bowl of Tea: A Novel of New York's Chinatown*. New York: Lyle Stuart/Carol Communications, [1961] 1995.

Chu, Patricia P. *Assimilating Asians: Gendered Strategies of Authorship in Asian America*. Durham, N.C.: Duke University Press, 2000.

Chuang, Hua. *Crossings*. Boston: Northeastern University Press, [1968] 1986.

Cixous, Hélène. *"Coming to Writing" and Other Essays*. Ed. Deborah Jenson. Trans. Sarah Cornell. Cambridge, Mass.: Harvard University Press, 1991.

Clark, Peter, and Anthony Davis. "The Power of Dirt: An Exploration of Secular Defilement in Anglo-Canadian Culture." *Canadian Review of Sociology and Anthropology* 26.4 (1989): 650–673.

Coe, Sue. *Dead Meat*. New York: Four Walls Eight Windows, 1995.

The Compact Edition of the Oxford English Dictionary. Vol. 1. Oxford: Oxford University Press, 1987.

Conboy, Katie, Nadia Medina, and Sarah Stanbury, eds. *Writing on the Body: Female Embodiment and Feminist Theory*. New York: Columbia University Press, 1997.

Corbin, Alain. *The Foul and the Fragrant: Odor and the French Social Imagination*. Trans. Aubier Montaigne. Cambridge: Cambridge University Press, 1986.

Counihan, Carole M. *The Anthropology of Food and Body: Gender, Meaning, and Power*. New York: Routledge, 1999.

Coward, Rosalind. *Female Desires: How They Are Sought, Bought and Packaged*. New York: Grove Press, 1985.

Creef, Elena Tajima. "Notes from a Fragmented Daughter." *Making Face, Making Soul/Hacienda Caras: Creative and Critical Perspectives by Women of Color*. Ed. Gloria Anzaldua. San Francisco: Aunt Lute Foundation Books, 1990. 82–84.

Crosby, Alfred W. *Ecological Imperialism: The Biological Expansion of Europe, 900–1900*. New York: Cambridge University Press, 1986.

Davis, Rocío G. " 'I Wish You a Land': Hawai'i Short Story Cycles and *Aloha 'Aina*." *Journal of American Studies* 35.1 (2001): 47–64.

Davis, Rocío G., and Sämi Ludwig, eds. *Asian American Literature in the International Context: Readings in Fiction, Poetry, and Performance*. Berlin: LIT Verlag, 2002.

Delaney, Janice, Mary Jane Lupton, and Emily Toth, eds. *The Curse: A*

Cultural History of Menstruation. Revised edition. Urbana: University of Illinois Press, 1988.

Diamond, Jared. *Guns, Germs, and Steel: The Fates of Human Societies.* New York: W. W. Norton, 1997.

Dirlik, Arif. "Asians on the Rim: Transnational Capital and Local Community in the Making of Contemporary Asian America." *Across the Pacific: Asian Americans and Globalization.* Ed. Evelyn Hu-DeHart. Philadelphia: Temple University Press, 1999. 29–60.

Douglas, Mary. "Deciphering a Meal." *Implicit Meanings: Selected Essays in Anthropology.* 2d ed. New York: Routledge, 1999. 231–251.

———. "Food as an Art Form." *Studio: International Journal of Modern Art* 188.969 (September 1974): 83–88.

———. *Purity and Danger: An Analysis of Concepts of Pollution and Taboo.* Boston: Routledge & Kegan Paul, [1966] 1980.

Downing, John D. H. " 'The Cosby Show' and American Racial Discourse." *Discourse and Discrimination.* Ed. Geneva Smitherman-Donaldson and Teun A. van Dijk. Detroit: Wayne State University Press, 1988. 46–73.

Eng, David L. *Racial Castration: Managing Masculinity in Asian America.* Durham, N.C.: Duke University Press, 2001.

Eng, David L., and Alice Hom, eds. *Q&A: Queer in Asian America.* Philadelphia: Temple University Press, 1998.

Enloe, Cynthia. *Bananas, Beaches, and Bases: Making Feminist Sense of International Politics.* Berkeley: University of California Press, 1990.

Epstein, Julia. *Altered Conditions: Disease, Medicine, and Storytelling.* New York: Routledge, 1995.

Fadiman, Anne. *The Spirit Catches You and You Fall Down: A Hmong Child, Her American Doctors, and the Collision of Two Cultures.* New York: Farrar, Straus, and Giroux, 1997.

Fernandes, Leela. "Reading 'India's Bandit Queen': A Trans/National Feminist Perspective on the Discrepencies of Representation." *Haunting Violations: Feminist Criticism and the Crisis of the "Real."* Ed. Wendy S. Hesford and Wendy Kozol. Urbana: University of Illinois Press, 2001. 47–75.

Frazer, June M., and Timothy C. Frazer. " 'Father Knows Best' and 'The Cosby Show': Nostalgia and the Sitcom Tradition." *Journal of Popular Culture* 27.3 (winter 1993): 163–172.

Fujikane, Candace. "Between Nationalisms: Hawaii's Local Nation and Its Troubled Racial Paradise." *Hitting Critical Mass* 1.2 (spring 1994). Retrieved October 25, 2001, from http://socrates.berkeley.edu/~critmass/v1n2/fujikane5.html.

Geis, Deborah R. "Feeding the Audience: Food, Feminism, and Performance Art." *Eating Culture*. Ed. Ron Scapp and Brian Seitz. Albany: State University of New York Press, 1998. 216–236.

George, Kathryn Paxton. *Animal, Vegetable, or Woman? A Feminist Critique of Ethical Vegetarianism*. Albany: State University of New York Press, 2000.

Gilman, Sander L. *Difference and Pathology: Stereotypes of Sexuality, Race, and Madness*. Ithaca, N.Y.: Cornell University Press, 1985.

Glenn, Evelyn Nakano. *Issei, Nisei, War Bride: Three Generations of Japanese American Women in Domestic Service*. Philadelphia: Temple University Press, 1986.

Goody, Jack. *Cooking, Cuisine and Class: A Study in Comparative Sociology*. New York: Cambridge University Press, 1982.

Gould, Stephen Jay. "An Evolutionary Perspective on Strengths, Fallacies, and Confusions in the Concept of Native Plants." *Arnoldia: The Magazine of the Arnold Arboretum* 58.1 (spring 1998): 2–10.

———. "Mickey Mouse Meets Konrad Lorenz." *Natural History* 88.5 (May 1979): 30–36.

Gray, Herman. *Watching Race: Television and the Struggle for "Blackness."* Minneapolis: University of Minnesota Press, 1995.

Greenblatt, Stephen. "Filthy Rites." *Daedalus* 3.3 (winter/fall 1982): 1–16.

Grimes, William. "Where the Deer and the Antelope Braise." *The New York Times*, Section F (January 14, 1998): 1.

Grosz, Elizabeth. *Volatile Bodies: Toward a Corporeal Feminism*. Bloomington: Indiana University Press, 1994.

Halpern, Rick. *Down on the Killing Floor: Black and White Workers in Chicago's Packinghouses, 1904–54*. Urbana: University of Illinois Press, 1997.

Halverson, John. "Animal Categories and Terms of Abuse." *Man: The Journal of the Royal Anthropological Institute* 11.4 (December 1976): 505–516.

Hamamoto, Darrell Y. *Monitored Peril: Asian Americans and the Politics of TV Representation*. Minneapolis: University of Minnesota Press, 1994.

Hardy, Quentin. "In Hawaii, the Wild Boar Hunt Ends with a Knife in Its Heart." *Star Tribune*, Section G (August 13, 1995): 5.

Hastings, Hester. *Man and Beast in French Thought of the Eighteenth Century*. Baltimore: Johns Hopkins University Press, 1936.

Herndl, Diane Price. *Invalid Women: Figuring Feminine Illness in American Fiction and Culture, 1840–1940*. Chapel Hill: University of North Carolina Press, 1993.

Hesford, Wendy S. "Defining Moments." *Haunting Violations: Feminist Criticism and the Crisis of the "Real."* Ed. Wendy Hesford and Wendy Kozol. Urbana: University of Illinois Press, 2001. ix–x.

Ho, Wendy. *In Her Mother's House: The Politics of Asian American Mother-Daughter Writing.* Walnut Creek, Calif.: AltaMira, 1999.

Holt, Patricia. "'Junglee Girl' Author Flouts Taboos." *San Francisco Chronicle.* April 30, 1995, Sunday Review: 2.

hooks, bell. "Desire and Resistance." *Eating Culture.* Ed. Ron Scapp and Brian Seitz. Albany: State University of New York Press, 1998. 181–200.

———. *Feminist Theory from Margin to Center.* Boston: South End Press, 1984.

Hoy, Suellen. *Chasing Dirt: The American Pursuit of Cleanliness.* New York: Oxford University Press, 1995.

Hu-DeHart, Evelyn. *Across the Pacific: Asian Americans and Globalization.* Philadelphia: Temple University Press, 1999.

Hunter, Kathryn Montgomery. *Doctors' Stories: The Narrative Structure of Medical Knowledge.* Princeton, N.J.: Princeton University Press, 1991.

Hwang, David Henry. *M. Butterfly.* New York: Penguin, 1989.

Inness, Sherrie A., ed. *Kitchen Culture in America: Popular Representations of Food, Gender, and Race.* Philadelphia: University of Pennsylvania Press, 2001.

Irigaray, Luce. *This Sex which Is Not One.* Trans. Catherine Porter with Carolyn Burke. Ithaca, N.Y.: Cornell University Press, 1985.

James, Jamie. "This Hawaii Is Not for Tourists." *The Atlantic Monthly* (February 1999): 90–94.

Kadohata, Cynthia. *The Floating World.* New York: Ballantine Books, 1989.

Kamani, Ginu. *Junglee Girl.* San Francisco: Aunt Lute Books, 1995.

Kaminsky, Amy K. *Reading the Body Politic: Feminist Criticism and Latin American Women Writers.* Minneapolis: University of Minnesota Press, 1993.

Keller, Nora Okja. *Comfort Woman.* New York: Penguin, 1997.

Kerr, William A., Kurt K. Klein, et al. *Marketing Beef in Japan.* New York: Food Products Press, 1994.

Kete, Kathleen. *The Beast in the Boudoir: Petkeeping in Nineteenth-Century Paris.* Berkeley: University of California Press, 1994.

Kilgour, Maggie. *From Communion to Cannibalism: An Anatomy of Metaphors of Incorporation.* Princeton, N.J.: Princeton University Press, 1990.

Kim, Elaine H. *Asian American Literature: An Introduction to the Writings and Their Social Context.* Philadelphia: Temple University Press, 1982.

Kingston, Maxine Hong. *The Woman Warrior: Memoirs of a Girlhood among Ghosts.* New York: Vintage, [1976] 1989.

Klein, Richard. "The Power of Pets." *The New Republic* (July 3, 1995): 18–23.

Kogawa, Joy. *Obasan.* Boston: David R. Godine, 1982.

Koshy, Susan. "The Fiction of Asian American Literature." *Asian American Studies: A Reader.* Ed. Jean Yu-Wen Shen Wu and Min Song. New Brunswick, N.J.: Rutgers University Press, 2000. 467–495.

Kraut, Alan M. *Silent Travelers: Germs, Genes, and the "Immigrant Menace."* New York: Basic Books, 1994.

Krishnamoorthy, K. *Kalidāsā.* New York: Twayne, 1972.

Kristeva, Julia. *Powers of Horror: Essays on Abjection.* Trans. Leon S. Roudiez. New York: Columbia University Press, 1982.

Kubie, Lawrence S. "The Fantasy of Dirt." *Psychoanalytic Quarterly* 6 (1937): 388–425.

Kurian, George T., ed. *A Historical Guide to the U.S. Government.* New York: Oxford University Press, 1998.

Law-Yone, Wendy. *The Coffin Tree.* Boston: Beacon Press, 1983.

Leach, Edmund. "Anthropological Aspects of Language: Animal Categories and Verbal Abuse." *New Directions in the Study of Language.* Ed. Eric H. Lenneberg. Boston: MIT Press, 1964. 23–63.

Lee, Karen A. "John Ford's *The Searchers* (1956) in Chuang Hua's *Crossings*: A Chinese American Woman's Categorical Liminality in a Cold War Society." *Hitting Critical Mass* 4.2 (summer 1997): 79–86.

Lee, Rachel C. *The Americas of Asian American Literature: Gendered Fictions of Nation and Transnation.* Princeton, N.J.: Princeton University Press, 1999.

Lee, Robert G. *Orientals: Asian Americans in Popular Culture.* Philadelphia: Temple University Press, 1999.

Legman, Gershon. *The Rationale of the Dirty Joke: An Analysis of Sexual Humor.* 2d Series. New York: Grove Press, 1975.

Lemonick, Brosing S. "Invasion of the Habitat Snatchers." *Time* 136.11 (September 10, 1990), 75.

Leong, Russell. *Asian American Sexualities: Dimensions of the Gay and Lesbian Experience.* New York: Routledge, 1996.

Li, David Leiwei. *Imagining the Nation: Asian American Literature and Cultural Consent.* Stanford, Calif.: Stanford University Press, 1998.

Li, Shu-yan. "Otherness and Transformation in *Eat a Bowl of Tea* and *Crossings*." *MELUS* 18.4 (winter 1993): 99–110.

Lim, Shirley Geok-lin. "The Center Can(not) Hold: American Studies and Global Feminism." *American Studies International* 38.3 (October 2000): 25–35.

———. "Introduction." *Transnational Asia Pacific: Gender, Culture, and the Public Sphere.* Ed. Lim, Larry E. Smith, and Wimal Dissanayake. Urbana: University of Illinois Press, 1999.

Lim-Hing, Sharon, ed. *The Very Inside: An Anthology of Writing by Asian and Pacific Islander Lesbian and Bisexual Women.* Toronto: Sister Vision, 1994.

Ling, Amy. "Foreword." *Crossings.* Chuang Hua. Boston: Northeastern University Press, 1986. 1–6.

———. "A Rumble in the Silence: *Crossings* by Chuang Hua." *MELUS* 9.3 (winter 1982): 29–37.

Liu, John M. "Asian Labor in Hawaii, 1850–1900." *Labor Immigration under Capitalism: Asian Workers in the United States before World War II.* Ed. Lucie Cheng and Edna Bonacich. Berkeley: University of California Press, 1984. 186–210.

Lowe, Lisa. "The International within the National: American Studies and Asian American Critique." *Cultural Critique* 40 (fall 1998): 29–47.

Ma, Sheng-mei. *The Deathly Embrace: Orientalism and Asian American Identity.* Minneapolis: University of Minnesota Press, 2000.

———. *Immigrant Subjectivities in Asian American and Asian Diaspora Literatures.* Albany: State University of New York Press, 1998.

MacCannell, Dean. *Empty Meeting Grounds: The Tourist Papers.* New York: Routledge, 1992.

MacClancy, Jeremy. *Consuming Culture: Why You Eat What You Eat.* New York: H. Holt, [1992] 1993.

Maira, Sunaina. *Desis in the House: Indian American Youth Culture in New York City.* Philadelphia: Temple University Press, 2002.

Marchetti, Gina. *Romance and the "Yellow Peril": Race, Sex, and Discursive Strategies in Hollywood Fiction.* Berkeley: University of California Press, 1993.

Maret, Elizabeth. *Women of the Range: Women's Roles in the Texas Beef Cattle Industry.* College Station, Tex.: Texas Agriculture and Mining University Press, 1993.

Mason, Jennifer. "Animal Bodies: Corporeality, Class, and Subject Formation in *The Wide, Wide World.*" *Nineteenth-Century Literature* 54.4 (March 2000): 503–533.

Mazumdar, Sucheta. "Asian American Studies and Asian Studies: Rethinking Roots." *Asian Americans: Comparative and Global Perspectives.* Ed. Shirley Hune, Hyung-chan Kim, Stephen S. Fugita, and Amy Ling. Pullman: Washington State University Press, 1991. 29–44.

McCarthy, Susan, and Jeffrey Moussaieff Masson. *When Elephants Weep: The Emotional Lives of Animals.* New York: Delacorte Press, 1995.

McClintock, Anne. *Imperial Leather: Race, Gender and Sexuality in the Colonial Contest.* New York: Routledge, 1995.

McDowell, Linda. *Gender, Identity, and Place: Understanding Feminist Geographies.* Minneapolis: University of Minnesota Press, 1999.

McHugh, Kathleen. "One Cleans, the Other Doesn't." *Cultural Studies* 11.1 (January 1997): 17–39.

McNally, Bob. "Days of Swine . . . and Noses." *Outdoor Life* 196.6 (December 1995): 17.

Melosi, Martin V., ed. *Pollution and Reform in American Cities, 1870–1930.* Austin: University of Texas Press, 1980.

Miller, Barbara Stoler, ed. "Two Classical Indian Plays: Kalidasa's *Śakuntalā* and Śudraka's *Little Clay Cart.*" *Masterworks of Asian Literature in Comparative Perspective: A Guide for Teaching.* Ed. Barbara Stoler Miller. Armonk, N.Y.: M. E. Sharpe, 1994. 201–208.

Modleski, Tania. *Studies in Entertainment: Critical Approaches to Mass Culture.* Bloomington: Indiana University Press, 1986.

Mohanty, Chandra Talpade, Ann Russo, and Lourdes Torres, eds. *Third World Women and the Politics of Feminism.* Bloomington: Indiana University Press, 1991.

Montanari, Massimo. *The Culture of Food.* Trans. Carl Ipsen. Cambridge: Blackwell, 1994.

Moraga, Cherríe. *Loving in the War Years. Lo que nunca pasó por sus labios.* Boston: South End Press, 1983.

Morrison, Toni. *The Bluest Eye.* New York: Knopf, 1993.

Muir, Frank. *An Irreverent and Thoroughly Incomplete Social History of Almost Everything.* New York: Stein and Day, 1976.

Najita, Susan Y. "History, Trauma, and the Discursive Construction of 'Race' in John Dominis Holt's *Waimea Summer.*" *Cultural Critique* 47 (winter 2001): 167–214.

Neuhaus, Jessamyn. "The Joy of Sex Instruction: Women and Cooking in Marital Sex Manuals, 1920–1963." *Kitchen Culture in America: Popular Representations of Food, Gender, and Race.* Ed. Sherrie A. Inness. Philadelphia: University of Pennsylvania Press, 2001. 95–117.

The New York Times. "Trash Tropes and Queer Theory: Decoding the Lewinsky Scandal." August 5, 2001, Sunday edition, Section 4: 7.

Nguyen, Viet Thanh. *Race and Resistance: Literature and Politics in Asian America.* New York: Oxford University Press, 2002.

Obeyesekere, Gananath. *The Apotheosis of Captain Cook: European Mythmaking in the Pacific.* Princeton, N.J.: Princeton University Press, [1992] 1997.

Ohnuki-Tierney, Emiko. "McDonald's in Japan: Changing Manners and Etiquette." *Golden Arches East: McDonald's in East Asia.* Ed. James L. Watson. Stanford, Calif.: Stanford University Press, 1997. 161–182.

Okada, John. *No-No Boy.* Seattle: University of Washington Press, [1957] 1976.

Okamura, Jonathan Y. "Why There Are No Asian Americans in Hawai'i: The Continuing Significance of Local Identity." *Social Process in Hawai'i* 35 (1994): 161–178.

———. "Aloha Kanaka Me Ke Aloha 'Aina: Local Culture and Society in Hawaii." *Amerasia Journal* 7.2 (1980): 119–137.

Oliver, Kelly. *Reading Kristeva: Unraveling the Double-Bind.* Bloomington: Indiana University Press, 1993.

———. "Nourishing the Speaking Subject: A Psychoanalytic Approach to Abominable Food and Women." *Cooking, Eating, Thinking: Transformative Philosophies of Food.* Ed. Deane W. Curtin and Lisa M. Heldke. Bloomington: Indiana University Press, 1992. 68–84.

Omi, Michael, and Howard Winant. *Racial Formation in the United States: From the 1960s to the 1990s.* New York: Routledge, 1994.

Omori, Miyako, dir. *Rabbit in the Moon. POV* broadcast. PBS. WGBH, Boston. June 1, 1999.

Ozeki, Ruth L. *My Year of Meats.* New York: Viking, 1998.

———. "There and Back Again." *The Independent* (October 1998): 40–42.

Palumbo-Liu, David. *Asian/American: Historical Crossings of a Racial Frontier.* Stanford, Calif.: Stanford University Press, 1999.

———. "Introduction." *The Ethnic Canon: Histories, Institutions, and Interventions.* Ed. Palumbo-Liu. Minneapolis: University of Minnesota Press, 1995. 1–27.

———. "Unhabituated Habituses." *Streams of Cultural Capital.* Ed. Palumbo-Liu and Hans Ulrich Gumbrecht. Stanford, Calif.: Stanford University Press, 1993. 1–21.

Parreñas, Rhacel Salazar. *Servants of Globalization: Women, Migration, and Domestic Work.* Stanford, Calif.: Stanford University Press, 2001.

Prashad, Vijay. *The Karma of Brown Folk.* Minneapolis: University of Minnesota Press, 2000.

Price, Darby Li Po. "'All American Girl' and the American Dream." *Hitting Critical Mass* 2.1 (winter 1994): 129–146.

Price, Janet, and Margrit Shildrick, eds. *Feminist Theory and the Body: A Reader.* New York: Routledge, 1999.

Priest, Robert Joseph. "Defilement, Purity, and Transgressive Power: The Symbolism of Filth in Aguaruna Jivaro." Ph.D. dissertation. University of California, Berkeley, 1993.

Ratti, Prakesh, ed. *A Lotus of Another Color: An Unfolding of the South Asian Lesbian and Gay Experience*. Boston: Alyson, 1993.

Ritvo, Harriet. "The Emergence of Modern Pet-Keeping." *Animals and People Sharing the World*. Ed. Andrew N. Rowan. Hanover, N.H.: University Press of New England, 1988. 13–31.

———. *The Animal Estate: The English and Other Creatures in the Victorian Age*. Cambridge, Mass.: Harvard University Press, 1987.

Roof, Judith, and Robyn Wiegman, eds. *Who Can Speak?: Authority and Critical Identity*. Urbana: University of Illinois Press, 1995.

Rosen, Ruth. "Who Gets Polluted? The Movement for Environmental Justice." *Taking Sides: Clashing Views on Controversial Environmental Issues*. Ed. Theodore D. Goldfarb. 7th ed. Guilford, Conn.: Dushkin/McGraw-Hill, 1997. 62–71.

Ross, Andrew. *The Chicago Gangster Theory of Life: Nature's Debt to Society*. New York: Verso, 1995.

———. "Cowboys, Cadillacs, and Cosmonauts: Families, Film Genres, and Technocultures." *Engendering Men: The Question of Male Feminist Criticism*. Ed. Joseph A. Boone. New York: Routledge, 1990. 87–101.

Ryan, Kathleen Jo. *Deep in the Heart of Texas: Texas Ranchers in Their Own Words*. Berkeley, Calif.: Ten Speed Press, 1999.

Ryan, Kathleen Jo, and Elmer Kelton. *Texas Cattle Barons: Their Families, Land and Legacy*. Berkeley, Calif.: Ten Speed Press, 1999.

Sagle, Lauri. "Reclamation of Historically Contextualized Identity Even Though *All I Asking for Is My Body*." *A Gathering of Voices on the Asian American Experience*. Ed. Annette White-Parks, Deborah D. Bufton, et al. Fort Atkinson, Wisc.: Highsmith Press, 1994. 225–233.

San Luis Obispo County Cattle Women. April 15, 1999. http://www.cattlewomen-slo.org/.

Scapp, Ron, and Brian Seitz, eds. "Introduction." *Eating Culture*. Albany: State University of New York Press, 1998. 1–10.

Schlosser, Eric. *Fast Food Nation: The Dark Side of the All-American Meal*. Boston: Houghton-Mifflin, 2001.

Scott, George Ryley. *The Story of Baths and Bathing*. London: T. Werner Laurie, 1939.

Serpell, James, ed. *The Domestic Dog: Its Evolution, Behaviour, and Interactions with People*. New York: Cambridge University Press, 1995.

Shah, Nayan. *Contagious Divides: Epidemics and Race in San Francisco's Chinatown*. Berkeley: University of California Press, 2001.

Shah, Sonia. "Tight Jeans and Chania Chorris." *Listen Up. Voices from the Next Feminist Generation*. Ed. Barbara Findlen. Seattle: Seal Press, 1995. 113–119.

Shell, Marc. "The Family Pet." *Representations* 15 (summer 1986): 121–153.

Simoons, Frederick J. *Eat Not This Flesh: Food Avoidances from Prehistory to the Present*. 2d ed. Madison: University of Wisconsin Press, 1994.

Simpson, James R., Yoichi Kojima, et al. *Japan's Beef Industry: Economics and Technology for the Year 2000*. Guildford, England: Biddles Ltd., 1996.

Sinclair, Upton. *The Jungle*. Cambridge, Mass.: R. Bentley, 1946.

Sivulka, Juliann. *Stronger Than Dirt: A Cultural History of Advertising Personal Hygiene in America, 1875–1940*. Amherst, N.Y.: Humanity Books, 2001.

Slotkin, Richard. *Regeneration through Violence: The Mythology of the American Frontier, 1600–1860*. Middletown, Conn.: Wesleyan University Press, 1973.

Sone, Monica. *Nisei Daughter*. Seattle: University of Washington Press, [1953] 1991.

The Statutes at Large of the U.S. of America, December 1915 to March 1917. Vol. 39. Part 1. Washington, D.C.: Government Printing Office, 1917.

Stewart, Susan. *On Longing: Narratives of the Miniature, the Gigantic, the Souvenir, and the Collection*. Baltimore: Johns Hopkins University Press, 1984.

Stoneley, Peter. "Sentimental Emasculations: *Uncle Tom's Cabin* and *Black Beauty*." *Nineteenth-Century Literature* 54.1 (June 1999): 53–72.

———. "Feminism, Fascism and the Racialized Body: *National Velvet*." *Women: A Cultural Review* 9.3 (1998): 252–265.

Sui Sin Far. *Mrs. Spring Fragrance and Other Stories*. Ed. Amy Ling and Annette White-Parks. Urbana: University of Illinois Press, [1912] 1995.

Sumida, Stephen H. "Sense of Place, History, and the Concept of the 'Local' in Hawaii's Asian/Pacific American Literatures." *Reading the Literatures of Asian America*. Ed. Shirley Geok-lin Lim and Amy Ling. Philadelphia: Temple University Press, 1992. 215–228.

Takacs, Stacy. "Alien-Nation: Immigration, National Identity and Transnationalism." *Cultural Studies* 13.4 (1999): 591–620.

Takaki, Ronald. *Iron Cages: Race and Culture in 19th-Century America*. New York: Oxford University Press, 1991.

Tamura, Eileen H. *Americanization, Acculturation, and Ethnic Identity: The Nisei Generation in Hawaii*. Urbana: University of Illinois Press, 1994.

Tan, Amy. *The Joy Luck Club*. New York: Ivy Book, 1989.

Tchen, John Kuo Wei. "Believing Is Seeing: Transforming Orientalism and the Occidental Gaze." *Asia/America: Identities in Contemporary Asian American Art*. The Asia Society Galleries. New York: The New Press, 1994. 12–25.

Thomas, Keith. *Man and the Natural World: A History of the Modern Sensibility*. New York: Pantheon, 1983.

Thomas, Nicholas. *In Oceania: Visions, Artifacts, Histories*. Durham, N.C.: Duke University Press, 1997.

Tomes, Nancy. *The Gospel of Germs: Men, Women, and the Microbe in American Life*. Cambridge, Mass.: Harvard University Press, 1998.

Tompkins, Jane. *Sensational Designs: The Cultural Work of American Fiction, 1790–1860*. New York: Oxford University Press, 1985.

Trask, Haunani-Kay. *From a Native Daughter: Colonialism and Sovereignty in Hawai'i*. Monroe, Me.: Common Courage Press, 1993.

Triechler, Paula. *How to Have Theory in an Epidemic: Cultural Chronicles of AIDS*. Durham, N.C.: Duke University Press, 1999.

Trinh T. Minh ha. *Woman, Native, Other: Writing Postcoloniality and Feminism*. Bloomington: Indiana University Press, 1989.

Truong, Monique. *The Book of Salt*. Houghton Mifflin Co., 2003.

Truong, Monique Thuy-Dung. "Kelly." *Asian American Literature: A Brief Introduction and Anthology*. Ed. Shawn Wong. New York: Longman, 1996. 288–295.

Tuan, Mia. *Forever Foreigners or Honorary Whites? The Asian Ethnic Experience Today*. New Brunswick, N.J.: Rutgers University Press, 1998.

Tuan, Yi-Fu. *Dominance and Affection: The Making of Pets*. New Haven, Conn.: Yale University Press, 1984.

Urry, John. *The Tourist Gaze: Leisure and Travel in Contemporary Societies*. Newbury Park, Calif.: Sage, 1990.

Uyemoto, Holly. *Go*. New York: Plume, 1995.

Vaughan, Megan. *Curing Their Ills: Colonial Power and African Illness*. Stanford, Calif.: Stanford University Press, 1991.

Vigarello, Georges. *Concepts of Cleanliness: Changing Attitudes in France since the Middle Ages*. New York: Cambridge University Press, 1988.

Wang, Vera C. "In Search of Self: The Dislocated Female Émigré Wanderer in Chuang Hua's *Crossings*." *Multicultural Literatures through Feminist/Poststructuralist Lenses*. Ed. Barbara Frey Waxman. Knoxville: University of Tennessee Press, 1993. 22–36.

White, E. B. *Charlotte's Web*. New York: Harper Trophy, [1952], 1980.

White-Parks, Annette. *Sui Sin Far/Edith Maude Eaton: A Literary Biography*. Urbana: University of Illinois Press, 1995.

Williams, Marilyn Thornton. *Washing 'The Great Unwashed': Public Baths in Urban America, 1840–1920*. Columbus: Ohio University Press, 1991.

Wilson, Rob. *Reimagining the American Pacific: From South Pacific to Bamboo Ridge and Beyond*. Durham, N.C.: Duke University Press, 2000.

Witt, Doris. "Soul Food: Where the Chitterling Hits the (Primal) Pan." *Eating Culture*. Ed. Ron Scapp and Brian Seitz. Albany: State University of New York Press, 1998. 258–287.

Won, See Hee. "Organic Foods Satiate the Senses and Soul." *The Minnesota Women's Press*. September 12–25, 2001: 5.

Wong, Jade Snow. *Fifth Chinese Daughter*. Seattle: University of Washington Press, [1945] 1989.

Wong, Sau-ling C. "Denationalization Reconsidered: Asian American Cultural Criticism at a Theoretical Crossroads." *Amerasia* 21.1–2 (1995): 1–27.

———. *Reading Asian American Literature: From Necessity to Extravagance*. Princeton, N.J.: Princeton University Press, 1993.

Wong, Sau-ling C., and Jeffrey J. Santa Ana. "Gender and Sexuality in Asian American Literature." *Signs: Journal of Women in Culture and Society* 25.1 (1999): 171–226.

Wood, Houston. *Displacing Natives: The Rhetorical Production of Hawai'i*. Lanham, Md.: Rowman and Littlefield, 1999.

Wright, Lawrence. *Clean and Decent: The Fascinating History of the Bathroom and the Water Closet*. London: Routledge and Kegan Paul, 1960.

Wu, William F. *The Yellow Peril: Chinese Americans in American Fiction 1850–1940*. Hamden, Conn.: Archon Books, 1982.

Wuerthner, George. "Alien Invasion." *National Parks* 70.11/12 (November/December 1996): 32–35.

Yaeger, Patricia. *Dirt and Desire: Reconstructing Southern Women's Writing, 1930–1990*. Chicago: University of Chicago Press, 2000.

Yamamoto, Hisaye. "Seventeen Syllables." *Seventeen Syllables and Other Stories*. Latham, N.Y.: Kitchen Table: Women of Color Press, 1988. 8–19.

———. "Yoneko's Earthquake." *Seventeen Syllables and Other Stories*. Latham, N.Y.: Kitchen Table: Women of Color Press, 1988. 46–56.

Yamamoto, Traise. *Masking Selves, Making Subjects: Japanese American Women, Identity, and the Body*. Berkeley: University of California Press, 1999.

Yamanaka, Lois-Ann. *Father of the Four Passages*. New York: Farrar, Straus and Giroux, 2001.

———. *Heads by Harry*. New York: Farrar, Straus and Giroux, 1999.

———. *Blu's Hanging*. New York: Avon, 1997.

———. *Wild Meat and the Bully Burgers*. New York: Farrar, Straus and Giroux, 1996.

Yamashita, Karen Tei. *Brazil-Maru*. St. Paul, Minn.: Coffee House Press, 1992.

————. *Through the Arc of the Rain Forest*. St. Paul, Minn.: Coffee House Press, 1990.

Yamauchi, Wakako. "And the Soul Shall Dance." *Songs My Mother Taught Me: Stories, Plays, Memoir*. Ed. Garrett Hongo. CUNY: Feminist Press, [1966] 1994. 19–24.

Index

abattoirs, 139, 145–46, 163n25
abjection, 5; of Asian Americans, 4, 25–28, 31, 38; triumph over, 167
abortion, 46, 57n17
Abrahams, Roger, 160n9, 164n31, 165n41
acromegaly, 66
Adams, Carol, 131n43, 140, 161n12, 163n30, 164n32, 164n34, 165n41
affirmative action, erosion of, 21n17
agency, 13; assimilation and, 14; loss of, 114
Aguaruna Jivaro, 125n20
allopathology, 64
America Is in the Heart, 38
American dream, 158
Andreas, Carol, 161n17, 163n26
animals: activism and, 139; anthropomorphizing of, 126n24; breeding of, 103–5, 128n29, 128n31, 128n32, 129n35; domestication of, 102, 105–6, 130n37; eating of (*see* meat); humane treatment of, 126n24; inhumane treatment of, 100–

101, 103–5, 131n43; language and, 131n44, 163n30; metaphors of, 85, 86; neoteny and, 108–9; pets, 108–9, 126n24, 127n25, 128n30; zoos and, 102
anorexia, 11, 153
Anzaldua, Gloria, 22n22, 27
Asian American studies, 26–27; denationalization of, 167, 168; dirt and, 167–70; evolution of, 4; future of, 23n33; politics of, 168
Asian Americans: abjection of, 4, 5, 26–28, 31, 38; body stereotypes of, 10; cultural disconnects of, 28, 35–36; displacement of, 29–31, 37, 42–48, 62; family issues of, 34–39, 48–51, 53–54; female identity of, 52–53; homosexuality among, 23n34; stereotyped as dirty, 5, 7; stereotyped as model minority, 21n17, 32; subjectivity of, 25, 29
Asian/Pacific American studies, 92
Asiatic Barred Zone, 32
assimilation, 4, 21n17, 27; myths of, 32

187

About the Author

Monica Chiu is an assistant professor of English at the University of New Hampshire, teaching courses in American literature, Asian American literature, Asian American film, and literature and the body. Her work has appeared in *MELUS, LIT: Literature Interpretation Theory*, the *Journal of American Studies*, and *Mosaic*.